TENSIONS AND TRANSITIONS IN THE MUSLIM WORLD

Louay Safi

University Press of America,® Inc.
Dallas · Lanham · Boulder · New York · Oxford

Copyright © 2003 by
University Press of America,® Inc.
4501 Forbes Boulevard
Suite 200
Lanham, Maryland 20706
UPA Acquisitions Department (301) 459-3366

PO Box 317
Oxford
OX2 9RU, UK

Library of Congress Control Number: 2003112593
ISBN 0-7618-2721-8 (clothbound : alk. ppr.)
ISBN 0-7618-2722-6 (paperback : alk. ppr.)

Table of Contents

Preface and Acknowledgments

Tensions and Transitions in the Muslim World examines the profound sociopolitical changes taking place in Muslim societies, and the social and political forces behind them. The book looks critically at the ideas and the developmental strategies espoused by both the nationalist and Islamist movements, and attempts to capture the dynamic nature of contemporary Muslim society. It underscores the pivotal role played by Islam in determining the direction of sociopolitical changes, and stresses the need to pay more attention to the forward looking agenda of Islamic reformists.

The ideas and arguments advanced in this work grew out of articles published in academic journals over the last decade, most notably the *American Journal of Islamic Social Sciences,* the *Middle East Affairs*, the *Intellectual Discourse,* and the *Journal of South Asian and Middle Eastern Studies.*

In putting this book together, I have been inspired and helped by so many friends and colleagues. The intellectual milieu that helped shape the ideas presented in this volume was formed through interactions and discussions with scholars, colleagues, and students with whom I have had the honor and opportunity to interact at the International Islamic University of Malaysia, the Association of Muslim Social Scientists, the International Institute of Islamic Thought, and the Center of the Study of Islam and Democracy.

I am thankful to Dr. Jamal Barzinji, for allowing me to use the resources of the International Institute of Islamic Thought to produce this volume, to Layla Sein for editorial assistance, and to Jay Willoughby for helping prepare the manuscript.

I am particularly grateful to my mother Hanna, whose big heart and encouraging words have always been a source of inspiration, and to my sisters Lina and Layla, and my brother Amir, for helping me see through their examples the importance of faith in making life worth living.

I am also grateful to my wife Razan for her encouragement and unfailing support, and to our children, Lubna, Rahaf, Munir, and Mackeen who constantly remind me, through their honesty, warm hearts, and great enthusiasm and hopes, of the value and importance of working for a better future.

My deepest and most profound thanks and appreciation remain with the source of all inspiration, meaning, and goodness, whose Mercy and Glory are revealed in the unceasing endeavors by people of all epochs and cultures to uplift the human spirit and improve the human condition.

Introduction

For many Westerners, the Middle East refers to that part of the world that arouses the deepest emotions, but which continues, despite hundreds of studies and countless efforts by researchers and research centers, to defy rational understanding. Westerners often perceive the Middle East as a region shrouded in mystery, as it frequently triggers too many conflicting emotions. For over a millennium, the Middle East has been the source of good and evil, love and hate, comfort and malaise, and confidence and fear.

The Middle East is home to the holiest sits of the two main religions long associated with the West: Christianity and Judaism. It is the land to which Christians turn their faces to reach out to God and perform their prayers, and where Christ lived and preached his message. It is also the land to which Jews dreamed for centuries to return, and they were lately able to fulfill their dream by establishing a modern Jewish state.

The Middle East is also the birthplace of Islam, which, though claiming lineage to the Abrahamic faith that gave birth to both Judaism and Christianity, has fought the Christian West for centuries. Despite marked moral and conceptual affinities between the followers of the three Abrahamic faiths, Judaism, Christianity, and Islam, the three religious traditions have memories of hostile encounters. The conflicts among the three religions have taken many twists and turns, and history records hostilities in which the followers of each of the three have fought the followers of the other two, as well as hostilities that united two of them against the other.

The term "Middle East," coined by Western powers, reflects Western geopolitical interests in the region. The boundaries of the Middle East continue to lack precise definition, as different statesmen and researchers use the term to denote different countries. The "Middle East" is frequently used in reference to the area which once was under the domain of the Ottoman Empire. It is occasionally expanded to include other Muslim countries, such as Iran, Pakistan, and North Africa. While the expansion and contraction of the Middle East is often governed by geopolitical interests, the underlying element that justifies the clustering of diverse cultures, ethnic and linguistic groups, as well as political regimes under the rubric of the Middle East is Islam and Islamic heritage. Islam has historically shaped the cultural values and social experiences of Middle Eastern societies, and continues today to inspire the thoughts and actions of an increasing number of Middle Eastern People.

The difficulties associated with understanding the Middle East are not limited to defining its boundaries, but also extend to determining the dynamics of development and change in an extremely volatile region. The emotional elements referred to above, undoubtedly, complicate the task of studying and explaining the region. The real complication stems, however, from the fact that the Middle East has historically had a markedly different social and political experience, and has been the catalyst for developing significantly different modes of organization and discourse. This has led to serious impediments in transmitting concepts and transplanting institutions across the cultural divide that separate the Western and Islamic worlds. The differences in experience and discourse across the historical divide that separate the two worlds make Middle Eastern-Western communication at times impossible, and call for greater attention to the problem of incommensurability that often plagues discussions and dialogues between the two historical blocs.

Take, for instance, the general attitude toward the process of secularization and the rise of the secular state. Secularization for most people in the West refers to the liberation of scientific research from the shackles of religious imposition, and the rationalization of public debate. Similarly, the secular state is seen in the West as providing an essential space for religious freedom and a vital structure for preventing the imposition of one religious tradition on a multireligious society. In the Middle East, however, secularization has been associated with the decline of individual autonomy and the disappearance of civil society, while the secular state is often associated with the control of public institutions and debates by dogmatic political elites, bent on imposing "modern" ideas and institutions on the larger society. We return to examine the impact of Western secularism on the Middle East in subsequent chapters.

Still, the fact that the term "secular" invokes quite different sets of experiences and memories points to the problem of incommensurability of terms and concepts between Western and Middle Eastern public discourses, and highlights the difficulties in communication and intellectual exchange between the two.

Western impact on the Middle East is not limited, though, to secularism and the secular state. The Middle East as we know it today has, in many ways, been shaped by Western ideas and actions. The political map of the Middle East was drawn by European powers around the turn of the twentieth century. The leading cultural, economic, and political institutions that govern Middle Eastern society today are modeled after those of the West. But similarities in institutions and practices between the two worlds are more apparent than real. The efforts of ruling elites to modernize society remain superficial, unable to penetrate into the moral core of Middle Eastern culture. Evidently, the governing political elites are more interested in enjoying Western lifestyles and products, and less in Western democracy and Western commitment to scientific creativity or due process and the rule of law.

Although the modernization of the Middle East has profoundly transformed Middle Eastern society along Western lines, it has, on the other hand, created deep tensions and resentments among substantial segments of society. The opposition to, and resentment of, Western hegemony over the Middle East manifests itself most vividly in traditional reactions engineered to relive historical experiences and revive historical modes of life, as well as in the backlash of radical groups against modernity and the West. Much of the images and narrations of the Middle East revolve around these two axises. Less familiar, however, are the reformist efforts aimed at evolving a creative synthesis of Islam and modernity.

Islamic Reform movements predate Western colonialism, and can be traced to the seminal works of mid-nineteenth-century Muslim intellectuals. As we will see in Chapter 3, all reform movements – the religious, the secular, and all in between – are indebted to the work of early Islamic reformers, most notably Jamaluddin Afghani, Muhammad Abduh, and Muhammad Rashid Rida, who are often subsumed in Arabic literature under the banner of Reform School (*Al-Madrasa al-Islahiyah*).

Even though the synthetic and inclusive reform message advanced by the Reform School was quickly bifurcated into the nationalist and traditionalist, and later into the radical Islamic movements, Islamic reform movements continue to exert the greatest and most profound influence in determining the direction of social and political reforms. They are, therefore, the key to understanding the cultural and sociopolitical dynamism of Middle Eastern society. Given the importance and centrality of the ongoing Islamic reform efforts to understanding the Middle East, it is unfortunate that the reformist movements are often overlooked and ignored by Western students of the Middle East.

Few scholars have provided us with useful insight into Islamic reform movements, most notably Edward Said, Leonard Binder, John Esposito, and Ibrahim Abu Rabi`.

I do, therefore, attempt in this study to focus attention on Islamic reform, to underscore the vitality of the reformist vision it espouses, and to reveal its unshakable commitment to evolving a pluralist society and participatory politics. As will be shown in subsequent chapters, the Islamic reform movement, though less numerous, constitutes the middle ground and the moral synthesis between the nationalist-secularist and the moralist-Islamist forces at the core of the great tensions that inspire Middle Eastern transformations. Its ideas and vision have galvanized people from both sides of the cultural debate, leading to a constant shift of the critical mass in the Middle East from the contending fringes to the moderate middle.

Unfortunately, there is currently little interest among American scholars and statesmen in recognizing the moderate and forward-looking vision of Islamic reformists. The efforts of Islamic reformists to advance a pluralist and democratically organized society are frequently dismissed by American critics as provisional and disingenuous. The sources of the dismissive attitude of the critics are multiple and complex, but can be reduced to two sets of factors: the inability of many in the United States to associate pluralism and democracy with religious traditions, and the tendencies to place the national interests of the United States above the moral autonomy and human rights concerns of Middle Eastern people.

Unfortunately, the failure to recognize Islam's capacity to evolve a pluralist and democratic society is the outcome of generalizations and extrapolations from Western experience, rather than a systematic and thorough examination of Islamic views and practices. Although putting the economic and geopolitical interests of the United States over and above the human rights and dignities of Middle Easterners may in the short-run boost up those interests, it is bound to spell disaster in the long-run for world peace and the United States.

The inability to understand the dynamics of Islamic resurgence is also due to the failure to differentiate the universal from the particular in both Western and Middle Eastern experiences. The universal represents the values and ethos inspiring actions and developments in both worlds, while the particular denotes concrete models and institutions that aspire to actualize universal ideals and values in specific historical circumstances. The failure to make the distinction between the universal and the particular is at the roots of the Islamic traditionalists' resistance to modernization, and is responsible for the anxiety, apprehension, and suspicions of Islam's ability to support democratic institutions and pluralist society. Both problems will be discussed at length in subsequent chapters.

The nine chapters that constitute this book are divided into four interrelated parts: (1) Democratization and the Islamic State, (2) Competing Visions of Reform, (3) Islamic Law and Human Rights, and (4) Islam in a Global Order. Each of these parts focuses attention on aspects of Middle Eastern politics and society, and the increasing role of Islam and Islamic values and ideas in Middle Eastern developments.

We begin in Part I by exploring the possibilities of bringing about a democratic order, rooted in Islamic values and beliefs, and the need to anchore political culture and structure in Islamic morality.

We then turn in Part II to examine the nature of the cultural dichotomy that gives rise to the Islamist-secularist tensions, and lay down the two nationalist-secularist and moralist-Islamist visions.

In Part III, we focus on Islamic law, and underscore its dynamic nature, and the need to position human rights within the Islamic moral and legal traditions. We argue that human rights should form the common ground on which Islamic and Western traditions converge. We stress, however, that convergence must be based on a process of cross-cultural dialogue, whereby the universality of human rights are established on objective (or intersubjective), rather than subjective grounds.

Finally, we take in Part IV the Islamic-secularist tension from the regional to the global level, by examining the evolving relationship between Islam and the West. We caution against the tendency to view Islamic movements as a monolithic bloc, and stress the importance of recognizing the liberating and progressive efforts of Islamic reformers. We particularly highlight the negative impact of the current approach of the United States foreign policy on the Middle East, and point to the need to resist the temptation to support autocratic regimes that display readiness to promote American economic and geopolitical interests at the expense of the freedom, dignity, and human rights of Middle Easterners. We argue that while such and approach might promote short-term interests, it is bound to spell disaster in the long run.

I. Democratization and the Islamic State

Democratization and the Islamic State

Modern democracy is the outcome of political debate and struggle within the modern West. Muslim societies have no historical experience of democracy as it is practiced today. This historical fact has led many to doubt Islam's capacity to generate a democratic order. The doubts are usually reinforced by an extrapolation from within the premodern West. Democratization is associated, in the Western mind, with the process of secularization that very much defines the dominant attitude toward the relationship between religion and politics, and determines the extent to which religion is allowed to venture to the political domain.

Still, Islam experienced a substantial participatory politics in its formative years. For over thirty years since the rise of the first Islamic polity in Madinah, the Muslim community continued to be extensively involved in selecting the head of state (caliph) and shaping public decisions. Further, historical Muslim society was a manifestly pluralistic society, providing ethnic and confessional communities with great political and legal autonomy, and tolerating a wide spectrum of lifestyles and intellectual opinions.

The question that concerns many students of Islam and the Middle East may be stated thus: Does Islam and Islamic values support a democratic rule and a pluralistic society? Or to put the question differently: Can democracy and pluralism – the two greatest political achievements of modernity – flourish in a society in which Islam and Islamic law command the allegiance of the majority?

The answer to the above question varies over a wide spectrum of positions from an emphatic yes to a definitive no. These positions are usually predicated on fragments of evidence derived from both practical Muslim experiences and theoretical arguments. We will have the occasion to address at length, in chapters 6 and 7, problems associated with the static and fragmental reading of Muslim history. The position we take in the next two chapters rejects both the emphatic yes and definitive no answers. I contend that Islamic values and principles favor a democratic and pluralistic political order. However, for such an order to be realized, a systematic cultural and legal reform is needed. The desired reform, I further argue, should approprpiate the universal elements embodied in the historical Muslim experience, and use them to transcend both classical and contemporary Muslim political and cultural institutions.

CHAPTER 1

Islam and the Secular State

The secular state emerged in modern times in response to religious infighting that plagued Europe for over a century, and put social life on a self-destructing path. The Hundred Years' War posed a serious threat to the then emerging modern Europe, underscoring the need to keep the state and church at a comfortable distance.

While the secular state was designed to prevent organized religion from controlling public institutions, it did not necessarily aim at undermining religiosity *per se*, or alienating religious communities. Rather, it was perceived as multireligious society's best defense against the imposition of the religious values and worldview of one community on others.

For many Muslims, however, the secular state is viewed as an instrument used to undermine religious heritage and deny the relevance of moral teachings to public life. While this perception has an element of truth, it does not necessarily depict the general nature of Western secularism. Evidently, the Muslim perception of secularism is not formed through an understanding of the original purposes and historical circumstances of Western secularism, but rather is influenced by the Muslim experience of secular dogmatism and the intolerance of the secular state in contemporary Muslim societies, most notably that of Turkey and many Arab and Central Asian states.

Reacting to secular dogmatism, populist Islamic groups have advanced a conception of the state that, while different in substance, is similar in purpose and form to the very secular state they oppose. Like Muslim secularists, Islamic populists see the state as an instrument in the hands of ruling powers for imposing a particular conception of the world on the rest of society. They insist, therefore, that the Islamic state should be charged with the duty of imposing Islamic law on the larger society.

I argue that the positions of contemporary Muslim populist movements stand in direct contradiction not only to Islamic values and beliefs, but are also contrary to political practices developed in historical Muslim societies. I also explore the extent to which religious beliefs and values were related to the political structures and public policies of the historical Muslim society. I contend that the political order that emerged under Islam was never perceived exclusively as Muslim, but rather was constructed on the basis of universal principles that transcend sectarian divisions.

I, therefore, conclude by underscoring the need to have a fresh Islamically-based conceptualization of political action and organization in ways that would help reclaim the moral core of social life, eroded with the advance of Western secularism, without sacrificing the important principles of freedom and equality.

The Origin of Secularism

Secularism refers to complex and multifaceted attitudes and practices that cannot be easily captured in a brief description or a simple definition. While one may find certain similarities between modern secularist attitudes and practices and those that existed in premodern societies, it is fair to say that secularism as we know it today is an essentially modern phenomenon that grew in the modern West, and later took roots in different societies.

In its essential sense, secularism denotes a set of notions and values whose aim is to ensure that the state is neither engaged in promoting specific religious beliefs and values, nor uses its powers and offices to persecute religion. To prevent state officials from using their political authority to impose a narrow set of religious attitudes and values on the larger society, and to foreclose the possibility of using religious symbols to agitate one religious community against another, Western intellectuals embarked on a project that aimed at separating political authority from religious affiliation. To do that, the Enlightenment scholars embraced a set of concepts and principles, and used them as the basis for reconstructing modern European consciousness. The new political ideology advanced by Enlightenment activists and thinkers emphasized concepts such as equality, freedom of conscience and conviction, and the supremacy of law, all of which were advocated by the Religious Reformation that put an end to the ancient regime of Europe.

The underlying sociopolitical morality advocated by the pioneers of the secular state in Europe was derived from the religious tradition delineated by the religious reformists of fifteenth-century Europe, but argued in rational terms and common good logic. Early advocates of the separation of church and state, such as Descartes, Hobbes, Locke, and

Rousseau, had no intention to undermine religion, or faith in the divine, but rather predicated their reformist ideas on the notions of God and civil religion. Descartes, for instance, argued "that the certainty and truth of all knowledge depends uniquely on my awareness of the true God, to such an extent that I was incapable of perfect knowledge about anything else until I became aware of him."[1] Similarly, Rousseau, while critical of the way religion was traditionally taught and practiced, recognized the need, even the necessity, of religious commitment and faith for the modern state to function properly. He, therefore, identified a number of "dogmas," and argued for their inclusion in the "civil religion" he advocated: "The existence of an omnipotent, intelligent, benevolent divinity that foresees and provides; the life to come; the happiness of the just; the punishment of sinners; the sanctity of the social contract and the law – these are the positive dogmas. As for the negative dogmas I would limit them to a single one: no intolerance."[2]

Even Kant, who limited the notion of truth to empirical experience and labored to set morality on a rational foundation insisted that "without a God and without a world invisible to us now but hoped for, the glorious ideals of morality are indeed objects of approval and admiration, but not springs of purpose and action."[3] However, by denying the possibility of transcendental truth, and as a result of the relentless attack on the authority of revelation as a source of ethical and ontological knowledge, secularist scholars have been able to successfully marginalize religion and undermine morality. The efforts to ground morality in utility and cost-benefit calculation, rather than truth, proved to be counter intuitive and futile, and gave rise to egoism and moral relativism.

There were, of course, intellectuals who have less sympathy to religion particularly among French intellectuals, but they did not represent the larger sentiments of the great majority in Europe. The French revolution displayed a clear anti-religious sentiment, but they were not, as Nietzsche was to discover later, directed against religion *per se*, but rather against organized religion represented by an official church. "Modern philosophy, being an epistemological skepticism, is," Nietzsche argued, "covertly and overtly, anti-Christian – although, to say this for the benefit of more refined ears, by no means anti-religious."[4]

The essential secularist sentiment is, therefore, rooted in the Religious Reformation; more specifically, it is rooted in the Protestant revolt against religious hierarchy and centralized religion. Secularism was not originally intended as a way to separate religion from society or religious consciousness from political action, but rather to isolate the state from the church structure and to separate religious and political authorities.

The tone started to change, however, a century later among progressive European intellectuals who saw in religion a negative force whose elimination, they believed, was essential for further emancipation and progress. Karl Marx, while agreeing that the secular state has success-fully neutralized religion and purged it from the public sphere, still saw a great danger in religious life. This is because, he argued, secularism re-duced religion into a private matter only insofar as the state is concerned. However, the privatization of religion gave it, in effect, more influence in the organization of civil society. Even in the United States where religion has been domesticated and individualized to the greatest extent, it contin-ues, Marx proclaimed, to divide society into distinct religious communi-ties, thereby allowing for the formation of internal solidarity with a clear bearing on economic life. Religion, Marx further thought, is an instru-ment in the hands of privileged classes to justify social misery and eco-nomic inequality. In *The Jewish Question*, Marx has the following to say about the need to emancipate humanity from religion:

> The decomposition of man into Jew and citizen, Protestant and citizen, religious man and citizen, is neither a deception directed against citi-zenhood, nor is it a circumvention of political emancipation, it is politi-cal emancipation itself, the political method of emancipating oneself from religion. Of course, in periods when the political state as such is born violently out of civil society, when political liberation is the form in which men strive to achieve their liberation, the state can and must go as far as the abolition of religion, the destruction of religion. But, it can do so only in the same way that it proceeds to the abolition of pri-vate property, to the maximum, to confiscation, to progressive taxation, just as it goes as far as the abolition of life, the guillotine.[5]

Nietzsche, like Marx, condemned religion as a negative social force responsible for preserving the meek and the weak, and hence, weakening the human race. By praising poverty and glorifying the tam-ing of the natural instinct, Nietzsche insisted, religion contributed to delaying the refinement of the human species. By giving "comfort to the sufferers, courage to the oppressed and despairing, a staff and sup-port to the dependent" Christianity, he contended, "preserved too much of what ought to perish."[6] Unlike Marx, who saw religion as an obsta-cle in the way to achieving universal equality, Nietzsche's rejection of Religion in general, and reformed Christianity in particular, was anti-democratic, directed against the egalitarian spirit it promoted, and hence against its failure to promote the "order of rank," a hierarchical social order which he believed to be both intrinsic to humanity and de-sirable to social life.[7]

Decoupling Islamic Law and the State

Many Muslim intellectuals insist today that Islam is an integral part of the state. The state in a society committed to Islam, they stress, is by definition an Islamic state since political authorities are bound to Islamic law, which has a direct bearing on constitutional law. This has created confusion about the nature of the Islamic state, and has given rise to apprehension on the part of modernist scholars who feared that remarrying Islam and the state is bound to give birth to theocracy.

The confusion is, of course, not only limited to outside observers and commentators who tend to extrapolate in their analysis from the historical experience of Western society, but has also affected those who advocate the formation of a political state on the basis of Islamic values. The difficulty arises from the efforts to combine the principle of popular government with that of a state bound by the rules of Islamic law. This confusion is, in my opinion, the result of equating the political structure of the *ummah* (Muslim community) with the political structure of the state, and consequently, mixing up Shari'ah *(Islamic law)* functions with that of the state. This confusion is not restricted to obscure works. Rather, it is found in the works of influential contemporary Islamic thinkers. Under the title *The Objectives of the Islamic State*, Abul Ala Mawdudi, for one, points out two kinds of objectives to be assigned to the Islamic state: negative objectives "like deterring aggression and preserving the freedom of people and defending the state,[13] and positive objectives such as banning all forbidden things which have been condemned by the Qur'an."[14] Mawdudi concludes by affirming the totality of the state's objectives on the basis of the comprehensiveness of the Shari'ah objectives. He writes:

> Obviously, it is impossible for such a state to limit its framework, because it is a totalitarian state encompassing the whole human life, and painting every aspect of human life with its moral color and particular reformist programs. So nobody has the right to stand up against the state and exempt himself from the liability by saying that this is a personal matter, so that the state does not intrude. In brief, the state encompasses the human life and every area of civilization according to its particular moral theory and particular reformist program. So, to some extent, it is similar to the communist and fascist state. But despite this totality the Islamic state is free from the color that dominates the totalitarian and authoritarian states of our age. Thus the Islamic state does not curtail the individual freedom nor has it much room for dictatorship or absolute authority.[15]

The above statement reflects the state of confusion to which we just pointed. In a single paragraph the author characterizes the Islamic state as totalitarian, likens it to the communist and fascist states, and stresses that no one has the right to stand up against the state and resist its intrusion into personal life. He then backs up, two sentences later, denying that the Islamic state may curtail individual freedom.

Certainly, the claim regarding the totalitarian character of the state is the result of mixing state functions relating to the Shari`ah's legal objectives with the objectives of the *ummah* concerning moral and educational dimensions. The differentiation between these two kinds of objectives is, thus, of vital importance to prevent the state from imposing on the larger society a normative order based on a narrow interpretation of the law. The Islamic state, it should be emphasized, is not conceived as an institution devoted to advancing the interests of the Muslim community, but as a political system based on universal principles, and one committed to maintaining peace, security, and welfare of all citizens, irrespective of their doctrines, religions, nationality, race, or gender.

As will be shown below, the Islamic system in the past did not lead, nor should it lead in the future, to imposing a narrow and limited concept or a particular opinion on society. This is because the principle of religious and doctrinal plurality has been considered since the very inception of the *ummah,* as a cardinal political principle. Here, the Qur'anic verses both Makkan and Madinan, clearly focus on the centrality of the principle of religious freedom in the Islamic concept.

Lately the concern over how religious commitments relate to the exercise of power reached into the ranks of Islamists. Mainstream Islamic groups have been moving gradually away from the early concept of centralized Islamic political order envisaged by such early leaders as Hasan al-Banna and Taqiyuddin al-Nabhani. Leaders of major Islamic movements in Egypt, Jordan, Pakistan, Syria, Turkey, and Tunisia, to name a few, have come openly in favor of a democratic, pluralistic political system in which freedom of speech and association is guaranteed for citizens, regardless of their political orientation or religious affiliation.[8]

The Formative Principles of the Madinah State

The notion of the Islamic state advanced today by populist writers is, as I tried to show above, a mixture of the nationalist structure of the modern state with the communal structure of historical Shari`ah. The concept of the state that emerges as a result is in complete contradiction with the nature and purpose of the polity found by the Prophet, or developed historically by successive Muslim generations. A quick review of the guiding principles of the first Islamic polity reveals the disparity between the two. The principles and structures of the early Islamic polity are epitomized in the Compact of Madinah (*Sahifat al-Madinah*) that formed the constitutional foundation of the political community established by the Prophet.[9]

The Compact of Madinah established a number of important political principles that, put together, formed the political constitution of the first Islamic state, and defined the political rights and duties of the members of the newly established political community, Muslims and non-Muslims alike, and drew up the political structure of the nascent society. The most important principles included in this Compact are:

First, the Compact declared that the *ummah* is a political society, open to all individuals committed to its principles and values, and ready to shoulder its burdens and responsibilities. It is not a reclusive one, whose membership rights and securities are restricted to a select few. The right to membership in the *ummah* is specified in: (1) accepting the principles of the Islamic system, manifested in the commitment to adhere to the moral and legal order; and (2) declaring allegiance to the system, through practical contributions and struggle to actualize the objectives and goals of Islam. Thus, allegiance and concern for public good are principles determining the *ummah's* membership as defined by the first article of the document: "This is a Compact offered by Muhammad the Prophet, (governing the relations) among the believers and the Muslims of Quraysh and Yathrib (Madinah), and those who followed, joined, and labored with them."[10]

Second, the Compact did not delineate only a general framework that defined individual norms and the scope of political action within the new society, but also preserved the basic social and political structures prevalent then in tribal Arabia. The Compact of Madinah preserved tribal structure, while negating tribal spirit and subordinating tribal allegiance to a morally based legal order. As the Compact declared that the nascent political community is "an *ummah* to the exclusion of all people," it approved a tribal division that had already been purged of tribal spirit epitomized by the slogan "my brethren right of wrong," subjecting it to the higher principles of truth and justice. The Compact therefore declared that the emigrants of the Quraysh, Banu al-Harith, Banu al-Aus, and other tribes residing in Madinah, according "to their present customs, shall pay the bloodwit they paid previously and that every group shall redeem its prisoners."[11]

The following three points explain how Islam avoided the elimination of tribal divisions. (1) The tribal division was not mere political divisions but also social divisions providing its people with a symbiotic system. Therefore, the abolition of the political and social assistance provided by the tribe before developing an alternative should have been a great loss for the people in society. (2) Apart from its being a social division, the tribe represented an economic division in harmony with the pastoral economy prevalent in the Arabian Peninsula before and after Islam. The tribal division is the ideal division of the pastoral production, as it provides freedom of movement and migration in search of pasture. Any change in this pattern requires taking an initiative first to change the means and methods of production. (3) Perhaps, the most important factor that justified the tribal division within the framework of the *ummah* after the final message had purged the tribal existence of its aggressive and arrogant content, is the maintenance of the society and its protection from the danger of central dictatorship that might come into existence in absence of a secondary social and political structure and concentration of political power in the hands of a central authority.

Hence Islam adopted a political system, based on the concept of the one *ummah* as an alternative to the divisional tribal system and upheld the tribal division having cleared it from its aggressive elements. It left the question of changing the political structure to gradual development of economic and production structures. Although Islamic revelation avoided any arbitrary directives, aimed at immediate abolition of the tribal division, it openly criticized tribal and nomadic life.[12]

Third, the Islamic political system adopted the principle of religious autonomy based on the freedom of belief of all of society's members. The Jews were granted the right to act according to the principles and rulings in which they believed: "The Jews of Banu Auf are one community with the believers. The Jews have their religion and the Muslims theirs." The Compact emphasized the fundamentality of cooperation between Muslims and non-Muslims in establishing justice and defending Madinah against foreign aggression. "The Jews must bear their expenses and the Muslims their expenses. Each must help the other against anyone who attacks the people of this Compact. They must seek mutual advice and consultation." It prohibited the Muslims from doing injustice to the Jews or retaliating for their Muslim brothers against the followers of the Jewish religion without adhering to the principles of truth and justice. "To the Jew who follow us belongs help and equality. He shall not be wronged nor shall his enemies be aided."[13]

Fourth, the Compact stipulated that the social and political activities in the new system must be subject to a set of universal values and standards that treat all people equally. Sovereignty in society would not rest with the rulers, or any particular group, but with the law founded on the basis of justice, goodness, and maintaining the dignity of all. The Compact emphasized repeatedly and frequently the fundamentality of justice, goodness, and righteousness, and condemned in different expressions injustice and tyranny. "They would redeem their prisoners with kindness and justice common among the believers," the Compact stated: "The God-conscious believers shall be against the rebellious, and against those who seek to spread injustice, sin, enmity, or corruption among the believers, the hand of every person shall be against him even if he be a son of one of them," it proclaimed.[14]

Fifth, The Compact introduced a number of political rights to be enjoyed by the individuals of the Madinan State, Muslims and non-Muslims alike, such as (1) the obligation to help the oppressed, (2) outlawing guilt by association which was commonly practiced by pre-Islamic Arab tribes: "A person is not liable for his ally's misdeeds;" (3) freedom of belief: "The Jews have their religion and the Muslims have theirs;" and (4) freedom of movement from and to Madinah: "Whoever will go out is safe, and whoever will stay in Madinah is safe except those who wronged (others), or committed sin."[15]

Religion and the State in Historical Muslim Society

Adhering to the guidance of revelation, the *ummah* has respected the principle of religious plurality and cultural diversity during the better part of its long history. Successive governments since the *Rashidun* period have preserved the freedom of faith and allowed non-Muslim minorities not only to practice their religious rituals and proclaim their beliefs, but also to implement their religious laws according to an autonomous administrative system.[16] Likewise, the *ummah* as a whole has respected the doctrinal plurality with both its conceptual and legal dimensions. It has resisted every attempt to drag the political power to take sides' with partisan groups, or to prefer one ideological group to another. It has also insisted on downsizing the role of the state and restricting its functions to a limited sphere.

Any one who undertakes to study the political history of Islam would soon realize that all political practices, which violated the principle of religious freedom and plurality, were an exception to the rule. For instance, the efforts of the Caliph al-Mamoun to impose doctrinal uniformity in accordance with the Mu'tazilite interpretations, and to use his political authority to support one of the parties involved in doctrinal disputes, were condemned by the ulama and the majority of the *ummah*. His efforts to achieve doctrinal homogeneity through suppression and force eventually clashed with the will of the *ummah,* which refused to solve doctrinal and theoretical problems by the sword. This compelled Al-Wathiq Billah, the third caliph after al-Mamoun to give up the role assumed by his predecessors and abandon their oppressive measures.

Obviously, Muslims have historically recognized that the main objective of establishing a political system is to create the general conditions that allow the people to realize their duties as moral agents (*khulafa*), and not to impose the teachings of Islam by force. We, therefore, ascribe the emergence of organizations to help compel the *ummah* to follow a narrow interpretation, and to call for the use of political power to enforce communal obedience to Islamic norms. This helps distinguish between the role and objectives of the *ummah* and those of the state. While the *ummah* aims to build the Islamic identity, to provide an atmosphere conducive to spiritual and mental development of the individual, and to grant him/her the opportunity to realize his/her role and aims of life within the general framework of the law, the state makes efforts to coordinate the *ummah*'s activities with the aim to utilize the natural and human resources to overcome the political and economic problems facing society.

Differentiating between the general and particular in the Shari`ah, and distinguishing between the responsibilities of the *ummah* and those of the state, is a necessity if we want to avoid the transformation of political power into a device for advancing particular interests. This distinction also prevents state agencies and institutions from blocking intellectual and social progress, or obstructing society's spiritual, conceptual, and organizational development.

Differentiating Civil Society and the State

Historically, legislative functions in Muslim society were not restricted to state institutions. Rather, there was a wide range of legislations related to juristic efforts at both the moral and legal levels. Since the major part of legislation relating to transactional and contractual relations among individuals is attached to the juristic legislative bodies, the judicial tasks may be connected directly with the *ummah*, not with the state. *The differentiation between civil society and the state can only be maintained by dividing the process of legislation into distinct areas that reflect both the geographical and normative differentiation of political society*

The importance of the differential structure of the law is not limited to its ability to counteract the tendency of centralization of power, which characterizes the Western model of the state. Rather, it is also related to guarantees extended to religious minorities. The Islamic model maintains the legislative and administrative independence of the followers of different religions, as the sphere of communal legislation does not fall under the governmental authority of the state. On the other hand, the majoritarian model of the democratic state deprives religious minorities of their legal independence, and insists on subjugating all citizens to a single legal system, which often reflects the doctrinal and behavioral values of the ruling majority.

The early Muslim community was cognizant of the need to differentiate law to ensure moral autonomy, while working diligently to ensure equal protection of the law as far as fundamental human rights were concerned. Thus, early jurists recognized that non-Muslims who entered into a peace covenant with Muslims were entitled to full religious freedom, and equal protection of the law insofar as their rights to personal safety and property were concerned. Muhammad bin al-Hasan al-Shaybani states in unequivocal terms that when non-Muslims enter into a peace covenant with Muslims, "Muslims should not appropriate any of their [the non-Muslims] houses and land, nor should they intrude into any of their dwellings. Because they have become party to a covenant of peace, and because on the day of the [peace of] Khaybar, the prophet's spokesman announced that none of the property of the covenanter is permitted to them [the Muslim]. Also because they [the non-Muslims] have accepted the peace covenant so as they may enjoy their properties and rights on par with Muslims."[16] Similarly, early Muslim jurists recognized the right of non-Muslims to self-determination, and awarded them full moral and legal autonomy in the villages and towns under their control. Therefore, al-Shaybani, the author of the most authoritative work on non-Muslim rights, insisted that the Christians who have entered into a peace covenant (*dhimma*) – hence became *dhimmis* – have all the freedom to trade in wine and pork in their towns, even though such practice is considered immoral and illegal among Muslims.[17] However, *dhimmis* were prohibited to do the same in towns and villages controlled by Muslims.

Likewise, early Muslim jurists recognized the right of *dhimmis* to hold public office, including the office of a judge and minister. However, because judges had to refer to laws sanctioned by the religious traditions of the various religious communities, non-Muslim judges could not administer law in Muslim communities, nor were Muslim judges permitted to enforce Shari`ah laws on the *dhimmis*. There was no disagreement among the various schools of jurisprudence on the right of non-Muslims to be ruled according to their laws; they only differed in whether the positions held by non-Muslim magistrates were judicial in nature, and hence the magistrates could be called judges, or whether they were purely political, and therefore the magistrates were indeed political leaders.[18] Al-Mawardi, hence distinguished between two types of ministerial positions: *plenipotentiary* minister (*wazir tafwid*) and *executive* minister (*wazir tanfiz*). The two positions differ in that the former acts independently from the caliph, while the latter has to act on the instructions of the caliph, and within the limitations set by him.[19] Therefore, early jurists permitted *dhimmis* to hold the office of the executive, but not the *plenipotentiary* minister.[20]

But while early Shari`ah law recognized the civil and political rights and liberties of non-Muslim *dhimmis*, Shari`ah rules underwent drastic revision, beginning with the eighth century of Islam. This was a time of great political turmoil throughout the Muslim world. It was during that time that the Mongols invaded Central and West Asia inflicting tremendous losses on various dynasties and kingdoms, and destroying the seat of the caliphate in Baghdad. This coincided with the crusaders' control of

Palestine and the coast of Syria. In the West, the Muslim power in Spain was being gradually eroded. It was under such conditions of mistrust and suspicion that a set of provisions, attributed to an agreement between the Caliph Omar and the Syrian Christians, were publicized in a treatise written by Ibn al-Qayyim.[21] The origin of these provisions is dubious, but their intent is clear: to humiliate Christian *dhimmis* and to set them apart in dress code and appearance. Their impact, however, was limited, as the Ottomans, who replaced the Abbasid as the hegemonic power in the Muslim world, continued the early practice of granting legal and administrative autonomy to non-Muslim subjects.

Islam, Civil Society, and the State

The modern state emerged to foster individual freedom and to protect the individual against arbitrary rule, and to ensure that the members of the political society assume full control over public institutions. To do so, the modern state found it necessary to free public institutions from the control of all exclusive groups, including organized religions. However, despite the clear desire of the pioneers of the secular state to replace religious morality with civic virtue as the moral foundation of the state, secularism gradually developed anti-religious tendencies, leading to the continuous erosion of the moral consensus. The continuous erosion of morality, and the rampant corruption in modern politics threatens to turn the state into an instrument in the hands of corrupt officials and their egoistic cronies.

This has prompted calls for the return of religion and religiously organized groups into the political arena. Nowhere are these calls louder and clearer than in Muslim societies where Islamic values have historically exerted great influence on the body politics. Unfortunately, the reunion envisaged by the advocates of the Islamic state is often presented in crude and simplistic terms, as it fails to appreciate the great care that was taken by early Muslims to ensure that the state incorporates, both in its objectives and structure, the freedom and interest of all intra- and inter-religious divisions.

This calls upon Muslim scholars to engage in new thinking that aims at redefining political principles and authority. In doing so, Muslim scholars should be fully aware of the need to transcend the historical models of political organizations in Muslim society. Political structures and procedures adopted by early Muslim societies are directly linked to their social structures, economic and technological developments, and political experiences. While historical Islamic models provide a mine of knowledge for contemporary Muslims to utilize, any workable formulation of the state's modern Islamic model that is true to Islamic values and ethos must emerge out of fresh thinking that takes into account the structure of modern society.

Islamic political thought, I believe, can make a profound contribution toward reclaiming the moral core of social life, and preserving religious traditions, without sacrificing the principle of freedom and equality promoted by the modern state.

The hallmark of Islamic political experience is the limitations that historical Muslim society was able to place on the actions of rulers, and the presence of a vigorous and robust civil society. Many of the functions the secular state assumes today were entrusted to civic institutions, including education, health, and legislation. The state was mainly entrusted with questions of security and defense, and was the last resort in questions relating to dispensation of justice. This understanding of state power would potentially free religious communities from intervention of the state and state officials, who tend to enforce their religiously based values and notions on the members of society, including those who do not share with them some of those values and beliefs.

The principles of individual freedom and equality which are intrinsic to Islamic political thought require that individuals have the basic civil liberties offered by the modern state. However, by freeing civil society from the heavy hand of the state, and by extending individual liberties to the community, and recognizing the moral autonomy of social groups, social and religious groups under the Islamic conception of law would have the capacity to legislate their internal morality and affairs in their communities. While the new sphere of freedom acquired under this arrangement allows for differentiation among citizens, equality would have to be maintained as the criterion of justice in the new area of public law, and in access to public institutions – i.e., matters that relate to sphere of shared interests and inter-communal relations.

CHAPTER 2

State and Society in Traditional Islam

The "Islamic State" is a new concept that entered our lexicon only recently. The phrase is used by some to denote the state in a predominantly Muslim society. While others use the term to indicate a state that has adopted Islamic law and endeavors to implement its dictates. Yet the phrase may also be used to refer to the specific political arrangements that transpired historically, and are likely to reemerge, in Islamically-dominant societies.

I delineate, in this chapter, the basic elements involved in the concept of the Islamic state and clarify the basis and scope of political power. More specifically, discussions focus on the purpose of the state in Islamic thought and experience, the source of political legitimacy, and the scope of state power. I intend to further elaborate the meaning and implications of the distinction between the role and purpose of the state and those of the *ummah*, for only through the separation of the responsibilities and objectives of the two can the injunctions of the Shari`ah and the principles of Islam be properly observed.

Delineating a general conception of the Islamic state, and defining its normative foundation through an extrapolation of Islamic values and historical experience, is very important to evaluate the stances of both the advocates of political Islam and their secularist critics. This chapter purports to provide a frame of reference to help analyze and demystify the notion of Islamic state.

Historical Background

Although the word "state" *(dawlah)* was first used in the Qur'an, almost six centuries had to elapse before the word was given its first technical definition by Muslim scholars. The word *dawlah* was mentioned once in the Qur'an (in 59:7)[22] in connection with the distribution of *fay'* (the property Muslims appropriated from the Banu al-Najjar upon the latter's expulsion from Madinah). The Qur'an justified this departure from the usual practice of dividing the spoils among the fighters by referring to the divine intention of preventing the circulation of wealth among a small group within the society.

Up until the late fifth century, one could hardly find any reference to the state in Muslim literature, or in Western literature for that matter. Other terms such as *al-amsar* or *dar al-Islam* were employed whenever a reference was made to the territories under Muslim control. Alternatively, the state as a political body was identified by its political organs, i.e., *khilafah, imamah,* or *wilayah.*[23] In the sixth and seventh centuries of the Muslim era, the term *dawlah* began to acquire a political connotation. Muslim scholars at this time, mainly historians, began to employ the word in reference to the various Muslim dynasties which emerged when the caliphal institution lost its executive power and was reduced to a nominal office symbolizing Muslim unity, while the real political and military power fell into the hands of strong clans and families. Ibn Manzur (630-711 AH), in his voluminous dictionary *Lisan al-Arab,* distinguished between two variations: *dawlah* and *dulah,* the former denoting the domination of one group by another through military power and the latter referring to economic domination.

Ibn Khaldun presented, in the eighth century of Islam (fourteenth century AD), the first empirical study of the state. He associated the concept of state with that of social solidarity or community spirit (*'asabiyah*) and contended that human beings were naturally inclined toward social organization. Such organization could be maintained only with the existence of an authority or a leadership that facilitates coordination and provides guidance. Ibn Khaldun distinguished between two types of authority: coercive and participatory. The former resembled the authority of a king who extracts obedience through coercive capacity, the latter that of a chieftain (*ra'is*) whose influence is ensured by the homogeneity of his interests and those of his followers.

Ibn Khaldun associated the state with the dominance of a powerful group whose power emanates from *'asabiyah* as well as the coercive capacity (*qahr*) it can bring to bear upon other groups. He, therefore, conceived of the state as a cyclical and recurring phenomenon – it comes into existence with the emergence of a social group enjoying a superiority of group spirit and coercive capacity and disappears when these two elements are lost after two generations.[24] Central to Ibn Khaldun's conception of the state is the emphasis on the heterogeneous nature of civil society and the domination of the political community by the most cohe-

sive and organized social group, an emphasis that makes him a forerun-
ner of modern theorists who stress the conflict-driven aspects of the state.

Defining the State

There is a tendency on the part of modern political theorists, including some Islamists, to define the state in terms of the major components
of the nation-state, the basic political unit in the contemporary international system. It is argued that the state is distinguished from other political systems by three elements: population, authority, and sovereignty.[25]
The problem with this approach is that it fails to provide any meaningful
explanation of the basis for political divisions in the international political system without relying extensively, and even exclusively, on the concept of power. Furthermore, defining the state in terms of the three
components cited above is of little help in identifying the essential elements which distinguish one form of state from another (liberal, socialist,
authoritarian, etc.). An alternative and probably more fruitful approach is
to identify the state with the order it purports to realize and which, in
turn, determines its goals and actions. By adopting this approach, the
Islamic state should be identified with the system of rules that determines
the quality of life in the political community as well as the political instruments necessary for the realization of the Islamic ideals.

Defining the Islamic state in terms of a system of rules and the organization responsible for their realization is crucial for avoiding confusion between the concept of state and that of *ummah*. The two may,
and often do, differ in their moral significance as well as in their territorial boundaries. Morally, the state and the *ummah*, as will be shown
later, operate on two different moral planes. Territorially, the geographical boundaries of the Islamic state need not coincide with those
of the *ummah*. This means that although the territorial component of
the state is important for determining the jurisdictional boundaries of a
specific state, it is not an intrinsic element of the state, since territorial
divisions mainly reflect the balance among the relevant powers in any
historical epoch.

A given state's population, in any society that has developed beyond tribalism, consists of a multiplicity of collectivities. Although
social groups in any society could be divided along different lines (i.e.,
linguistic, ethnic, or racial), the Islamically significant and politically
relevant element of social differentiation is the ultimate purpose that
brings the community members together and unites them with one another. The organization of purposes attains its highest expression in the
state, the central organization of any society. The cohesion of collectivities is maintained by a system of norms (normative system) that determines the socially acceptable behavior of individual members.

Likewise, the cohesiveness of the state is guaranteed by a political consensus *(ijma')* on a set of principles and values which constitute the fundamental law of society.

The Nature of State Power

The state is not the only organization of purpose in society, and state law is not the only system of rules. However, what distinguishes the state and its laws from other social associations and norms is the supremacy it enjoys over all other social organizations and the overriding power of its rules. As the bearer of political power in a specific society, the state is endowed with the authority to regulate all forms of association and determine the general social and economic conditions which have a direct bearing on the quality of life in that particular society. The authority of the state, society's central organization, signifies the recognition by individuals as well as social groups of its right to regulate social behavior, and hence, the citizens' obligations to comply with state regulations. The state's ability to enforce its decisions, and hence ensure conformity, is crucial for the integrity of the political community and the functioning of society. The state's failure to enforce law or implement public policy is a signal that the political community is on the verge of disintegration or that the social order is about to collapse.

We need not conclude, however, that force is all that the state requires to ensure compliance, for after all, its authority is contingent upon the support and cooperation of a significant portion of the active social forces of society, i.e., a system of purposes representing the normative foundation of state law. Political authority, on the other hand, represents the system that brings about the realization of dominant social purposes.

In other words, force is a necessary but insufficient condition for enforcing the law, unless the state is willing to use brute force against defiance and dissension. The state is unlikely to be able to effectively enforce a law when a significant proportion of society is vehemently opposing it. Its coercive power is needed, under ideal conditions, only to deter and punish those individuals whose unprincipled egocentricity drives them to violate the rights of others and ignore the demands of justice. "Ideal conditions" refers to the availability of two elements: a general consensus over the fundamental values of society (i.e., the conception of the desired society to be realized) and a political authority representing society's common interests and working for their realization. Therefore, in the absence of a set of fundamental values unanimously accepted by the majority of society to guide and enlighten the decisions of political leaders, and of a political leadership providing a true representation of society's common interests, law may well become an instrument of exploitation and repression. Furthermore, in the absence of a true moral commitment on the part of society's members, the state's coercive power cannot be employed as a substitute for the self-motivation required for the realization of social goals.

Political Consensus *(Ijma` Siyasi)*

It is conceivable that a system of rules, including the Islamic legal system, could be maintained through the excessive use of naked and brute force, at least for a while, against the will of the state's population. A stable and effective order, however, requires the masses' cooperation and support. The imposition of a legal system by a powerful group on the rest of society through the use of violence would inevitably lead to the alienation of other social groups, giving rise to animosity, and would eventually lead to disorder and violent confrontations. The effectiveness of the Islamic order and the stability of the state therefore require political consensus *(ijma` siyasi)*.

The concept of consensus *(ijma`)* was regarded by classical jurists *(al-fuqaha' al-usuliyun)* as the fundamental principle which confers legitimacy on the state. Al-Juwayni, for instance, contended in his book *Ghiyath al-Umam* that political legitimacy could not be derived directly from any textual source, since a firm textual statement *(nass qat`i)* was lacking. Consequently, political legitimacy had to be achieved through the principle of consensus:

> The question of *imamah* should not be sought in the rules of reason, but should rather be subordinated to textual evidence *(dalil nassi)*. But since no specific Qur'anic statement exists (on the subject), and a confirmed tradition *(khabar mutawatir)* is lacking, the validation of the doctrine of *(imamah)* falls under the principle of *ijma`*.[26]

In their attempt to develop a model of legitimate authority, classical jurists confined the exercise of consensus to the first generation of Muslims. The limitation placed on the principle of *ijma`* was not induced by constraints provided by the Shari`ah but by practical considerations stemming from historical conditions. The principle of *ijma`* itself, devised by earlier *fuqaha'* was employed for the purpose of establishing the authenticity of statements and practices attributed to the Prophet and his Companions. Malik and al-Shafi`i, for instance, respectively defined *ijma`* as the consensus of *ahl al-Madinah* (people of Madinah) and the consensus of the *ummah*. The principle was later used as a means for substantiating the rules of the Shari`ah arrived at through individual *ijtihad*.

In the absence of definite *dalil nassi* concerning the form and scope of government, the first generation's consensus on a specific method of selection for the head of state reaffirms the idea that the *ummah* is the source of political power and legitimacy. The consensus of the Companions on certain political institutions and practices does not give these institutions and practices an absolute legitimacy; it only shows that the early Muslims were able, using their fallible judgment and contemplating the particular conditions of their society, to agree on a set of mechanisms for the selection and exercise of political authority.

But if the principle of *ijma`* is the basis of political legitimacy, the question arises as to what are the proper ends of consensus? Consensus occurs when all members of a community unanimously agree on the meaning or desirability of certain issues. Since unanimity on all questions confronting the community is virtually impossible, the objects of consensus should be narrowed down to those which are fundamental for the realization of the Islamic order and relevant to the goals and proper functions of the state. What we need to achieve is a consensus on the basic parameters which permit the individual to lead a meaningful life while respecting the moral integrity and collective well-being of the community.

Before delineating the area of essential consensus for establishing a viable Islamic political order, we need to recognize that consensus is a multidimensional concept involving three distinct areas of agreement – agreement over the basic values and principles of the desired order: (a) value consensus *(ijma` qimi),* therefore, represents an agreement on the general purpose of the state and the essential moral foundations of social life. Since disagreement is bound to arise within the general framework of value consensus, a society will need to establish mechanisms which permit a peaceful resolution of social conflict; (b) regime or procedural consensus *(ijma` ijra'i)* represents an agreement on political processes and institutions; and (c) even after agreeing on the political regime or the structure of authority, a society must agree on the scope of authority, i.e., the limits to be imposed upon the exercise of political power. We will call this final area of agreement policy consensus *(ijma` siyasi).* The three areas of consensus are respectively discussed below under the headings purpose, organization, and power of the Islamic state.

The Purpose of the State in Islam

We saw in the previous section that value consensus refers to the general agreement between social groups over the purpose of the state. In this section we will turn to the fundamental question: What is the proper purpose of the Islamic state? To begin with, the Islamic state is not a political community whose population is mainly composed of Muslim individuals, but rather one whose legal order is based on and derived from the principles of the Islamic law.

This should not, however, be interpreted to mean that the Islamic state's purpose is to impose a narrowly defined code of behavior on society. Far from it. Religious autonomy and toleration of differences in beliefs and doctrinal commitments are established Islamic principles. Both the Makkan and Madinan Qur'anic revelations ascertain in unequivocal terms the principle of religious autonomy.[27] The principles of religious freedom and confessional diversity were respected by the *ummah* throughout the better part of Muslim history. Differences in belief were tolerated by Muslim governments throughout history. The right of non-Muslim minorities to express their beliefs and practice their own legal codes was given full recognition.[28] Likewise, doctrinal differences among ideological and doctrinal groups were for the most part respected and kept out of the state's domain. Incidents involving the violation of religious and doctrinal tolerance represented the exception rather than the rule. As we saw in the previous chapter, al-Mamoun's efforts to bring the state into the doctrinal domain were resented and condemned by the majority of the *ummah*, and the practice was quickly abandoned by the rulers who succeeded al-Mu`tasim.[29]

The purpose of the state is not to impose Islamic teachings on society, but rather, to establish the general conditions that will facilitate the realization of the human mission *(khilafah)*. It is important here to distinguish between the role and purpose of the Islamic state and those of the *ummah*. While the latter purports to foster the Islamic character and help the individual grow morally and spiritually, allowing him/her to define his/her role and objectives in life within the general framework of the Shari`ah, the former attempts to coordinate the activities of the *ummah* in ways that will enable a society to cope with economic and political challenges and to enhance the quality of life in the community.

The distinction between the roles and purposes of the *ummah* and the Islamic state should not be taken to mean that one could be isolated from the other. Both are closely interconnected, and the functional existence of one presupposes the other. The creation of the Islamic state presupposes the emergence of a society committed to Islamic principles and norms; in a word, it presupposes the existence of the *ummah*. On the other hand, although the *ummah qua* the moral Islamic order could exist and has existed without an Islamic state, the creation of the state is imperative if the *ummah qua* the legal Islamic order is to be realized. As such, the Islamic state is indeed a supreme moral goal, because Islamic moral life can never be complete in the absence of the Islamic state. The Islamic state, being the political dimension of the *ummah*, comes into existence when the *ummah* becomes centrally organized for the purpose of pursuing Islamic goals and ideals. Yet the purpose of the state, as the moral expression of the higher objectives of the Shari`ah, transcends the domain of the Muslim community to encompass the whole of humanity. The humanistic and global purpose of the state is derived from the overall purpose of the Shari`ah, as it is expressed in different parts of the Qur'an and articulated by eminent Muslim scholars.[30]

The Organization of State Power

Historically, classical scholars and jurists *(al-`ulama' wa al-fuqaha' al-usuliyun)* endorsed the caliphate as the only legitimate institution for the *ummah's* governance. Though rejecting the concept of divine commission advanced by Shi`i jurists, classical scholars looked at the first political system, the consultative caliphate, as a model from which they derived their theories and argumentations.[31] The first model of Islamic government existed during the reign of the four rightly-guided caliphs who succeeded the Prophet. During this period, the Muslim community was involved in the selection of its leader either directly or through its local leaders. The selection *(ikhtiyar)* of political authority, however, was transformed gradually during the reign of the Umayyad dynasty from the community at large to an increasingly smaller group of Muslims, and was eventually confined to the ruling family and a few other influential government officials. Al-Baqillani (d. 403/1013) summarizes the views of the major political groups of his time on the selection of the leader:

> There is disagreement also on the method whereby the imamate is established, whether it is by designation or by election. The vast generality of our associates and of the Mu`tazilah, Khawarij, and the Najjariyah hold that the method of its establishment is by election on the part of the community, through the exercise of responsible judgment *(ijtihad)* by those qualified to do so and their selection of one who is fit for the office.
>
> . . . there is a further disagreement among the partisans of election as to the number of actual electors of the leader. Al-Ash`ari held that the imamate is validly contracted on behalf of one who is fitted for it by the contract of a single pious man who is qualified to exercise *ijtihad*. . . . the Zaydi and certain of the Mu`tazilah held that the least number . . . is two persons of piety and *ijtihad*. . . . Al-Qalanisi [an Ash`ari contemporary] and those of our associates who follow him hold that the contract . . . is validly made by the ulama of the community who are present.'[32]

Despite the fact that the caliphate had become a hereditary system after the establishment of the Umayyad dynasty, it was never sanctioned or recognized as such by Muslim jurists. They maintained that the leader could be either elected *(ikhtiyar)* or designated *(`ahd)* and that the selected head of the community should meet certain physical, moral, and intellectual requirements. Al-Mawardi (d. 450/1058), for instance, predicated the foregoing two modes of selection on the practice of the Muslim community during the time of the four rightly-guided caliphs. He based the election of the leader on the precedent of the choice of Abu Bakr (the first caliph) by election and that of Omar (the second caliph) by nomination. Al-Mawardi also stated that the leader should receive confirmation *(bay`ah)* from the community or its representatives as it was practiced during the early caliphate. This practice was modeled after the *bay`ah* of al-Aqabah, in which people expressed their allegiance to the Prophet and acknowledged his commission and leadership."

Classical jurists divided the selection process into two stages: nomination and confirmation. While most leading jurists and schools of law agreed that the leader may be nominated by one competent individual, they differed as to what constituted confirmation. However, the widely accepted proposition was that it was the right of the community, through its local leaders *(ahl al-hall wa al-`aqd)* and scholars (ulama)[33] to confirm the leader. Muslim scholars disagreed, however, on the number required for the nomination stage and how the people of *ikhtiyar* were to be chosen. The vast majority of classical jurists settled for the number one. They, nevertheless, insisted that this one person could not be chosen arbitrarily, but that he had to represent and be supported by the majority of society:

> I contend that if Omar's nomination of Abu Bakr had been challenged by others; I would have argued that the nomination (of the head of state) by one individual was insufficient (under the circumstances). Similarly, if the nomination by two or four was challenged by many others, it would not have been binding. But when Omar made the *bay`ah* others followed suit, (eventually) the community declared its allegiance (to the new caliph).[34]

Although the model adopted by classical jurists was designed to correspond with the practice of the Prophet's Companions, it was evidently founded on the belief that the *ummah*, being the bearer of divine revelation, was the ultimate source of political power and that the community's approval of the head of state was essential for the legitimation of state actions. Clearly, the political model of the Islamic state is secondary to the principle which justifies it, and it should, therefore, be modified and even changed when it fails to realize the principle which justifies its existence. In fact, classical jurists and the Muslim community before them were willing to endorse different variations of the model so long as these variations continued to reflect the fundamental principle.

Two questions regarding the method of selection went unanswered by classical jurists. The first question had to do with the nature of the *ahl al-hall wa al-`aqd,* and the other with the mechanisms to be used in the confirmation stage of elections. Classical jurists were content with spelling out the basic qualifications that the *ikhtiyar* people had to meet while overlooking the important question of how these individuals were to undertake their extremely important tasks. This was probably due to the fact that there was then no urgent need to clarify this question, for by the time classical jurists developed the *khilafah* theory, political power was practically under the tight control of powerful families and clans. Evidently, the *ahl al-hall wa al-`aqd* was not conceived of as a clearly defined body with formal duties, but rather as a group of influential persons interacting loosely among themselves. As a system of representation, the *ahl al-hall wa al-`aqd* could be reduced to one person whenever the choice made by this one individual reflected the will of the *ummah*. The number had, however, to be increased until this body became reflective of the entire *ummah*:

> We consider that one person should be sufficient (for the selection of the leader) so long as this individual is obeyed and esteemed (by the people) and so long as his inclination to one side coincided with the inclination of the masses. . . . But if achieving this objective (popular support of the leader) required that two or three persons (should agree), then their agreement is necessary.[35]

The Scope of State Powers

Historically, classical jurists gave the head of state a wide array of executive powers, including an indefinite term of office, unlimited appointive power, and tight control over all appropriations and the budget. The head of state was indeed supreme on the executive side, but he was never an absolute ruler. Beyond his executive supremacy, he was subordinate to the Shari`ah and limited by its rules and principles. The Shari`ah was the ultimate source of law, and both the community and the jurists acted as a check on the ruler. Ordinary members of the Muslim community were able to curb the ruler's power in their capacity as trustees of the divine revelation, and believers were religiously obliged to obey the ruler only so long as he abided by the Shari`ah's rules. Jurists could also act as a barrier to the ruler's abuse of power because they were seen as the repository of knowledge and the only segment of society which had the capacity to interpret the law.

Furthermore, not only did the ruler lack any legislative power, but his influence over the judiciary as well as educational and social welfare institutions was minimal or nil. Judges who were appointed by the caliph had to apply civil and criminal codes developed by the jurists, whereas schools, universities, and social welfare institutions were completely independent from government control and were run by both private citizens as well as the ulama. Notwithstanding the tremendous power which the *ummah* and the ulama exerted over the government, their influence remained informal and loosely channeled to the political system; indeed, both failed to transform their political function into that of well-defined and organized institutions.

In short, the power to enact law (i.e., legislative power) remained historically in the domain of the *ummah*. Admittedly, the head of state and his ministers could occasionally establish public rules, but these rules were more like executive orders than laws, and they had to conform to the rules of the Shari`ah developed by Muslim jurists in order to be considered valid by the community.

In recent years, contemporary Muslim leaders and intellectuals have started to call for the establishment of legislative bodies, stressing the need to add a legislative function to the state. It is argued that the witholding of legislative power from the state was understandable when political power was usurped by tribal dynasties. But an elected government should be entrusted with the responsibility to legislate, instead of keeping this important function unorganized.[36] Some prominent scholars have even argued that since the purpose of the state is to implement the Shari`ah, and since the Shari`ah addresses various aspects of life, the Islamic state is in a sense totalitarian.'[37] Such statements underscore confusion between the concept of *ummah* and that of state, a confusion that mistakes the role of the *ummah* as the moral manifestation of the Shari`ah with the role of the state as the bearer of political power. However, the distinction between the roles of the state and those of the *ummah* should not be interpreted to mean that the political is to be separated from the moral; far from it. From an Islamic perspective, the political and the moral are inseparable. The Islamic state, as we saw earlier, presupposes the existence of the Islamic normative order, i.e., the *ummah* with its unique set of values and beliefs whose realization requires the establishment of specialized political organs. The distinction is rather one of scope and degree. That is, state activities are distinguished from social activities in that they reflect a commitment to the higher objectives of the Shari`ah and, consequently, a broader basis of consensus.

The difference between commitments associated with the *ummah* and those identified with the state can be better understood by considering the structure of the Shari`ah. The Shari`ah's rules may be divided into three categories: (a) rules identifying moral principles and personal obligations. These mainly involve teachings intended to promote individual character and to help the Muslim grow spiritually and hence improve his/her relationship with his/her Creator *(akhlaq* and *`ibadat);* (b) rules intended to regulate individual behavior in respect to other members of society. These include rules regulating interpersonal relations among the members of society *(mu`amalat);* and (c) rules intended to regulate individual behavior in relation to society as a whole. These are essentially general guidelines outlined in broad terms. Many of the rules in this area fall within the realm of the Shari`ah known as *masalih mursalah* (public good). Rules of this sort are subject to reasoned judgments in line with the guiding principles of the Shari`ah. It is only this last category of rules that should be delegated to the state.

Personal and interpersonal rules should fall under the control of the *ummah*, because individual character and morality can be better influenced by inspirational and educational means, while personal exchange should be regulated by communities because it is subject to local considerations. Only intergroup behavior and questions concerning the general well-being and quality of life in society should come under the state's control.

Whereas economic and contractual relations involving members of the community should be left to the *ummah* and civil society in general, economic and contractual relations involving classes[38] of citizens must be regulated by the state so as to prevent the formation of a closed economic elite and to ensure that public resources are equitably distributed among the society's members. The state's authority to regulate intergroup economic and contractual relations is derived not only from its overall responsibility to ensure that social relations are structured pursuant to the principles of justice and human dignity, but is also prompted by Qur'anic injunctions which emphasize fairness, decency, and compassion.[39]

Conclusion

It is argued in this chapter that the Islamic state should be identified with two elements: the system of rules that determines intergroup activities and the general social and economic conditions, as well as the political organs necessary for the realization of Islamic ideals. A distinction is made between the Islamicity of the state and the legitimacy of state power. The former is connected with the source of law, the latter with the source of authority. The state is Islamic insofar as its rules and laws are based on and derived from the principles of the Shari`ah. The legitimacy of the state, on the other hand, depends upon the extent to which state organization and power reflect the will of the *ummah*, for as classical jurists have insisted, the legitimacy of state institutions is not derived from textual sources but is based primarily on the principle of *ijma`*.

It is further argued that a distinction should be drawn between the role and purpose of the Islamic state and those of the *ummah*. The latter purports to facilitate the moral and spiritual growth of the individual and to provide the environment that would allow the individual to define and then realize his/her role and objectives in life within the general framework of the Shari`ah, while the former aspires to establish the general conditions that would enhance the quality of life in the political community.

The distinction between the role and purpose of the state and those of the *ummah* translates into two distinctive spheres of moral and social responsibility. On the one hand, control over personal and interpersonal behavior should be localized; decisions regarding interpersonal social and economic activities should be handled by local communities, and hence should fall under the domain of the *ummah*. The state, on the other hand, should focus on global questions concerning the quality of life in society as well as intergroup activities.

II.   Visions of Reform

INTERLUDE II

Visions of Reform

There are too many visions competing for the future of Middle Eastern society. Despite the diversity of the views and blueprints offered by contending social groups, they can be reduced to two main visions: Islamic, informed by Islamic tradition, and secularist, inspired by Western experience.

The Islamic-secular dichotomy greatly simplifies the complexity of the ongoing struggle for the soul of Middle Eastern society. Still, the dichotomy is very useful, because it highlights the nature of the tensions that drive sociopolitical developments in the Middle East. As we saw in the previous chapters, the labels of Islamic (traditional) and secular (modern) are exceedingly misleading when they are understood through a process of analogy with Western traditionalism and secularism. For here, "Islamic" need not denote a desire to maintain traditions, and "secular" does not necessarily connote liberal, democratic, or pluralist commitments.

The above paradox makes any attempts to employ conventional language and terms to understand the Middle East prone to misunderstanding and misjudgment. The Middle East must be understood through its own language and terms.

In the next two chapters, I examine two main visions competing for defining and redefining the modern Middle East. I argue that the two visions, the nationalist-secularist and moralist-Islamist, suffer from serious partialities and inconsistencies, as each seems to evolve in the process of negating the other. The end result has been a developmental process in which the modern is detached from its historical foundation that forms the moral/affectional basis of Middle East consciousness, while the later is unable to benefit from the achievements of modernity.

CHAPTER 3

Competing Visions of Reform

For almost two centuries now, development has been one of the most pressing questions confronting Middle Eastern leadership. Since the Ottoman sultan Salim III introduced his modernization program, many models and projects aimed at bringing about better social, economic, and political conditions have been produced.

In this chapter I examine the two contending models of development in Muslim society: the secular and the Islamic. The examination is done with the aim of discovering the historical patterns that govern the process of social change in Muslim societies. I contend that while the dominant Islamic model of development draws on the Qur'anic model, it fails to study the history of human development in order to gain further insight into the phenomenon of progress. The chapter concludes that while moral reform is essential to social progress, genuine progress requires, as well, intellectual and organizational development. Thus any project of development, which neglects to recognize the dialectical relationship between the psychological, cultural, and material aspects of social life is bound to fail in achieving real progress.

Historical Patterns of Islamic Reform

Like all other religions, Islam brought an essentially moral message with far-reaching social implications. The message of Islam soon captured the imagination of the people of Madinah, and transformed the otherwise marginal community into a center of growing Islamic civilization that lasted for over a millennium, and exceeded in its expansion, resilience, and achievement all previous civilizations, including the Roman.

Although the causal linkage between Islamic reform and Islamic civilization cannot be denied, the patterns of progress from the moment of initiating the reform to the moment of reaching the climax of Islamic civilization are quite complex. While providing a detailed account of this process is beyond the scope of this study, identifying the general profile of early Islamic development is useful for the purpose of understanding the general patterns of the rise and fall of the Islamic civilization. The following four points underscore some of the essential patterns of the rise of Islamic society.

First, Islamic Revelation rejected the polytheist beliefs and values of Arab pagans, and promoted a pure form of monotheism that emphasized equal dignity of all peoples, individual moral responsibility, the rule of law, and social justice.

Second, by committing people to egalitarian values and social justice, Islam reformed both individual actions and societal institutions. Further, Islam set the foundation of a multicultural and multireligious society by recognizing the moral and legal autonomy of an ethnic and confessional community. We return to examine communal pluralist society in chapter 4.

Third, by freeing people from superstition and social bondage, and by mobilizing individual and collective energies and channeling them toward productive and creative activities, Islam established the psychological and societal conditions conducive to progress.

Fourth, in building a distinctively Islamic civilization, Muslims did not start from scratch, but built on the achievements of earlier civilizations. In natural science, technology, commerce, and administration, Muslim physicists, technicians, traders and administrators appropriated many of the theories, techniques, and practices developed and perfected by earlier civilizations.

The foregoing patterns of change suggest that while Islam was the major source contributing to the value-orientation of Islamic civilizational action, technical rules were borrowed, with some modification, from other civilizations. However, as the process of civilizational exchange progressed, it gradually proved to be problematic, especially in these areas where the value orientation and technical orientation of action could not be easily distinguished. To illustrate this point, I will single out two areas in which Muslim failure to develop technical rules capable of actualizing the Islamic values was decisive in relegating these values into the realm of pure theoretical discussion.

Distortions in the Political Sphere

Political organization is the first area where Islamic values were compromised due to the absence of practicable rules or structures. The Qur'an established the principle of *shura* (consultation) as the cornerstone of political decision-making within the *ummah*. Similarly the Prophet of Islam, and later his Companions, exemplified the principle of *shura* in their practices. Gradually, however, the practice of *shura* was undermined, and was eventually abandoned as the Muslim community embraced the hereditary model of political organization during the reign of Mu`awiyah bin Abu Sufyan. Historically, the establishment of hereditary rules was attributed to Mu`awiyah's desire to maintain the caliphate within the Umayyad branch of Quraysh. While this may or may not be a true assessment of Mu`awiyah's psychological disposition, the eclipse of the practice of *shura* from the early Muslim society should be initially attributed to the inability of the early Muslims to institutionalize the principle of *shura*. In other words, Madinah's leadershihp role was destabilized due to the Muslim community's inability to institutionalize the principle of *shura* in ways which would have given the provincial Muslim leadership equal access to the decisioin-making process. This led to a state of anarchy and disorder, thereby justifying the imposition of the monarchical rule for maintaining order.

Indeed the Islamic leadership continued, throughout the *Rashidun* (the rightly-guided caliphs) period, to deal with the emerging problems of a vast state by using decision-making procedures borrowed from the Arab tribal system. Thus, the caliph at Madinah depended exclusively on the *Muhajirun* (Makkah immigrants) and *Ansar* (Madinah natives) leaders, while provincial leaders were excluded from such important decisions as selecting provincial governors. The exclusion of Muslims residing outside Madinah from decision-making led gradually to a widespread discontent, culminating in civil disturbance during the reign of the third caliph, `Uthman bin `Affan.

While the interpretations of the nature of the armed conflict which plagued the Muslim community after the assassination of the third caliph may vary, one aspect of the conflict is quite clear, viz., the march from the provinces was instigated by the desire of the provinces to have more control over their own affairs, including the selection of provincial governors.[40]

The conflict quickly escalated into a civil war due to the absence of established procedures for a peaceful resolution of the conflict that erupted between the central government and the provinces.

. . . And in the Scientific Sphere

The field of scientific research is the second area where Islamic values were undermined because Muslim scholars failed to maintain appropriate technical rules for their actualization. In their drive to perfect the natural sciences and their technologies, Muslim scholars studied works produced by previous civilizations, most notably the Greek and Hellenistic. But because Greek sciences and technologies were not completely isolated from Greek values and beliefs, the interaction between Greek and Islamic cultures led to the emergence of the science of *Kalam,* a science whose main aim was to defend and purify the Islamic faith from Greek influences. But rather than limiting its purification efforts to the normative aspects of Muslim culture, *Kalam* scholars ended up condemning all sciences which were rooted in Greek civilization, including natural sciences.

Historically, the tension between the Islamic-rooted and the Greek-rooted worldviews was manifested in the clash between Muslim theologians *(mutakallimun)* and Muslim philosophers *(falasifah).* As a result of this clash, the *Mutakallimun* gradually developed an antagonistic outlook toward natural (or rational, to use their own term) sciences. This antagonism is apparent in the writings of eminent Muslim scholars, such as al-Ghazzali or al-Shatibi. Al-Ghazzali's antagonistic attitude toward natural sciences is revealed in his important work *Tahafut al-Falasifah.* Al-Ghazzali set out in this work to demonstrate the impossibility of grounding metaphysical knowledge in purely rational arguments. And as far as this objective of his work was concerned, he was quite successful. Although he did not intend to refute physical (or rational) sciences, and cautioned against any attempt of such refutation on the basis of semantic disagreement over the usage of certain terms, or on the basis of apparent disagreement between Qur'anic statements and physical knowledge, he ended up undermining the foundation of physics, i.e., the principle of causality.[41]

Al-Ghazzali denied the necessity of causal connections among natural phenomena, attributing the regularity of natural behavior to customary habituation *(`adah).*[42] Evidently, his rejection of the principle of causality was motivated by his fear that one's belief in causality would undermine one's faith in God as the ultimate author of all things. As Ibn Rushd was able to demonstrate, while accepting the necessity of causal relations need not lead to undermining one's faith, as long as the human mind is capable of accepting a necessary connection willed by the divine, the rejection of the connection between cause and effect is bound to undermine the very notion of reason, and to reduce the scope of science to science of divinity.[43] While understanding the full ramifications of the *mutakallimum-falasifah* schism falls outside the scope of this study, it is important to realize here that by undermining causality the *mutakallimun* destroyed the foundation of rational sciences; hence science was gradually reduced to legal science, while non-Shari'ah sciences were valued only insofar as they directly contributed to advancing Shari'ah sciences. This legalistic tendency, i.e., the equation of science with legal science, is apparent in the writings of leading Muslim scholars who were influenced by the Ash`ari system. This legalism can be discerned in the writings of al-Ghazzali himself. In his *al-Mustasfa*, al-Ghazzali divided sciences into three categories: rational *(`aqli),* narrative *(naqli),* and rational-narrative, and declared the rational as useless. As he put it:

> Sciences are of three types. Purely rational, which Shari`ah does not encourage or require, such as arithmetic, geometry, astronomy, and the like. These sciences [may be divided, in turn, into] useful but based on false speculation, and sometimes speculation is sin; and into useless, though it may be predicated on reason ... [The second type is] purely narrative, like Hadith, or *Tafsir,* or rhetoric *(Khatabah).* . . . Finally the noblest of sciences is the one that combines both the rational and narrative, and joins both opinion and Revelation, and the sciences *of fiqh* and its principles and of this kind.[44]

The antagonistic attitude toward rational sciences, which we can discern in al-Ghazzali's works, was elevated into an intellectual principle in al-Shatibi's writings. In discussing the fifth prelude in his *al-Muwafaqat,* al-Shatibi declared that "discussing a matter which does not lead to action is a discussion of something the Shari`ah does not approve."[45] He went on to explain his statement by arguing that studying all kinds of objects for the purpose of gaining knowledge is something that Muslims should reject and avoid because it is contrary to the Sunnah. He further proclaimed that these kinds of research were the "practice of the philosophers who are condemned by the Muslims."[46] Anticipating that his argument could be objected to on the basis that Islam requires learning and sciences, he claimed that this requirement was limited to the learning and study of questions connected with action.[47]

Culture-Structure Interplay

We saw in the foregoing section that the relationship between the theoretical (ideal) and practical (actual) aspects of collective life is such that the ability of Islamic principles and values to shape actual practices of society is limited, first, by the availability of practical means for their implementation, as well as the development of social structures which permit their institutionalization, and, second, by their interpretation and systematization into a comprehensive set of beliefs and values.

If the foregoing analysis is correct, then sources of civilizational decline cannot be confined to moral corruption, but should include also distortions in the original worldview which brought social and material advancement in the first place, as well as the failure on the part of the intellectual and political leadership to translate ideals and principles into workable models and effective institutions. Therefore, an effective project of development should take note of the close interrelationship among three strata of social life, alluded to earlier: the psychological, the cultural, and the material. That is, for material development to take place, a set of cultural and psychological conditions must be obtained first.

Psychologically, in order for the peoples' energies to be channeled to develop their social and material environment, three conditions must be met: (1) their actions must be oriented toward work, both mental and physical; (2) they must be willing to postpone immediate gratification, so as to reinvest part of what they produce to further develop and perfect their act of production; and (3) they should have a firm belief in the positive values of innovation and creativity.

Culturally, a number of sociocultural conditions must prevail in order for the psychological orientation of individual members to have a significant effect. These conditions which are aspects of social morality that foster an atmosphere of social trust and cooperation include: (1) mutual respect manifested in toleration of differences in interpretation and strategy; (2) political order conducive to meaningful popular participation, as well as self-criticism and self-correction; (3) a just and efficient system of law to command the respect of the majority of people; and (4) vibrant intellectual and scientific movements.

The intimate relationship between the theoretical and practical aspects of social life, alluded to above, means that the development of the practical (e.g., organizational, economic, etc.) cannot be attempted apart from that of the theoretical (e.g., moral, intellectual, etc.). Indeed, the slow pace of progress in many Muslim countries should be, at least partially, attributed to the failure of political and intellectual leaders to appreciate the dialectical relationship between the development of the cultural and structural levels of social life. A comparative study of the strategies of the two main forces in Muslim societies, the secularist and the Islamist, can show that while the secular and Islamist projects stand in direct opposition in terms of the substantive issues, both approach the issues of their concern with the same one-sidedness which emphasizes one aspect of social life at the expense of the other. Therefore, secularists seem to be consumed with structural, procedural, and organizational change, while Islamists are completely devoted to the moral, the legal, and the confessional.

Decoupling Civilization and Culture[48]

The debate and conflict over developmental approaches in Muslim societies may be traced back to the early years of the nineteenth century, when political and military leaders at the highest levels within the Ottoman ruling circles felt the need to reform military institutions along with educational and administrative systems.

Up until the eighteenth century, the Ottoman Empire was considered a Great Power, with a formidable military capacity and vast territories, stretching over the bulk of Eastern Europe and the Middle East. Yet by the end of the eighteenth century, it became apparent that the Empire was on a course of rapid decline. The state of decline was felt by sultan Salim III (reigned 1789-1808), who was especially concerned about the deteriorating conditions of the Ottoman army, and the decline in the Empire's capacity to meet military threats from the rising European powers, most notably the Russian Empire. The modernization of the Ottoman army was completed during the reign of Salim III's successor, Mahmud II, who utilized the services of West European military officers to restructure the Ottoman army.

The efforts to modernize the military were not confined to those of the sultan at Constantinople. Muhammad Ali, the ambitious governor.[49] Egypt, shortly followed in the footsteps of the Ottoman sultans, embarking on a project of military modernization. Muhammad Ali began his efforts to build a modern military force by hiring ex-officers of European armies, mainly French and Italian. He established several military academies to teach modern military doctrines and techniques, and built a new industrial base to supply the military with modern weaponry systems." However, he went farther than the Ottoman sultans when he decided to send missions of Egyptian nationals to receive training in Europe. He started sending students in small groups to receive training in Italy as early as 1813. The first large mission, consisting of forty-four students, was sent to France in 1826. This unprecedented move to send Muslim students to study in the West encouraged the Ottoman sultan Salim II to follow suit, sending Ottoman nationals to study in Western Europe, mainly in Prussia.[50] Undoubtedly, sending Muslim students to the West marked the beginning of profound cultural changes in Middle Eastern society.

Although the early reforms led by the Ottoman sultan and his governor were directed almost exclusively toward the military establishment, the two Muslim rulers soon realized that to keep the Ottoman military forces competitive with their European rivals, they had to introduce modern sciences to the educational system, and hence decided to establish technical schools to teach pure sciences, such as mathematics and physics, since these sciences were excluded from the curricula of regular schools. Evidently both Muhammad Ali and his patron were driven toward reform by the desire to maintain or expand their power base. For not only were their reformist efforts directed, almost exclusively, at the military and the bureaucracy, but they showed no interest whatsoever in social and political reform.[51]

Yet despite the many precautionary measures taken by the Ottoman rulers' to confine modernization to technical spheres and safeguard the

Empire against European cultural influences, the separation between the technical and cultural spheres of Western civilization proved untenable. Quickly, European ideas, customs, and habits began to penetrate the Ottoman society, creating social divisions and cultural tensions. Cultural tension and polarization became increasingly evident when those who received training in Europe came back to assume leading positions in the Ottoman bureaucracy. Having been exposed to a superior civilization, the European-educated students were deeply impressed by the advanced political and social institutions of Europe, and by the vigor and skills of Europeans.

The first Muslim intellectual to point out the flaws of the Ottoman and Khedivate project of modernization was Jamaluddin Afghani. While emphasizing the need for developing the scientific and technological capacities of the Muslims, Afghani realized that scientific development could not be achieved merely by training Muslims to use Western technology. For technology and scientific innovations are but artifacts, reflecting the ethos of a people and their philosophical outlook. What was needed by the Muslims to progress was a new spirit and direction. As he put it:

> If a community did not have a philosophy, and all the individuals of that community were learned in the sciences with particular subjects, those sciences could not last in that community for a century. . . . The Ottoman government and the Khedivate of Egypt have been opening schools for the teaching of the new sciences for a period of sixty years, and they are yet to receive any benefit from those sciences.[52]

Afghani ascribed the Muslim failure to catch up with the West in science and technology to their deficient outlook and faulty perspective, arguing that Islam had created in the early Muslims the desire to acquire knowledge. Thus, they quickly assumed a leading role in scientific research, first by appropriating the sciences of the Greeks, Persians, and Indians, and later by moving these sciences to new frontiers.[53] He accused contemporary Muslim scholars (ulama) of wasting time and energy on trivial matters, instead of addressing the important questions and issues of the time.

Evidently, Afghani, along with those who supported his reformist project, most notably Muhammad Abduh and Muhammad Rashid Rida, believed that genuine technological and economic reforms must be combined with cultural reform. People's attitudes and conceptions have to be reformed if the locus of the organizational and technological development was to be located within the Muslim society itself. Afghani endeavored, therefore, to combat fatalism, which plagued the majority of Muslim societies by the turn of the nineteenth century. It was widely accepted then that Muslim decadence was natural, as it reflected an advanced stage in the continuous moral decline since the time of the Prophet. It was also believed that this trend was inevitable and beyond human control.[54] Afghani rejected this interpretation of history, which was advocated by traditionalists, insisting that Muslim decadence has been precipitated by moral and intellectual decline, and that the superiority of the West, and its triumph over the Muslims, was a temporary stage in the continual struggle between the East and the West.

The reformist school put the blame for Muslim backwardness in particular on Muslim scholars, traditionalist ulama. Afghani, for instance, argued that the ulama, rather than providing strong leadership for the community, had become obstacles hindering its development. By dividing the universal nature of science into Islamic and European subdivisions, the ulama had deprived the *ummah* of technology, allowing the West to surpass the Muslims in military capacity. "Ignorance had no alternative but to prostrate itself humbly before science and to acknowledge its submission."[55]

Similarly, Muhammad Abduh held the ulama responsible for the Muslim decline by failing to confront the serious problems facing the *ummah,* and to enlighten the people as to how they can go about solving them.[56] Even worse, the ulama adopted a fatalistic outlook, believing that nothing can be done to overcome the plague encompassing the Muslim community. Abduh explains:

> Those idle and stagnant say, repeating the saying of the enemy of the Qur'an: the end of time has arrived, and the day of judgment is about to start, and that corruption which has befallen the people and the recession which has inflicted religion are only signs of the age. It is, therefore, useless to work to [rectify these deviations], for all efforts [in this regard] are fruitless, and all movements [in this direction] are pointless.[57]

The fatalistic attitude of Muslim scholars was reflected in their resistance to innovation and creativity, and their blind adherence to their forefather's opinions. By raising the early generation of Muslims to the level of sanctity and infallibility, and resorting to all repressive measures to combat original minds,[58] the traditionalist ulama prevented contemporaryy Muslims from resorting to original reasoning and inhibited fresh readings of the divine revelation. Abduh went farther to openly accuse traditionalist ulama of being the enemies of Islam; they kept the Muslims weak by depicting natural sciences as perverted, admonishing Muslims to refrain from learning them. "The truth is where there is proof," Abduh wrote, "and those who forbid science and knowledge to protect religion are really the enemies of religion."[59]

But rather than bringing about an Islamic reform, the critique of Muhammad Abduh led to strengthening the forces of secularization in

Egypt. This is due mainly to the fact that the work of Abduh helped reveal the flaws of the traditionalist models without offering an alternative. His students and followers, including Sa`d Zaghlul and Mustafa Kamil, substituted Western models for the traditional.

The Nationalist-Secularist Model

The secular model of development is epitomized in the work of Taha Hussein. Hussein, and other secularists, shared the reform school's belief in the need for cultural reform in order to achieve organizational and technological development. His solution, however, was not geared toward developing contemporary social forms on the basis of Islamic principles and norms, but to wholeheartedly embracing Western forms and institutions. To achieve this objective Hussein endeavored to prove that Egypt belonged culturally to the West, and to deny the significance of Islamic influence on Egyptian society.

In *Mustaqbal al-Thaqafah fi Misr,* Hussein set out to demonstrate the Western nature of the Egyptian culture. Stressing historical continuity and the interrelationship between past and future historical conditions, Hussein wrote: "I do not want us to contemplate the future of culture in Egypt except by reflecting on its distant past, and near present. Because we do not want, and cannot afford, to sever linkage between our past and present."[60]

To demonstrate that the Egyptian culture was historically part of the European culture, Hussein argued that Pharaonic Egypt was in harmonious relationship with the "Western" nation of Greece, while it was engaged in a bloody conflict with the "Eastern" nation of Persia.[61] He pointed to the cultural exchange that took place between the Egyptians and the Greeks during the reign of Alexander the Great. "The Egyptian mind, during the reign of Alexander," he contended, "influenced, and was influenced by, the Greek mind, sharing many, if not all, of the latter's characteristics."[62] This is what happened in the distant past, but what about the near past? Hussein recognized that Pharaonic civilization was superseded by over one millennium of continuous Islamic civilization, but rejected the notion that the Islamic culture had restructured the Egyptian mind. He rather contended that just as Christianity was forced to readjust to fit into the European culture, failing thereby to reshape the European mind, which continued to be faithful to its Greek roots, Islam was also compelled to change so as to conform to local cultures, thereby failing to change the Egyptian mind, or for that matter, what Hussein called the "Mediterranean mind." "If it is true that Christianity did not change the European mind, and was not able to deprive it of its Greek heritage, or strip it of those characteristics it acquired by being part of the Mediterranean region, it should be [equally] true that Islam did not change the Egyptian mind, or the minds of other Mediterranean people."[63] Hussein conceded that most Egyptians saw themselves as part of the East, not only the geographical, but the cultural as well.[64] He, however, dismissed this belief as a misconception, arguing that religious similarity among Middle Eastern societies can be the "basis of economic exchange, is not sufficient to be a basic of cultural unity."[65]

Hussein returned from the distant past to the present to find that the old close ties between the Egyptian and European society have been renewed in the last few decades. He noted that the Egyptians have copied the European life in all aspects.

> Europe built railroads and telegraphs and telephone lines, so did we. Europe uses tables [for dinning], and produces [different kinds] of dining wear, utensils, and food, so do we. We have gone further to emulate Europeans in their clothing, and even their lifestyle, without being selective or cautious; nor have we distinguished between what is good and what is not, nor what is appropriate and what is inappropriate [when emulating the European]. Our political system is purely European, we have copied it from Europe without being cautious or hesitant.[66]

If the Egyptian society had already become in practice a European society, as Hussein asserted, why is it necessary, then, for him to prove the obvious? Hussein realized that the Europeanization of the Egyptian society was incomplete. For one thing, only the "upper" social classes *(al-tabaqat al-raqiyyah)* had been Europeanized, while the vast majority of Egyptians had not. But for another, Hussein recognized that the development of the upper classes, and the Europeanization of the Egyptian society, and by implication, of other Middle Eastern societies, had been superficial. What had been Europeanized is people's taste, not their intellect. They had acquired European appetite, but not the European assertiveness, creativity, productivity, or scientific curiosity. Even the parliamentary system and the democratic rule, a source of great pride to Hussein, which he thought were so entrenched in society that no Egyptian would be willing to give them up,[67] were after all not so deeply rooted in pre-1950 Egypt. Hussein himself was allowed to live enough to see Egyptian democracy vanishing in the air in 1952.[68]

Be that as it may, Hussein contended that Western culture remained at the surface, unable to penetrate deep into the heart of the Egyptian society, because Egyptians have been reluctant and selective in adopting European culture. In order to reap the fruits of modern civilization, Egyptians would have to follow the example of the Japanese, who, although exposed to Western civilization for a shorter period of time, stand today on equal footing with the West, because they have not been hesitant in adopting Western ideas and practices.[69] In short, to stand on competitive ground with the Europeans, the people of Egypt, Hussein contended, have to become Europeans themselves; they have, that is, to embrace the European culture in all of its aspects, both the "good" and the "bad."

> The road to [civilization] cannot be traveled on empty words, super-
> ficial semblance, or compromised positions. The road is rather
> straightforward, with no alternatives. The road is this: we have to fol-
> low in the footsteps of the Europeans, and adopt their ways, in order
> to become their equals; we have to become their partners in modern
> civilization], in its good and evil, in its sweetness and bitterness, in its
> attractive and repulsive aspects, and in its elements which can be
> celebrated and those which should be faulted.[70]

The model of modernization *qua* Westernization was carried vigorously by almost all Muslim secular regimes that had dominated Muslim
societies since the middle of this century. The result has been a very slow
pace of material growth without development. Surely, for all appear-
ances, life in most Muslim capitals seems to be as modern as it is in
Western capitals. But beneath the facade of modernity lies an eerie emp-
tiness. For as soon as one delves deeply to examine modern practices,
one finds that Muslim elites have acquired only Western taste, but not
Western industriousness and creativity. That is to say, Muslim elites'
interest in modernity lies for the most part in consuming modern goods,
and imitating Western lifestyles. Even when one encounters modern institutions and technologies in Muslim societies, one finds them lifeless
and dysfunctional. Hence, only the procedural element of vote-casting,
but not the spirit of popular political participation is shared by parliamentary systems in most Muslim countries and their Western counterparts.
Although factories may produce products similar to those manufactured
in developed societies, the technologies and the innovative ideas behind
them are made abroad.

The failure of the secular project of modernization lies primarily in
the fact that secular elites thought they could impose Western culture and
practices through an act of bare force. They failed to understand that the
mode of change lies ultimately in the psychological and cultural aspects
of society, which can only be influenced through an open debate aimed at
persuasion, and not through compulsion and harassment.

The Moralist-Islamist Model

It was against the background of the violent model of secularization
that the current Islamic model of development emerged and matured. The
model of change, which continues to be dominant within the rank of
Islamists, is epitomized in the writings of Sayyid Qutb. Qutb organizes
his system of ideas around three key concepts: *"jahili* society," "Islamic
society," and "the Islamic vanguard." He contends that all societies could

be subsumed under one of two, mutually exclusive, societies: Islamic and *jahili*. Qutb developed the concept of *jahiliyyah* or *jahili* society, to analyze modern society and expose its shortcomings and deficiencies. The term *jahiliyyah* was first introduced in the Qur'an in reference to the faithlessness of the pre-Islamic Arab society and its ignorance of divine guidance. Sayyid Qutb, however, adapted the term and gave it a new definition. According to Qutb, the *jahili* society is one that has been established on rules, principles, and customs that have been founded by man without regard to, or in ignorance of, divine guidance. In such a society, Qutb argues, man's unrestrained greed and self-aggrandizement become the overwhelming forces that dominate social, economic, and political relationships among its members, leading to injustice and exploitation of some persons, classes, races, or nations by others.

> *[Jahiliyyah]* roots are in human desires, which do not let people come out of their ignorance and self-importance, or in the interests of some persons or some classes or some nations or some races, whose interest prevails over the demand of justice, truth and goodness.[71]

Islamic society, on the other hand, is based on harmony between God and man, and the unity of religious and sociopolitical principles, and on man's duty to his fellow man and his duty to God. Qutb defines Islamic society as one in which Shari`ah rules, and where Qur'anic and Prophetic injunctions are observed and practiced.

> [The] Muslim community does not denote a land which is the abode of Islam, nor is it a people whose forefathers lived under the Islamic system at some earlier time. It is the name of a group of people whose manners, ideas and concepts, rules and regulations, values and criteria, are all derived from an Islamic source.[72]

But how does this process of resurrection of Islamic society begin? How can *Islam replace jahiliyyah*? Qutb's answer was that bringing an Islamic society to life requires the emergence of an Islamic vanguard.

The transformation of the *jahili* society to an Islamic one is not a natural process that takes place apart from human efforts, Qutb stresses. Nor is it a supernatural process carried out directly by divine power in isolation of human agency. Rather, changing the prevailing conditions from *jahili* to Islamic is a long and tedious process that requires the struggle of the Muslim masses. The struggle to establish an Islamic society, Qutb contends, should be initiated and led by a vanguard. The vanguard must confront the *jahili* society on two levels: theoretically, by refuting the ideas and arguments of the *jahiliyyah* and exposing its corruption; and practically, through a well-organized movement, equipped with all the strength it can acquire, to combat a powerful *jahiliyyah*.

When *jahiliyyah* takes the form, not of a 'theory' but of an active movement in this fashion, then any attempt to abolish this *jahiliyyah* and to bring people back to God, which presents Islam merely as a theory, will be undesirable, rather useless. *Jahiliyyah* controls the practical world, and for its support there is a living and active organization. In this situation, mere theoretical efforts to fight it cannot even be equal, much less superior, to it.[73]

What is troubling about Qutb's model is that it reduces the problems facing the Muslim society to a simplistic struggle between good and evil, faith and infidelity, or morality and immorality. These problems no longer appear as cultural and civilizational problems, resulting from a drastic decline in the intellectual, industrial, and organizational capacities of the Muslim people, alongside the moral decline in the Muslim character. With Qutb, the problems of the Muslim society became exclusively moral problems, and could be solved simply when a significant number of people declare their commitment to the "Islamic worldview."

Qutb went further to redefine the terms "development" and "underdevelopment," and to introduce new criteria for advancement and progress. A developed society, Qutb insisted, is not a society that is on the cutting edge of material production, but one which displays moral "superiority." A society, which is high on science and technology but low on morality, is backward, while a society, which is high on morality but low on science, and material production is advanced. By so defining the question of development, Qutb was able to take away the guilt associated with underdevelopment, and provide a quick fix to a seemingly complex and intricate situation. The feeling of relief and self-confidence was obtained, however, at the expense of sacrificing clarity and sound judgment. As a result, many Islamist groups began to see their role in terms of converting the *jahili* society to "Islam," and engaging in a fierce, and frequently bloody struggle with political authorities. Advancement and progress are no longer to be accomplished solely by emphasizing science, industry, innovation, education, and social reform, but rather through revolution.

While the currently dominant Islamic model draws its conception of reform from the Qur'anic framework of historical change, the model is completely oblivious to the interconnectedness between the moral sphere and other spheres of collective life. Thus, the dominant Islamic model articulated by Qutb separates moral development from material advancement, while portraying social change in terms of growth in the number of individuals who renounce their allegiance to *jahili* society and declare their commitment to Islam.

The simplistic nature of the model stems from the fact that it neglects to study the impact of social structure on the process of institutionalization of moral principles. The advocates of the model failed to take note of the structural differences between the society that witnessed the early institutionalization of the Islamic ideals and the one in force today. As a result of this ahistorical approach to understanding social change, the dominant model almost completely ignores the need for identifying the patterns of historical change, so as to develop a model that allows organizational and technological development, along with the moral one.

Conclusion

We saw early in this chapter that the contemporary historical experience of the Muslim society has demonstrated the futility of bringing about real progress by concentrating on the structural and material aspects of social change, *à la* the secular model. However, contemporary experience also shows the impossibility of changing society by focusing on the moral sphere of individual life, *à la* the moralizing model embodied in the dominant Islamic approach. Both contemporary and historical experiences of the Muslims show that piety and good will do not suffice by themselves for building an advanced social life capable of fulfilling the requirement of *khilafah*. For while moral commitments are essential to progress, they have to be supplemented by scientific, technological, and organizational skills.

The complementarity of moral and technical elements of social life reemphasizes the importance of our observation that Islamic civilization was developed by building on the accomplishments of earlier civilizations. That is, cultural exchange and civilizational appropriation have always been essential aspects of human progress. And so while a people cannot advance its material conditions merely by learning technical skills from others, it cannot, by the same token, bring about order and progress by asserting its moral commitment to a higher vision.

The challenge before the Muslim society today is to produce a developmental model capable of integrating the moral and technical elements of collective life, while taking into account the specificities of the structural and organizational aspects of contemporary society.

Chapter 4

Arab Nationalism:
Forging a New Political Identity

The tension between indigenous modes of thinking that have been influenced by the Islamic historical experience of Arab societies on the one hand, and ideas developed by the modern West on the other, is epitomized in the efforts to restructure the foundation of political unity in the Arab world after the collapse of the Ottomans. Arab nationalism, and the forging of Arab nation-states, was presented as the only viable alternative to the communal pluralist system, better known as the millet system, which held sway for centuries in the Middle East.

A product of Europe's historical experience, nationalism found its way to the Muslim world and gained many adherents and advocates. The nationalistic mindset has become an intrinsic part of the political thinking of many Muslim individuals and groups. As a result of the discontinuity in historical political thinking and practice affected by the European cultural and political domination of Muslim life for the last two centuries, many Muslims are unaware of the political structures which existed – albeit in rudimentary, distorted, or compromised forms – before Western penetration.

In this chapter, I will discuss the origin and development of the concept of nationalism, and contrast it with the communal pluralist system that existed during the Ottoman period. I argue that nationalism is a European phenomenon invented by German intellectuals and employed by Prussia in order to bring about a united German state. Its adoption by Arab nationalists to bring political unity to the Arab region was ill-conceived. I conclude by discussing, in general terms, the model of communal pluralism that flourished under the system of caliphate that lasted for over a millennium in the region.

European Roots of Arab Nationalism

The conceptual framework elaborated by Arab nationalists to justify a new political order based on nationalist ethos was borrowed from the nationalist ideas advanced by German nineteenth-century philosophers, most notably J. G. Herder and J. G. Fichte. Two Arab intellectuals exerted far-reaching influence and were instrumental in the formation of the nationalist movement in the Arab World: Sati al-Husari and Michael Aflaq.

Al-Husari's theory of Arab nationalism was a replica of the one advocated by Herder and Fichte. In a lecture delivered in 1928 before the Baghdad Teacher Club, Baghdad, Iraq, he discussed at some length the basis of Arab nationalism, addressing the question: "What are the elements that comprise nationalism and constitute a nation?" His answer was short and straightforward: "unity of origin and stock."[74] Al-Husari argued that "unity of origin" does not mean unity based on blood relations or pure ethnicity, for such purity could not exist in modern times. Rather, "unity of origin" refers to affinity inspired by shared outlook and mindset.[75] What is important, therefore, is not the actual "unity of origin," al-Husari contended, but rather the mere belief in this unity. The belief in the unity of a people is, however, not purely ideological, for its bases are embedded in society itself, and these bases, he argued, are two: the commonality of language and history.[76] Language is the spirit of a nation, he insisted, because by establishing communication within a linguistic group, it brings them together and prevents their dissolution in other groups. History, likewise, is the memory of a nation and its consciousness. The commonality of historical experience gives the people who share this experience a distinct national character.

Eager to transcend the Ottoman experience, he insisted that "Muslim unity" cannot replace "Arab unity," for history shows that Muslim unity failed, under the Abbasid Caliphate, to unite all Muslim peoples under one political banner.[77]

Al-Husari's arguments for a nationalist foundation of Arab political unity recall those of Herder and Fiche. Herder advanced the notion that God intended the world to be composed of diverse cultural groups, each of which would have its own unique national character. Therefore, he concluded, it was the duty of the members of the various cultural groups (or nations) to preserve their unique national heritage and to make sure that the cultural qualities of their groups remained pure. Since the preservation of the community's national character is possible only when the nation in question is ruled by a national government, Herder theorized, the realm of the state must coincide with that of the nation. Multinational states were thus unnatural, not because Herder feared that one nation may dominate another, but rather because states containing more than one nation posed a threat to the principle of diversity. Nations that were politically united under one state risked losing their national identity and, hence, of being extinguished.[78]

Fichte, following in Herder's footsteps, proclaimed that the German people constituted one nation and that the German nation had to be ruled by one sovereign state. In the play *Patriotism and Its Opposite*, published in 1807, Fichte expressed his nationalist sentiments through one of the play's characters. "Understand me rightly," the character says. "Separation of the Prussians from the rest of the Germans is purely artificial ... the separation of the Germans from the other European nations is based on Nature."[79]

In the same year, Fichte delivered a series of lectures in Berlin in which he called for the unification of the German-speaking people into one independent state. Fichte was addressing his Prussian audience at a time when the German people where divided into numerous states and municipalities. "The German-speaking parts of Europe had the most diverse political arrangements, and the fact that Prussians and Bavarians, Bohemians and Silesians all spoke German was not considered a great political moment.[80]

It was natural for the Prussian proponents of nationalism to chose linguistic ties as the criteria of nationhood, for their dream was to unite all German-speaking peoples under the leadership of Prussia. Herder, and later Fichte, insisted that language was not simply a means of verbal and written communication; it was rather the repository, as it were, of a people's national character and heritage. The way individuals think and perceive the world was determined, to a great extent, by their language.[81]

By inventing a political doctrine connecting language and political divisions, Prussian nationalists found a powerful way to get back at the Austro-Hungarian Empire and to justify Prussia's expansion at the empire's expense. At the turn of the nineteenth century, the Austro-Hungarian Empire was the largest state in Europe, its rule extending over vast territories in central and Eastern Europe. This empire was composed of many different nations, and people who spoke German as their native language represented a significant portion of its subjects. The empire itself was ruled by the House of Hapsburg, a German dynasty dating back to the twelfth century, and was the main rival to the Prussian monarchy. It was also the major obstacle confronting the ambitions of a Prussia seeking to expand beyond its borders.

The nationalist ideology advanced by Prussian political philosophers was almost completely alien to the majority of Europeans living around the turn of the nineteenth century. Of course these people were aware of their ethnic and linguistic differences, but only a tiny minority of them would go so far as to equate ethnic and linguistic divisions with political divisions.

"A nation, to the French revolutionaries," argues Kedourie, meant a number of individuals who have signified their will as to the manner of their government. A nation, on this vastly different theory (i.e., the nationalist theory), becomes a natural division of the human race, endowed by God with its own character, which its citizens must, as a duty, preserve pure and inviolable. Since God has separated the nations, they should not be amalgamated. "Every nationality," proclaims Schleiermacher, "is destined through its peculiar organization and its place in the world to represent a certain side of the divine image."[82]

It is often argued that the nation-state system dates back to the Treaty of Westphalia, which, in 1648, ended the Thirty Years' War in Europe.[83] Yet on closer examination, one could see that this event did not establish a system of nation-states. Rather, it recognized the sovereignty of the state and its independence from papal authority. As Kedourie observed, modern proponents of nationalism tend to confuse the state with the nation, and hence use one to justify the other. Long after the Treaty of Westphalia was signed, Europeans continued to attach their loyalties to political and religious institutions rather than to their fellow nationals.

Up until the nineteenth century, Europe rarely had political divisions predicated on national identity. People's resistance and acquiescence to political orders had always been in response to state institutions and to the agitation of local leaders who had inspired them to support or oppose one dynastic rule or the other. The proponents of nationalism seem to forget that nations are the outcome of long and persistent efforts by established states governed by ambitious and calculating statesmen whose skills and policies, and frequently their luck, helped them expand their hegemony and prevent foreign encroachment into their spheres of influence.

Furthermore, the nation-state system allegedly established by the Treaty of Westphalia appears, under close scrutiny, more of a myth than a reality. Despite numerous wars, including two world wars, not all German-speaking people have been integrated into one united German nation. Substantial German populations still live in Poland, the Czech Republic, Hungary, and France, let alone Austria, whose population is overwhelmingly of German stock. On the other hand, many states in Europe and elsewhere continue to demonstrate, even in our own time, the futility of talking about a system of nation-states in any meaningful and coherent way. Multinational Switzerland, Turkey, and Canada could hardly be classified as nation-states.

Apparently, al-Husari, and other advocates of Arab nationalism, found a neat match between the formation of the German state on the ashes of the Austro-Hungarian Empire, and their drive to form Arab unity out of the fragments of the collapsed Ottoman Empire. He believed that with the collapse of the Ottomans, and the division of the Arab world into small territorial (*qutri*) states, the Arabs were in need of a new nationalist ethos to replace the Islamic ones that united them for four centuries with the Turks under the Ottoman state. They were in need, that is, of a nationalist ideology which could unite them together, and allow them to join the club of nation-states.

Al-Husari was especially inspired by the unification projects carried out successfully by German and Italian nationalists in the nineteenth century, and made his admiration explicit in various articles and speeches. In an introductory lecture delivered in Cairo before the faculty and student body of the then newly established Institute of Advanced Arab Studies, al-Husari told his audience that modern European states have all been established on what he termed the "nationalist principle," while the Arabs were divided into small fragments. "Why? Why have we been, thus far, lagging behind?" he asked and immediately went on to cite two reasons for the lack of national awareness and unity among the Arabs. First, Arab nationalism was always subdued throughout the Ottoman rule because of the Arabs' commitment to the "state of Islamic Caliphate."[84] Second, since the Arabs' early exposure to Western civilization was through their contacts with the British and French cultures, Arabs were influenced exclusively by the political ideas and practices of these two European cultures. Although the French and British were both well established powers, with global imperialistic ambitions, they disdained and discouraged nationalist ideas and sentiments so that other European nations would remain divided and be easily dominated. Ultimately, the "nationalist principle" triumphed, despite the resistance of the British and French, transforming both Italy and Germany into two great powers.[85]

The Romanticist Substance of Arabism

Arab nationalism emerged out of the immediate need and desire to fill the gap created by the collapse of the Ottoman Empire. Its early advocates adopted a model that did not fit well into the demographic and historical context of Arab society. In their zeal to invent a new ideology, Arab nationalists reverted to various tactics, including reinterpreting history and introducing romantic notions, remnants of European romanticism. Al-Husari, for one, insisted that unity of premodern Arab society was based on an Arabist rather than Islamic foundation. The Abbasid Caliphate, he contended, failed to unite all Muslims under one political banner.[86] Yet it could be shown that a consistent reading of Arab history does not allow any historical inference in support of Arab national unity. Al-Husari ignores, for instance, that the Abbasids were able to unite four Muslim nations (Arabs, Persians, Kurds, and Turks) while failing to unite all Arabs.

The romanticist tendencies of Arab nationalism can be seen very vividly in the ideas of Michael Aflaq, the founder of the Baath Party, one of the main political forces driving toward pan-Arab unity. In a statement addressed to the youth in 1940, Aflaq denied that the concept of Arab nationalism has its roots in the nationalist theory developed by German philosophers, arguing that "Arab nationalism is not a theory, but the source of all theories; nor is it an artistic expression, but art's spirit and source. It does not stand in opposition to freedom, for it is freedom itself."[87] He contended, likewise, that Arab nationalism required no rational justification, since it was, in the first place, a "sentiment" and "love," proclaiming that "he who falls in love does not search for the reason for his love. And when a person becomes incapable of love unless he can find obvious reasons, this clearly means that the love he once had in his heart has either diminished or vanished."[88]

Using the same romanticist tone, he equivocates in two separate statements made in 1950 and 1956 the meaning of the Baathist slogan: "One Arab nation with an eternal mission." This mission is in the first place, he argued, a faith and conscience. "The Arab mission," he proclaimed, "is faith, before being anything else. It does not diminish of its importance that faith is its deep core, for faith always precedes clear knowledge. And indeed there are things which are innate to humans, desiring no proofs or studies."[89] Aflaq, then, goes on to argue that the Arab mission, though eternal, is not fixed. In the past, the eternal mission was embodied in the moral values of Islam, values whose influence was deeply felt by non-Arabs as well. However, the mission of Arabs is no longer universal, but has to be understood today as a mission of a people unto themselves. He proclaimed that the Arabs' mission today is to form a united political community, with advanced social and economic structures.[90]

Among the most serious and profound challenges confronting the Arab nationalist movement has been the articulation of a vision capable of motivating its followers and providing the moral core to be shared by the Arab masses. Evidently, Aflaq was aware of this predicament, at least intuitively, and tried to address it by introducing notions such as the eternal mission of the Arab nation, as well as the Baath's cardinal objectives of "unity, freedom, and socialism." Aflaq recognized the importance of Islamic values in the historical unity of Middle Eastern society, but was ambivalent as to how those values can relate to a nationalist movement. He, thus, asserted that the Arab past, especially during its Islamic phase, cannot, and should not, be repudiated. It has inspired, and will continue to inspire the Arab spirit, and must be utilized to propel the Arabs forward. "The movement of Arab Baath inherits from Islam," he contended, "its renovative spirit and revolution against traditionalistic values. It also acquires from Islam the virtues of faith and excellence, and detachment from personal interests and earthly temptations."[91]

Yet Islam which inspired the admiration of Aflaq was a historical experience, a bygone glorious period in the history of the Arabs which they can recall with pride and which serves as an inspiration to them, but not as a set of living principles which may command the present or guide social progress toward the future. Islam, Aflaq insisted, played a leading role in the past, and should be praised and commended for that. But today, it is Arab nationalism, and only Arab nationalism, which may qualify as an ideology capable of leading the Arabs on the road to economic prosperity. As he put it:

> If we look at the Arab past, we find that religion was the driving force at the advent of Islam. . . . Economic reformation, then, was a consequence of deep religious faith. Today, however, nationalism is the driving force in this period of Arab life. And as the Arabs responded, in the past, to religious calls, and were, hence, able to accomplish economic reform, they can today achieve social justice, and equality among citizens, and can ensure freedom among all Arabs, by putting their faith in nationalism alone.[92]

Both al-Husari and Aflaq were oblivious to the impact of introducing nationalism into an essentially multinational society that historically developed under a system of communal pluralism. The impact of the new foundation of political unity on the numerous ethnic and religious groups that constitute Middle Eastern society was completely lost in the rush to find a new basis for unity borrowed from the experiences of other societies. In a national state, everyone has to observe one code of law and completely submit to the rules and regulations enacted by the national government. In such states, rules of law as well as political arrangements carry the imprint of the dominant ethnic group. Ethnic minorities are thus placed in an unfavorable condition; at best, they have to give up their historical identity (ethnicity, language, religion, etc.) or suffer alienation and oppression.

Nationalism, which rejects the coexistence of autonomous or semi-autonomous ethnic groups in the state, encourages national leaders to devise policies aimed at assimilating ethnic minorities in order to achieve national integration. This meant that ethnic minorities that have social and religious practices incompatible with those of mainstream society would have to give up their ethnic identity or become an outcast and undesirable social group. Thus Arabs, Kurds, and Armenians had to suffer under Turkish nationalism, while Kurds, Armenians, Turks, Berbers, Copts and other minorities were reduced to peculiar and underprivileged groups in Arab countries.

Communal Pluralism

In a diverse and heterogeneous society, one can recognize two types of minorities: ethnic and confessional. Ethnic minorities are subgroups distinguished from the dominant group by physiognomic, linguistic, or cultural characteristics. Confessional minorities, on the other hand, are subgroups distinguished by their values and ideologies, as well as the resulting practices. The classical Muslim world was divided into a multiplicity of confessional groups along ideological lines. Society was differentiated, under classical Islamic organization, into a dominant Muslim community and a variety of non-Muslim minorities. Each confessional community was allowed to maintain its own code of law and an autonomous local administration run by local notables and religious leaders. Confessional communities had, however, to declare their allegiance to the Muslim authorities and to pay an annual tribute in the form of poll tax *(jizyah)*. This pattern of communal pluralism was later adopted by the Ottomans and continued to be the basic social organization in the Middle East until the collapse of the Ottoman Empire in 1919.

Communal pluralism has been criticized for its tendency to revert to hierarchy. Rodinson termed this pattern of social organization as "hierarchical pluralism," since, despite their relative autonomy, confessional minorities were subordinated to the dominant Muslim majority.[93] Rodinson argues that under the communal system that prevailed in the Ottoman Empire (a similar system flourished in the Austro-Hungarian Empire), the central government was controlled by the Muslim majority. Yet he and other critics seem to forget that even under modern democratic systems, state institutions are usually run by members of the dominant social group. In those countries where the population is differentiated along religious lines (i.e., India, Pakistan, or Israel) the dominant religious group tends to control state institutions. Likewise, countries where ethnicity is the basis of social differentiation (i.e., Canada and England), the state is run for the most part by the ethnic majority. The difference between the communal and national systems, however, is that while in the latter the majority imposes its values and ideas on the rest of society, the former system protects its minorities from the majority's ideological and moral encroachment

The communal system that flourished under the Ottomans was not without its own problems. Yet the transformation from a multinational empire into a system of nation-states fashioned after the European model has proven to be disastrous. It is true that the Ottoman Empire's problems had become so large by the beginning of the twentieth century that one could hardly begin to imagine how they could be solved without dissolving the empire. Nevertheless, the creation of numerous nation-states out of the ruin of the Ottoman Empire did not solve the problems, but rather gave rise to a host of new problems that tended to exacerbate the ones already in existence.

In *The Making of the Modern Near East,* Yapp takes issue with the widely accepted description of the Ottoman Empire as the sick man of Europe. He argues that contrary to the claims of many Western historians, the Ottoman Empire was engaged in a process of profound reform. Yapp contends that some Western sources tend to perpetuate this image of the Ottomans for four reasons: (1) The Ottomans' image has been constructed mainly on biased information obtained from the archives of their enemies; (2) The Ottomans' history has been written by Christians who are either prejudiced against Islam or have little insight into the functioning of the Ottoman system; (3) Authors of books on the Middle East are committed to nationalism and liberalism and, therefore, have a negative view of multinational empires; and (4) Those Europeans primarily responsible for giving the final blow to the Ottoman Empire wanted to believe that it was doomed to extinction anyway.[94]

It is beyond the scope of this work to determine whether the Ottomans would have been able to reform their empire if the Allied forces had left them alone (I tend to think that the Ottomans were already on an irreversible course toward dissolution). I do think, however, that Yapp's last two points are relevant to this discussion. The British and French, prejudiced by their own nationalist and liberal thought, were neither able nor willing to recognize the incompatibility of the nation-state system and the social reality of the Middle East. In the following section, I will discuss the social structure of the Ottoman Empire and highlight the peculiar features of Middle Eastern society in general.

The Ottomans and Their Heirs

When Osman I (`Uthman) died in 1326, the Ottoman state was still a small but expanding municipality in Western Anatolia. In less than a century, this state expanded its hegemony into the Balkans and the greater part of Anatolia (Turkey proper). It was, however, not until 1453 when Muhammad II (known also as the Conqueror) seized Constantinople and made it the Ottoman capital that the Ottomans became a world power recognized and feared by the great powers of the time in the Christian West and Muslim East. Muhammad the Conqueror was, in addition to being a brilliant military leader, an astute statesman and gifted reformer. He is remembered not only for his military achievements but also for the many reform measures he introduced into the Ottoman system.[95] Having consolidated Ottoman control over the Balkans and Anatolia, he moved quickly to organize the state and codify relations between the capital and local communities and municipalities, a significant proportion of which were composed of non-Muslims.

The administrative system employed by the Ottomans was known as the *millet* system. This system did not originate with the Ottomans but was in fact borrowed from classical Islam. The term *millet* was derived from the Arabic word *millah,* meaning confessional community. Under this system, confessional communities were regarded as autonomous social units that enjoyed both administrative and legal independence.[96] In addition, Ottoman rulers introduced a series of regulations aimed at protecting peasants against abuse by the local authorities.

> To understand the superiority of the Ottoman to the local Balkan administrations one has only to compare Ottoman laws with the code of the Serbian monarch, Stephen Dusan. For example, Dusan's code required the peasant to work for his lord two days a week; Ottoman regulations required the *raeya* to work only three days a year on the sipahi land. Protection of the peasantry against the exploitation of local authority was a basic principle of Ottoman administration.[97]

Ottoman administration, with its tolerant attitude toward religious minorities and noninterventionist policy, was seen by local communities throughout the Balkans as a major improvement over the heavy-handed policies of their former patrons. The *millet* system of communal pluralism continued to function for almost five centuries, being abandoned only in 1909 by the Young Turks. The same system was later applied to the Empire's Arab provinces after the Ottomans incorporated Syria and Egypt, in late 1516 and early 1517, during the reign of sultan Salim II.

The Ottomans entered Syria in the latter part of 1516 after defeating the Mamluk army at Marj Dabiq, a site located to the north of Aleppo. After this decisive battle, in which the Mamluk sultan Qansaw al-Ghawri perished, the Ottomans were able to advance to Cairo, the Mamluk capital, meeting with only little if any resistance.[98] With the fall of Cairo, all of the Arab provinces under Mamluk control (including Arabia) became part of the Ottoman Empire. The new rulers recognized local authorities and, with the exception of a few minor changes, kept the internal organization of the various local communities intact. The Arabs did not seem to resent their new rulers partly because of the wide measure of local autonomy accorded to them, and partly because the Turks were regarded as Muslim *ghazis* (warriors) and champions of the Islamic cause. Furthermore, Ottoman strength assured the Arabs that they would be protected against internal disorder and foreign encroachment.[99]

Unlike Christians residing in the Balkans, Muslim Arabs had another reason for welcoming the new Turkish rulers. Being coreligionists, the Turks were willing to employ qualified Arabs in the administration of the state. Muslim Arabs played an important role under the Ottomans, especially in the judicial administration. Since a good command of Arabic was essential for mastering the Shari`ah, many judges, jurists, and legal scholars came from the Arabic-speaking peoples of the Ottoman Empire.[100] It was, therefore, only a matter of time before Arabs became partners with the Turks in running the state. Nuri al-Sa'id Basha, a high-ranking officer in the Ottoman army and later several times prime minister of Iraq, observed that:

> In the Ottoman Empire, Arabs and Muslims were regarded as partners of the Turks. They shared with the Turks both rights and responsibilities, without any racial distinction: the higher appointments in the state, whether military or civil, were open to the Arabs; they were represented in both the upper and the lower houses of the Ottoman parliament. Many Arabs became Prime Ministers, Sheikh-al-Islams, Generals and Walis, and Arabs were always to be found in all ranks of the state services.[101]

For almost four centuries, Muslim Arabs and Turks were bound together under the banner of Islam. Throughout this period, the question of Arab nationalism was never an issue. Although Arabs were aware of the fact that they were ethnically different from the Turks, they had never considered a specifically Arab nationalism as a political doctrine or a basis for political organization. The Turks themselves "made no attempt to assimilate non-Turkish elements in their Empire."[102] Pan-Arabism was mainly a reaction to the pan-Turanism movement that flourished after 1909. The beginning of a nationalist ethos among Arabs and Turks was the result of their exposure to European culture. Some Arab intellectuals, troubled by the continuous economic and political deterioration of the empire, came to see nationalism as a powerful tool that could be used to mobilize their fellow Arabs against the increasingly intrusive policies of the Young Turk leaders. In addition, such nationalism could also be used to justify the Arabs' secession from the Ottoman Empire. Arab nationalists eager to achieve independence from Istanbul apparently never considered the consequences of establishing national states in a region as non-homogeneous as the Middle East.

By the turn of the twentieth century, Middle Eastern society was already highly diverse and heterogeneous. Yapp eloquently describes the social structure of Ottoman society on the eve of the Empire's collapse. "Another valuable concept which has been applied to Near Eastern society," writes Yapp,

> is that of the mosaic. In this view Near Eastern society *is* seen as a mosaic of autonomous corporations existing side by side and not arranged in any particular order of eminence, or at least not an order accepted throughout the society. Government itself may be regarded as one such corporation and, like the others, [is] defined partly by inheritance and partly by function, the provision of defense and some modest administrative services.[103]

The Ottoman central government was only one of a multiplicity of organizations that permeated the Middle East. The state was not the monstrous apparatus it was depicted to be. On the contrary, the state had a minimal amount of control over the lives of individual subjects and interacted with them only indirectly through various local and regional intermediate organizations. Thus, the traditional image of an oriental despot presiding over the state, intruding into the lives of his subjects, and closely controlling their activities, was more of a fiction than reality.[104] Intrusion and tight control were introduced later by the Young Turks in their attempt to "modernize" state institutions by adopting nationalist policies. The Committee of Unity and Progress, a group of Ottoman nationalists that took charge after the abdication of `Abd al-Hamid II, the last Ottoman sultan, in 1909, opted for the Turkification of all non-Turkish provinces as well as the centralization of state institutions. It was the implementation of these developments that triggered Arab indignation and the subsequent Arab revolt.

Nation-States in Multinational Society

With the increased centralization of political decision-making under the Young Turk regime, Arab demands for political participation were intensified. The Young Turks were, however, reluctant to give Arab leaders a more active role in running the state and instead began implementing a new set of policies aimed at the Turkification of the Arab population'. These new policies met with strong resistance from the Arabs, and those Arab leaders who were alarmed by this new development quickly began mobilizing the Arab population against the Young Turk regime. Several clandestine organizations were formed in Lebanon, Syria, and Iraq.

Although Arab demands for reform were aimed initially at fixing abuses within the system, the reformist tone was quickly replaced by calls for an independent Arab commonwealth. Plans for joint action against the Turkish government were negotiated between local Arab leaders in Syria and Sharif Hussain, the governor of Makkah, on the one hand, and between the latter and the British authorities on the other. In 1909, Hussain's army, composed of Arab warriors and British soldiers, entered Damascus. Three days later, Amir Faysal, the son of Sharif Hussain, was declared king of Syria, thereby ending the Turkish rule of Arab lands.

Arab independence was encouraged by the Allies, especially England, which were in a state of war with the Ottoman Empire. Under the banner of self-determination, the Allies pledged to support the aspirations of all nations struggling for independence. The principle of self-determination was, however, one of those ambiguous concepts open to wide interpretation. Interestingly enough, "the pursuit of self-determination in 1919 produced a peculiar institution known as the mandate."[105] According to the mandate concept, the newly independent territories were to fall under the direct control of European nations until such time as the Arabs would be able to govern themselves. It appeared that the advocates of self-determination concluded that the Middle East's political boundaries and institutions had to be determined not by the inhabitants, but by the occupation forces of the Allies.

After the collapse of the Ottoman Empire, the former communal system (the millet system) was replaced by several nation-states fashioned after the Western liberal model. Ethnic minorities at first demanded equal treatment for all confessional groups, but soon realized that equal treatment required a uniform legal system applied to all communities equally. This meant that confessional communities had to give up their own systems of rules, which had been recognized and sanctioned by a higher law under the Ottomans, and submit to a homogeneous system determined by the dominant confessional community. Under the new system, confessional groups would be reduced into associations of groups sharing common values and views, i.e., to philosophical societies.[106]

In the absence of the former system of communal pluralism, which had prevailed for centuries in the Middle East, members of various minority groups began to recognize that the new system of nation-states would take away their autonomy and impose upon them a new legal system formulated by the dominant social groups.

> To an imperial government the groups in a mixed area are all equally entitled to some consideration; to a national government they are a foreign body in the state to be either assimilated or rejected. The national state claims to treat all citizens as equal members of the nation, but this fair-sounding principle only serves to disguise the tyranny of one group over another. The nation and all of its citizens must be animated with the same spirit.[107]

Conclusion

Historical evidence shows that nationalism derives from eighteenth- and nineteenth-century German philosophical thought. This doctrine was first used by German, and later Italian, nationalists to inspire their countrymen to bring about national integration. Arab nationalists adopted German ideas and implemented them to forge a new political unity after the collapse of the Ottomans.

Nationalism, through its rejection of the coexistence of autonomous or semiautonomous ethnic groups within the state, encourages national leaders to devise policies aimed at assimilating ethnic minorities in order to achieve national integration. This means that ethnic minorities having social and religious practices viewed as incompatible with those of society's mainstream must either give up their ethnic identity or become an outcast and undesirable social group.

As long as nationalism was exclusively confined to Western European states, all of which enjoy relatively homogeneous societies, its flaws and defects were not readily apparent. But even in Europe, nationalism was not free from defects: anti-Semitism in Germany and elsewhere in Europe was partially a consequence of nationalism. However, as soon as it began to spread to other parts of the world, especially those with highly mixed and diverse populations, its defects became extremely obvious. Arab nationalism, with its elitist and centralizing tendencies, set the stage for the politicization of ethnicity and religion in the Arab World. One consequence of the intrusive nationalist policies is the rise of political Islam, i.e., the employment of Islamic notions and concepts to counteract the secularist and nationalist policies of the modern Arab state, a question to which our attention will be devoted in the next chapter.

CHAPTER 5

Islamic Reform and Radicalism

For over a century now, Muslim intellectuals and activists have been attempting to revitalize Muslim society and establish Islamic rule. The century-long efforts have manifested themselves in a growing movement that aspires to replace the present sociopolitical system with a new one based on Islamic principles and ideals. Although the Islamic movement has yet not been able to achieve its goals, several indicators suggest that its popularity is on the rise. Does this mean that the movement is destined to attain the goal it set out to achieve? Given the setbacks the Islamic movement has been dealt in recent years, even in countries where Islamic parties claim strong popular support, it is too early to give a definitive answer to the above question. We can, therefore, do better by undertaking a critical evaluation of the objectives of the movement and the types of strategies employed to achieve these objectives, as well as the nature of the problems and difficulties it faces.

In dealing with these questions, equal emphasis will be given to both the theoretical framework of the movement and its operational activities. Three phases in the evolution of the movement will be recognized and discussed. As will be argued later, these phases have been colored by the ideas and thoughts of three eminent thinkers. The first phase was shaped by the writings of Jamaluddin Afghani, the chief agent in the inception of the Islamic movement in modern times. The second phase was influenced by the ideas of Hasan al-Banna, the founder of the Ikhwan movement. Finally, the third phase carries the imprints of Sayyid Qutb's revolutionary thoughts.

In discussing modern Islamic movement, the arguments will be confined primarily to the Islamic movement in Egypt. Egypt has been chosen because it is the country which has witnessed the creation and development of the first modern religio-political organization, which later became a model to be emulated by similar organizations elsewhere in the Muslim world; Egypt is also the country where a great deal of contemporary Islamic ideas have originated. Perhaps with the exception of Turkey's Islamists, the Islamic movement in Egypt may be regarded as a microcosm of the modern Islamic movements.

The underlying premise in this chapter is aimed at employing Islamic principles to construct a new reality for the modern Islamic movement, although its theoretical framework is transcendental in its nature and intent. The movement's operational activities have been the outcome of a dialectical process in which the transcendental ideas and views are confronted with, and compromised by, their antithetical traditionalist ideas. The latter aspires not to apply Islamic principles to a changing reality, but to recreate detailed historical models developed by early Muslims.

The term *modern Islamic movement* is used here to denote the activities of intellectuals and political activists who take Islam as a reference point and basis to analyze social problems and provide remedies for them. The movement emerged in the second half of the nineteenth century in response to European colonial powers, which had by then already captured parts of the Muslim world, such as Tunisia and India, and were persistently expanding their hegemony into the Muslim heartland. Since its inception, the movement has had to deal with two principal problems: Western colonialism and the shock waves it created throughout the Muslim land, on the one hand, and the backwardness of the Muslim societies which created the pervasive sense of helplessness and defeat that overwhelmed the Muslim masses, on the other.

Initially, the Western impact caused strenuous shock and almost complete confusion. However, Muslim intellectuals began to gradually develop new ideas and strategies to meet what they considered a cultural invasion and ideological menace threatening the very existence of Islam. The European triumph, Muslim intellectuals asserted, was the result of the gradual decline of Islamic values and practices. Therefore, independence and sovereignty, they proclaimed, could be achieved only when the Islamic spirit and ethos are restored to the Muslim community.

In addition to dealing with the effects of colonial rule, Muslim intellectuals have been concerned about the overwhelming sense of helplessness and defeat which permeated the Muslim world in modern times, and which was reflected in the passive and indifferent attitude of the average Muslim toward political participation, an attitude inherited from centuries of quietism. They stress that Muslim decline has resulted from the deficient doctrines and practices that prevailed during recent centuries. To deal with this problem, they provide a worldview that depicts history as a continuous struggle between Islamic and anti-Islamic forces, emphasizing the role of the believer in this struggle and the inevitability of the eventual triumph of Islam.

The ideological framework of the modern Islamic movement is for the most part revolutionary in its intent and approach. As does all revolutionary thought, it involves evaluation and assessment of the current society's nature and conditions, as well as a vision of a more promising one, and a strategy for the transformation of the former to the latter. Contemporary Islamic ideologies thus provide the Islamic movement with a goal and direction as well as a framework for analyzing and understanding state and society. The ideological framework as it stands today has been shaped for the most part by the ideas of three leading thinkers: Jamaluddin Afghani, Hasan al-Banna, and Sayyid Qutb. In addition to their political activism, these three Muslim intellectuals are distinguished by the new vision and insight they brought to the movement. Furthermore, the life of each of them can be seen as a turning point, marking the beginning of a new phase in the development of the Islamic movement in Egypt.

For the sake of simplifying an otherwise very complex movement, we divide the evolution of the Islamic movement into three phases: Intellectual, populist, and radical. The division of the growth of the movement into phases does not denote a complete and comprehensive transformation from one mode of thinking and action to another. Rather, each phase points to the emergence of new modes and approaches without negating earlier ones. Therefore, the radical phase points to the emergence of radical thinking and action without negating intellectual and populist tendencies. Indeed, radical groups continue to claim a small following today in comparison with intellectual and populist groups.

The Intellectual Phase

Afghani, the chief agent in the inception of the modern Islamic movement in Egypt, was born in 1839 at Asadabad, in Afghanistan. He studied Islamic sciences in different parts of Afghanistan, Persia, and Iraq.[108] When eighteen years of age, he went to India, where he was exposed to European sciences. Afghani led a highly active life traveling throughout the Muslim world and Europe, propagating his reformist ideas, and searching for fertile soil in which his ideas could flourish. He arrived in Cairo in March of 1871, where he stayed until his expulsion by Khedive Tawfiq in September 1879 because of his political activism. Despite the relatively short period of time Afghani spent in Egypt, he left a lasting impact, for his ideas were embraced and nurtured by Egypt's leading figures, the most prominent of whom was Muhammad Abduh.

Afghani, along with his eminent disciple Abduh endeavored to combat fatalism, which plagued the majority of Muslim societies by the turn of the nineteenth century. It was widely accepted then that Muslim decadence was natural, as it reflected an advanced phase in the continuous moral decline since the time of the Prophet. It was also believed that this trend was inevitable and beyond human control.[109] Afghani rejected this interpretation of history, advocated by traditionalists, insisting that Muslim decadence had been precipitated by moral and intellectual decline, and that the superiority of the West and its triumph over the Muslims, was a temporary phase in the continual struggle between the East and the West. He attributed Western military superiority to its scientific advancement, arguing that the French and English had been able to conquer Muslim lands not by virtue of being French or English, but because of their superior and more advanced scientific capabilities.[110] Furthermore, Afghani saw a positive aspect of the rivalry between the East and the West, contending that Western invasion of Muslim lands had a stimulating effect on the Muslims, and would eventually awaken them from the state of slumber that had dominated their lives for centuries.[111]

Afghani recognized, however, that scientific development could not be achieved merely by training Muslims to use Western technology. Technology and scientific innovations are but artifacts, reflecting the ethos of a people and their philosophical outlook. To make scientific progress, Muslims needed to adopt a new spirit and directions.

Afghani blamed the Muslims' failure to catch up with the West in science and technology on their deficient outlook and faulty perspective, arguing that Islam had created in the early Muslims the desire to acquire knowledge. He accused contemporary ulama of wasting time and energy on trivial matters, instead of addressing the important questions and issues confronting the *ummah*. He, therefore, called upon the ulama to probe into the causes of Muslim decline, instead of occupying their minds with minutiae and subtleties.[112]

Muhammad Abduh the most influential Egyptian scholar in the nineteenth and early twentieth century, joined his teacher in his attack on traditionalist ulama who depicted "European" sciences as perverted, and admonished Muslims to refrain from learning them. "The truth is where there is proof," Abduh proclaimed, "and those who forbid science and knowledge to protect religion are really the enemies of religion."[113] Abduh agreed with Afghani that the decline of the Muslim community stemmed from its deficient educational system, which discouraged rational reasoning and suppressed intellectual curiosity. He emphasized that such an educational system was incompatible with Islamic teachings, which honor reason to the extent of giving it the authority to judge the validity and truth of religious claims.[114]

But if the ulama were partly responsible for the decline of the *ummah*, the rulers also shared in this responsibility, for they had placed their self-interests before those of the *ummah*, and hence allowed the division of the Muslim world into small entities. It is incumbent upon Muslims by their faith, he asserted, to come together under one banner, and join forces to meet the challenge of imperialism. Afghani contended that the division of the Muslim world into small units defies the teachings of Islam, and thus should not be condoned by Muslims.[115] He placed the blame for the schisms and divisions squarely on the shoulder of Muslim rulers who, he insisted, deviated from the solid principles on which the Islamic faith is built and stray from the path followed by their early ancestors.[116]

The division of the Muslim world into small states, he maintained, was artificial, induced by the struggle for power among various rulers. As such, this division did not reflect the real sentiments of the Muslim masses that had been, on the contrary, united from the very beginning only by the bonds of Islam, disregarding any other type of bonds such·as race or ethnicity.[117]

The unification of the Muslim peoples under one Islamic government was Afghani's chief goal throughout his life. Establishing a unified Islamic state, he thought, could be the first step toward reforming the decadent conditions of the Muslims. He believed that such a state could revitalize the Muslim *ummah* and mobilize the masses to meet the European challenge. To achieve this goal, Afghani tried first to persuade the rulers of India, Persia, and Egypt, as well as sultan Abdulhamid, the head of the Ottoman state (with whom he had a close personal relationship) to Islamicize the practices and the policies of their governments. He soon realized that Muslim rulers were neither receptive to his ideas nor interested in Islamic reform. Gradually, he began to address his reformist ideas to Muslim intellectuals in particular, and the public in general. In 1879, he established the first Egyptian political party, which was known as al-Hizb al-Watani al-Hurr (the National Liberal Party). Evidently, Afghani's political activities invoked the wrath of Tawfiq, the Khedive of Egypt, who expelled Afghani from Egypt in the same year.[118] Leaving the country which provided him with his most receptive audience, Afghani spent two years in India before moving to Paris, where he was joined by Muhammad Abduh; together they established an Arabic newspaper called *al-Urwah al-Wuthqa* (The Indissoluble Bond). The newspaper was distributed throughout the Muslim world, especially in Egypt and India. Apparently, *al-Urwah* was also the name of a clandestine organization headed by Afghani himself. This organization helped in financing and distributing the newspaper, and was dedicated to two objectives: the struggle against imperialism and the unification of the Muslim community. The newspaper was forced to stop after publishing eighteen issues when the British authorities in Egypt and India enacted severe measures to prevent its distribution. For instance, the possession of one issue of the newspaper was punishable in India by £100 and two years' imprisonment.[119]

The government Afghani advocated was based on, and limited by, Islamic law. Under such government, the ruler was obliged to consult the *ummah* and to work toward promoting the common good.[120] The ruler's principal task was to safeguard the Islamic law.

> ... the ruler of the Muslims will be their religious, holy, and Divine law that makes no distinction among people. This will also be the summary of the ideas of the nation. A Muslim ruler has no other privilege than that of being the most ardent of all in safeguarding the sacred law and defending it.[121]

Afghani's concerns with political reform notwithstanding, his emphasis was primarily on educational reform as a prerequisite for any sociopolitical change. Ironically, however, most of those inspired by him were interested in political reform, and had thus paid little, if any, attention to reforming the ideas and practices underlying Muslim backwardness. Perhaps the only exception was Muhammad Abduh, who devoted the later years of his life to reforming religious ideas and practices, emphasizing education as the principal approach to social change.

The Populist Phase

The modern Islamic movement continued to be confined to intellectual circles up until the late 1920s, when Hasan al-Banna founded al-Ikhwan al-Muslimun (the Muslim Brethren). Al-Banna was a charismatic leader who received both traditional Islamic and Western education. From an early age, al-Banna was alarmed by the deteriorating conditions of the Muslims in Egypt and elsewhere throughout the world. He attributed the backwardness of Egyptian society in particular, and Muslim societies in general, to the spiritual and moral decline of the Muslim individual. Al-Banna, the chief ideologue of the Ikhwan, declared that the mission of his organization was to accomplish two objectives: the independence of the Muslim land from foreign domination, and the establishment of an Islamic sociopolitical system.[122] He believed that reviving and resurrecting the *ummah* must inevitably begin with the individual, stressing that those able to rebuild the Muslim community must have three qualities: spiritual strength manifested through the determination of the individual and his integrity and self-sacrifice, knowledge of the principles of Islam, and the ability to relate the Islamic principles to real life and apply them effectively to practical circumstances.[123]

In less than twenty years, the Ikhwan organization grew from a small association, in the city of Ismailiyah, to a major political power with numerous branches scattered throughout Egypt. Al-Banna employed an elaborate structure to organize the Ikhwan. The various Ikhwan branches in each province were headed by an Administrative Board *(maktab idari)* composed of the members of the Executive Council *(majlis idari)* of the central branch in a province, as well as representatives of all branches in that province. Administration boards were, in turn, connected together through the Ikhwan headquarters *(al-markaz al-`amm)*, located in Cairo. The headquarters was divided into a number of specialized committees and departments: General Committee, Education Committee, Department of Labor, Department of Scouting, Department of Propaganda, Department of Phalanxes, Department of Families, Department of Social Services, Department of Communication with the Muslim World, and Department of Muslim Sisters. The leadership of the Ikhwan was divided among three bodies: the Founding Assembly *(al-hay'a al-ta'sisiyah)* composed of one hundred members representing the various provinces and branches, (the Assembly was the policy-making body which set the general policy, of the movement); the executive power was assigned to the Executive Office *(al-maktab al-tanfidhi)*, which was composed of twelve members and headed by the Supreme Guide *(al-murshid al-`amm)*; the members of the Executive Office were selected by a special committee, which was known as the Membership Committee *(maktab `udwiyah)*. The committee was also responsible for investigating all charges made against the members of the Founding Assembly, and if need be disciplining them.[124]

To achieve the Ikhwan's goals, al-Banna called for a gradualistic approach in which the desired reform could be attained through three stages. First is the stage of communication and propagation, aimed at exposing the Egyptian society to the true Islamic principles. Second is the stage of mobilization and organization in which the movement would select and train its active members. Finally comes the stage of executing and implementing the Islamic rules and principles in which a society is completely transformed into an Islamic one.[125] Although al-Banna did not explicitly spell out the characteristics of each of these stages, or when and how each of them begins and ends, he stressed time and again that the Ikhwan had a long way to go before they could achieve Islamic reform, and that they were not interested in any revolutionary tactics. He also warned those among the Ikhwan who were looking for fast results that they would either have to learn to be patient and persevering or leave the movement.

> O Muslim Brethren, especially those of you who are impatient. Listen to these clear and blunt words I address to you from this platform in this spectacular conference of yours. Your plan has been determined step by step. I will not modify this plan after I have become quite convinced that it is the safest plan to follow. Yes, it might take a

longer time (to execute), but it is the only (effective) plan. Clearly, manliness manifests itself through patience, persistence, diligence, and hard work. So let those of you who are in a hurry to reap the fruits before they are ripe, or snatch the roses before they are fully grown, (know that) I do not agree with them in this respect, and that it is better for them to leave this movement and look for another (suitable to them).[126]

Indeed, during its early years, the Ikhwan movement, rejecting violence, adopted a peaceful approach aimed at the gradual reform of society through two types of measures. First, by propagating the Islamic message, and raising the consciousness of the people about current social and public issues; and by offering better solutions and alternatives. The Ikhwan therefore placed a great deal of importance on publication and issued a number of newspapers, magazines, and periodicals. The second type of measures employed by the Ikhwan for achieving reform included sponsoring social welfare projects, such as hospitals, schools, charities, clubs, and the like.[127] But within one decade the reformist tone of the Ikhwan was gradually replaced by a militant one. This was reflected in the statements of al-Banna and in the establishment of a paramilitary wing as well. In an editorial published in May 1938 in the first issue of *al-Nadhir,* a new weekly magazine of the Ikhwan, al-Banna stated:

Till now you have not confronted a political party or organization. You did not join them, either ... Your position was passive in the past. But today, in this new stage, it will not be that way. You will strongly oppose all of those, whether they are in power or not ... if they do not respond to you by accepting the teachings of Islam as their program for action... [The choice] is either loyalty or animosity ... It's not our fault that politics is part of religion.[128]

In another statement delivered before the Fifth General Conference of the Ikhwan, al-Banna made similar assertions.

... the time when you will have, O Muslim Brethren, ... three hundred phalanxes, each one of them equipped spiritually with faith and principles, mentally with science and culture, and physically with training and exercise; at that time ask me to plunge with you into the depth of the seas, to rend the skies with you, and to attack every tyrant; then God willing, I will do it.[129]

The Ikhwan's increasing militancy was also reflected in the establishment in 1940 of a paramilitary wing known as the Special Organization, sometimes referred to as the Secret Apparatus. Al-Banna named Saleh al-`Ashmawi as the first director of the Special Organization, and instructed him to recruit and train its members so they could carry out paramilitary operations in defense of the Ikhwan movement when they were called upon.[130] However the Special Organization was later to become a source of problems and devastation, rather than safety and security.

In January 1948, the government of Prime Minister Mustafa al-Nuqrashi, under pressure from the British government, which was alarmed by the rising anti-British sentiments and activities on the part of the Ikhwan, cracked down on the Ikhwan, closing their offices and publications and confiscating their properties. Twenty days later, al-Nuqrashi was assassinated by members of the Ikhwan. In a communiqué issued right after al-Nuqrashi's assassination, al-Banna strongly condemned the assassins and their act, proclaiming that they were neither Ikhwan nor Muslim. Yet two days after the Ikhwan leadership issued their communiqué, another Ikhwan member was apprehended while attempting to place explosives in the building housing the Court of Appeal. Henceforth, Ikhwan members were involved in a number of paramilitary operations including an unsuccessful attempt to assassinate the new prime minister, Ibrahim 'Abd al-Hadi (who escaped the attempt), the assassination of a senior judge in the criminal court of Cairo, and other violent acts.[131]

Apparently, these paramilitary operations were carried out by the Special Organization of the Ikhwan without the knowledge and approval of al-Banna, or any of the executive officers for that matter. In his memoir, Mahmoud Abd al-Halim, one of the early members of the Ikhwan and a close aide of al-Banna, narrated that Hassan al-Hudaybi, al-Banna's successor, once called him to complain about the Special Organization, and to ask him to intervene with their leaders. Addressing Abd al-Halim, al-Hudaybi said:

> I do not care about those Ikhwan who like to show off, nor those who are vocal and outspoken, nor those who are fervent and zealous. You may know that I first declined the Supreme Guide post because of these people ... I have learned later about the rebellion of the Special Organization against the movement. I also learned that a number of attempts to persuade them and curb their uncontrolled behavior have failed. I was about to resume my old stance (of refusing to be the Supreme Guide) – for I do not wish to be the head of a movement controlled by shadowy figures, threatening to destroy and shatter it apart ... had it not been for those who told me: give us time to call for a brother who is admired and respected by the members of the (Special) Organization ... then he added: ... (al-Banna) told me about the conversation between you and those Brethren, and how they eventually succumbed and ended their rebellion.[132]

It is clear from this passage that the formal organization of the Ikhwan had lost control over the Special Organization since it was headed by al-Banna, and that the latter continued to work independently during the time of al-Hudaybi. This situation continued to be a source of frustration for al-Hudaybi until he finally resigned from his post as the

Supreme Guide of the Ikhwan, after the unsuccessful attempt to assassinate Nasser in 1954, which was again blamed on the Special Organization. Reflecting on the sequence of events initiated by the assassination of al-Nuqrashi, one may conclude that the Special Organization was committed to a campaign of violence aimed at dismantling the old regime in spite of the strong objection of al-Banna. Abdul Halim described the reaction of al-Banna to one of the paramilitary operations carried out by Ikhwan members against the ruling regime; the operation was seemingly in retaliation for the government's harsh measures against the Muslim Brethren. According to this account, al-Banna is said to have compared the loyalty of these people to their movement to the loyalty of a bear to his trainer; to relieve the trainer from a fly that landed on his face while he was sleeping, the bear threw a rock that missed the fly but killed the trainer.[133]

The bloody confrontation between the monarchists and the Ikhwan finally culminated in the assassination of Hasan al-Banna by the Egyptian secret police in 1949.[134] Shortly before his assassination, al-Banna expressed his desire to withdraw the Ikhwan movement from the political arena and confine its operation to religious, educational, and economic activities, while allowing a number of outstanding members to engage in politics using the platforms of other political parties.

> The thought which occurred to me is that our organization should take upon itself the task of raising the standards of the community, religiously, socially and economically – neglecting the political aspects – and to permit outstanding members of the association to present themselves for the elections under the auspices of whatever political parties they see fit to join; provided that they do not join any one party and provided they undertake the spreading of the mission of the association within these parties.[135]

Generally speaking, although the Ikhwan's approach appeared to be for the most part peaceful and gradualistic, it was potentially violent. While Article IV, section 2 of the Ikhwan's 1945 basic regulations stated that "the Brethren will always prefer gradual advancement and development ..." several statements by the Ikhwan's leadership showed that they were inclined to resort to violence in such circumstances as those which transpired under al-Nuqrashi Pasha's government. Al-Banna, for example, clearly asserted that he would not hesitate to use violence if he were forced to do so, or when the Ikhwan were ready to seize power: "The Brethren will use practical force whenever there is no other way and whenever they are sure the implement of faith and unity is ready."[136] The ambivalent stance of the Ikhwan leadership gave confusing signals to the rank and file, leading some to take it upon themselves to carry out a series of violent attacks against the ruling regime, and perhaps believing that the monarchists' crackdown on their organization had left them with no other choice but to literally fight back.

Despite the Ikhwan's active involvement in Egyptian politics, al-Banna did not see his organization as a political party, but as a proto-type of an Islamic society. Nor did he consider the Ikhwan's political participation within the context of sharing power with other parties. Rather, he believed that it was imperative that the Ikhwan movement grew until it encompassed the entire Egyptian society. In this sense, al-Banna regarded his political activities as a struggle against those forces which were working to hinder the growth and development of the Is-lamic movement.[137] In fact, al-Banna looked with contempt and disdain on all political parties in Egypt, accusing them of corrupting social and political life. He repeatedly condemned political parties, charging them with being interested only in increasing the wealth and power of their members, failing thereby to offer any meaningful platforms or pro-grams geared toward promoting the well-being of Egyptian society.[138] In a speech delivered before the Ikhwan Fifth Conference, al-Banna called upon the king to dissolve all political parties, arguing that a rep-resentative system could survive without parties.

> [The Muslim Brethren] believe . . . that in a representative, and even a parliamentary, system there is no need for a party system (espe-cially if it is) like the one that exists today in Egypt. [This is true be-cause] otherwise coalition governments in democratic countries could not survive. Therefore, the notion that a parliamentary government could only exist with a party system is unwarranted; for many consti-tutional and parliamentary countries are based on a one-party system, and that is possible ... [the Muslim Brethren] have also asked His Majesty to dissolve all the existing (political) parties, so that they could be consolidated altogether into one popular assembly, which will work for the common good of the *ummah* in accordance with the principles of Islam.[139]

Al-Banna strongly believed that political parties had become a real menace, hindering the development of Egyptian society. He was thus convinced that by dissolving these parties, Egypt would stand a better chance to grow and advance. What al-Banna, and other Ikhwan leaders, failed to see was that by giving the state the right to prohibit party activi-ties, he would enable it to use the same right against any other groups actively involved in public affairs, including the Ikhwan themselves. In-deed, when Nasser came to power in 1952, he immediately dissolved all political parties, sparing the Ikhwan organization. Nasser's measure against political parties was hailed by the Ikhwan leadership, who thought that Nasser was going to grant the Ikhwan a greater role in run-ning the country. But in less that two years, the Ikhwan themselves were added to the list, after Nasser consolidated his power and purged the army of all officers who were sympathetic to the Ikhwan, or unreceptive to his views.

The death of al-Banna was tragic for the Ikhwan movement, for he was the central figure in the movement, and a respected Egyptian leader who was able through his charisma and leadership skills to elicit the sympathy and support of many influential people. Shortly after al-Banna's assassination, the Executive Office of the Ikhwan selected Hasan al-Hudaybi, a well-known and respected judge, to lead the movement. Apparently, the selection of al-Hudaybi, who was not a member of the movement, was influenced by the Ikhwan leadership's desire to find a person with high credibility and a good reputation. Being an outsider, however, al-Hudaybi could not control the movement, especially the paramilitary wing of the Ikhwan, the Special Organization.[140] In October 1954, al-Hudaybi submitted his resignation to Abd al-Qadir Awda the Ikhwan deputy, shortly after the unsuccessful attempt to assassinate Nasser.

The attempt to assassinate Nasser on October 26, 1954, marked the beginning of a devastating period in the history of the Ikhwan that characterized most of Nasser's rule until his death in 1970. The attempt was immediately blamed on the Ikhwan, and the government authorities moved quickly to arrest two members of the Special Organization, Hindawi Duwayri and Muhammad Abd al-Latif, charging them with an attempt to assassinate the president, and charging the Ikhwan organization with an attempt to overthrow the government. Without wasting time the government cracked down on the Ikhwan organization, arresting its members and closing its branches. By the end of 1954, the formal organization of the Ikhwan was completely liquidated. Thousands of Ikhwan members were sent to concentration camps, while four high-ranking leaders, as well as the two members implicated in the assassination attempt, were executed.[141] Most Ikhwan writers maintain that the alleged assassination attempt was invented by Nasser, who used the incident as a pretext to liquidate the Ikhwan and consolidate his power. Salih al-`Ashmawi, the spokesman of the Supreme Guide during al-Hudaybi's tenure, for instance, narrated in his memoir that Yusuf Tal`at, the head of the Special Organization and one of the five Ikhwan leaders who were executed by Nasser's government in 1954, assured him in a private meeting that the Special Organization had nothing to do with the attempt to assassinate Nasser.[142] Yet al-`Ashmawi himself had his suspicions concerning the Special Organization's involvement, characterizing the Ikhwan's situation during that period as chaotic, if not in complete disarray.[143]

The Revolutionary Phase

Among the Ikhwan imprisoned during this period was Sayyid Qutb. Qutb joined the Ikhwan in the late 1940s after an active career as a writer and journalist. He was arrested in 1954 and sentenced to fifteen years' imprisonment, but was freed in 1964 after serving ten years of his sentence. While in prison, Qutb was appointed as the head of the Ikhwan and continued to serve in this capacity until he was executed with other Ikhwan leaders in 1966, after being charged with the attempt to assassinate Nasser and overthrow the government.[144]

Unlike his predecessors who for the most part spoke softly, Sayyid Qutb gave the modern Islamic movement a revolutionary tone. Despite the fact that many of the ideas presented by Qutb were borrowed from Afghani, al-Banna, Mawdudi, and other Muslim writers, he was able to develop these ideas into more refined concepts, and linked them together in a systematic way to create a more or less comprehensive ideology. The political ideology developed by Sayyid Qutb was built around three core concepts: The concept of "*jahili* society," the concept of "Islamic society," and the concept of "movement" as a mechanism for transforming the former into the latter.

Like many other Muslim intellectuals, Qutb was concerned about the overwhelming sense of helplessness and defeat which permeated the Muslim world in modern times, and which was reflected in the passive and indifferent attitude of the average Muslim toward political participation, an attitude which had been inherited from centuries of political quietism. To deal with this problem, he provided a worldview which depicted history as a continuous struggle between *jahiliyah* and Islam, emphasizing the role of the believer in this struggle and the inevitability of the eventual triumph of Islam over *jahiliyah*. For Qutb, historical changes occur not as a result of contradiction between traditional and modern forces as modernization theory states, nor between the bourgeoisie and the proletariat as Marxist theory insists. Rather, changes occur because of the contradiction between faith *(iman)* and infidelity *(kufr)*, justice and injustice, Islam and *jahiliyah*.[145] Islamists perceive the current struggle in the Muslim countries as one between the Islamic forces and those of the imperialists and their agents or client regimes.[146] Most Muslim writers agree that Westernization is a major threat to Muslim countries, and blame imperialism for the backwardness and economic dependency of the Muslim world;[147] all of them see Islam as the only viable alternative for independence and development.[148]

Qutb also stresses the intimate relationship between one's values and beliefs and his attitude and behavior, emphasizing that the latter stems from, and depends on, the former. Islamic values must manifest themselves through tangible actions. For only by acting upon Islamic principles, can one begin to appreciate the meaning and value of these principles.[149] Islam, therefore, is not a set of ideals that a Muslim admires or identifies with, but rather a sober commitment to a system of life that requires complete devotion. Furthermore, because of the all-encompassing nature of the Islamic commitment, the struggle for the establishment of an Islamic society, Qutb advises, must be carried out on two levels. First, on the collective level by joining the Islamic movement and strengthening its forces. Second, on the individual level by purifying oneself through practicing Islamic morality and adhering to the ordinances of the Shari`ah.[150]

By reinterpreting Islam as an all-encompassing system where religion and politics intermingle, and by depicting history as the outcome of the struggle between the forces of Islam and those of *jahiliyah*, Qutb was able to portray the 'Muslim as an active political agent who is religiously obliged to get involved in the sociopolitical activities of his community. It is incumbent on the Muslim, he stresses, as part of his covenant with God, to enjoin the good and forbid evil *(al-amr bi al-ma`ruf wa al-nahy `an al-munkar)*, and to struggle for the establishment of Islamic rule even at the expense of life itself. To die in the cause of Islam, Qutb proclaims, is considered martyrdom *(shahadah)*, which the Qur'an recognizes as the ultimate honor for the believer in this life, leading to paradise in the hereafter.[151]

Despite his revolutionary ideas and sharp criticism of the prevailing sociopolitical system, Qutb rejects the use of violence to change it. He insists that a truly Islamic state can only be established among people who are properly educated in the teachings of Islam, and who are self-motivated to implement these teachings in their daily life. Any attempt to use violent tactics to overthrow the ruling elite and install an Islamic elite in its stead, he contends, would be a grave strategic mistake. First, because Islam is a belief system in the first place, and a sociopolitical system afterward. Second, such an approach would inevitably violate the tenets of the Islamic ideology.

During his interrogation in 1964 – in connection with an alleged plot to assassinate Nasser, and to overthrow the incumbent government – Qutb told his interrogators that "establishing an Islamic system requires a prolonged effort of education and propagation, and could not be done through a *coup d'etat.*" Qutb went on to say that "the overthrowing of the established regime does not bring about Islamic rule. Clearly, the obstacles that stand before the establishment of an Islamic system are big enough to require a long time, and elaborate preparations which might take one or several generations."[152]

Qutb strongly believed in a gradualistic approach in which the Islamic movement would struggle to expand its power base and gain support of the masses through communication and mobilization. He further advised the Islamists not to become impatient and rush their efforts to bring about a revolution before the sociopolitical conditions warrant such a move, warning that any premature attempt to overthrow the ruling power could lead to bloodshed, and would eventually culminate in a disaster.[153] Yet, by using certain conceptions and categories, such as *mufasalah* (distinction), *jahiliyah* (ignorance), *kufr* (blasphemy), and *dar al-harb* (territory of war), Qutb unwittingly paved the way for radical groups, providing them with a terminology which they could use to justify an all-out war against current society. He argued, for instance, that the Islamic movement must distinguish itself from the surrounding *jahili* society. Such a distinction, he maintained, was necessary so that the Islamists could become independent from the prevailing *jahiliyah*, channeling their energies to build the growing Islamic movement, rather than support the *jahili* regime.[154] Although Qutb tried elsewhere to shed more light on how a distinction could be maintained between the two, his statements remained equivocal, lacking a clear and practical expression.

> This [replacing *jahiliyah* with Islam] cannot come about by going along a few steps with *jahiliyah*, nor by now severing relations with it and removing ourselves to a separate corner, never. The correct procedure is to mix with discretion, give and take with dignity, speak the truth with love, and show the superiority of the Faith with humility.[155]

Likewise, by stripping the Islamic identity from modern Muslim societies, and by subsuming them under peculiar categories, such as *jahili society* and *dar al-harb*, Qutb helped Muslim radicals to use classical solutions, initially designed to tackle different circumstances, to deal with a society that can be classified as un-Islamic, and a state that could be called a territory of war. In fact, some of the passages of Qutb's last book, *Milestones,* could easily be interpreted as an open invitation to use violence against current Muslim society, especially if they are read apart from the few passages in which Qutb emphasizes a gradual approach and a long-term strategy.

> Any country which fights the Muslim because of his belief and prevents him from practicing his religion, and in which the Shari'ah is suspended, is *dar al-harb* (territory of war), even though his family and his relatives or his people live in it.[156]

The 1970s brought about a new development, namely, the proliferation of Islamic organizations and groups. During the Sadat administration which succeeded Nasser's upon the latter's death in 1970, the Ikhwan movement reemerged as one of the major political forces in Egypt. Evidently, the new Ikhwan organization under the leadership of Umar al-Tilmisani, and most recently that of Muhammad Hamid Abul al-Nasr, renounced the old revolutionary tactics, once employed by the Special Organization, adopting a gradualistic approach. However, a number of Muslim radical groups, known collectively as the Jama`at, entered the political scene; the most influential of which were: Shabab Muhammad, Jama`at al-Muslimun, and the Jihad organization.[157] Unlike the neo-Ikhwan who advocate peaceful and gradualistic approach, the Jama`at calls for revolutionary tactics and the use of violence against the state.

Although the majority of Ikhwan activists shun the revolutionary tactics of radical groups, the latter have been able to appropriate the theoretical framework of the movement, putting the former on the defensive. The reformist Ikhwan, deprived of the benefit of an ideology which would explain and justify their strategy, could only invoke pragmatic arguments in support of their gradualism. In contrast, radical groups, by appropriating the ideology advanced by Qutb, are able to project themselves as the legitimate heirs of the Islamic movement. It is for this reason that we turn now to briefly outline the strategy of radical groups, and discuss their basic views. Such a discussion is essential for assessing the post-Qutb trends within the Islamist forces.

Islamist Radicalism

The principle of revolution adopted by the Jam`at finds its roots in the writings of Qutb, who reinterpreted Islam as a revolutionary ideology and forcefully emphasized that the Islamic movement cannot afford to make compromises with the *jahili* society and yet remain faithful after that to the Islamic principles.[158] Indeed, radical Muslim groups maintain many of the core concepts of the Ikhwan's ideology – their reading of history, their ultimate goals, and their worldview.[159] They sharply disagree, however, with the Ikhwan on the question of identifying the best and most effective strategy to transform the present society from *jahiliyah* to Islam.

Jama`at al-Muslimin (the Muslims' Group) was established in the early 1970s by Shukri Mustafa, a veteran of the Ikhwan who served several years in prison during Nasser's rule because of his political activism. The group described modern society as *jahili* suffering from corruption and injustice. Their manifesto *al-Khilafah* (the Caliphate) divided the group's mission into three stages. In the first stage, the group was to involve itself in communication activities aimed at educating the public about the true Islamic principles and beliefs. The second stage is distinguished by the concentration on organization and mobilization activities, the purpose of which is to prepare the group to the third and final stage, the jihad stage.[160] The group was charged with kidnapping and murdering Shaykh Husayn al-Dhahabi, former Minister of *Awqaf* (religious affairs). Consequently, the group's leadership as well as 400 of its members were arrested after a bloody confrontation with government forces. On March 19, 1979, Shukri Mustafa, along with other members, was executed.[161]

Shabab Muhammad (Muhammad's Youth) was also established in the early 1970s by Saleh Sariyah, a Palestinian by birth who was a member of a Jordanian-based organization known as the Islamic Liberation Party (Hizb al-Tahrir al-Islami). Unlike the Jama`at al-Muslimin which viewed both the state and society as an integral whole, Shabab Muhammad differentiated between the two, condemning the former while regarding the latter as a victim of cruel and godless rulers. The group was short-lived, for it quickly came into major military confrontation with the government when it carried out an unsuccessful attack on the Military Technical College in Cairo. Saleh Sariyah and a number of the Shabab's leaders were executed on November 10, 1976, while other members were imprisoned. The remaining members of the group formed a new group known as al-Jihad which was responsible for the assassination of Sadat in 1981.[162] Al-Jihad's ideology and strategy were expressed in the organization's manifesto, *Al-Faridah al-Gha'ibah* (The Neglected Duty), written by al-Jihad's ideologue, Muhammad Abd al-Salam Faraj (1954-1982).

In *The Neglected Duty,* Faraj dismisses propaganda *(da'wa)* as an ineffective means for the transformation of the current Egyptian *jahili* society into Islamic, and insists that armed struggle should be the paramount method for this transformation. To prove his point, Faraj quotes a verse from the Qur'an stating that a small band may conquer a large band."[163] Faraj concludes from this Qur'anic verse that "Islam does not triumph by the majority."[164] He cites also the struggle of the Prophet and early Muslims, emphasizing that it was a struggle of a righteous minority over a corrupt majority.

> Some of them [the Muslim gradualists] say that the right road to the establishment of an [Islamic] state is (nonviolent) propaganda *(da'wa)* only, and the creation of a broad base. This, however, does not bring about the foundation of an [Islamic] state. Nevertheless, some people make this point the basis for their withdrawal from (true) jihad. The truth is that an (Islamic) state can only be founded by a believing minority ... Those who follow the straight path that is in accordance with the command of God and the example of the Apostle of God – may God's peace be upon him – are always the minority.[165]

Faraj also rejects the neo-Ikhwan's strategy to work through other political parties on the grounds that it produces the opposite of what is desired, "since it means building the pagan state and collaborating with it."[166]

Muslim radical groups, which tend to have a simplistic outlook and dichotomous worldviews, have failed to appreciate the complexity of modern society. The simplicity of their thought stems from their failure to distinguish Islamic norms and values from their historical applications. What the Muslim radicals attempt to achieve is not a modern society based on the principles of Islam or a society that embodies Islamic values, but rather a society which is an exact image of the first Islamic society and which literally imitates the first society in all aspects of life.[167]

Conclusion

Over a century ago, Jamaluddin Afghani set in motion a new Islamic trend and movement. The basic mission of this movement, Afghani envisaged, was to revitalize and reform the backward conditions of the *ummah*. Afghani strongly believed that Muslim decadence was precipitated by faulty interpretations of Islam and the misperception of the meanings and intents of Islamic principles. He, therefore, insisted that the Muslim decline was intrinsically intellectual in nature, reflecting the failure of Muslim scholars to apply the principles and teachings of Islam to an ever-changing reality. The military defeat of the Muslims at the hands of Europe was only the symptom of the spiritual and intellectual decline of the *ummah*, and never its cause. Although Afghani, and later Muhammad Abduh emphasized proper Islamic education as the ultimate means for the revitalization of Muslim conditions, he believed that establishing a united Islamic state was the best and shortest approach to achieving the desired reform. Toward this end, Afghani tried unsuccessfully to employ his influence and personal relationships with Muslim rulers to convince them to adopt his reformist ideas. While his endeavor to bring about change through rulers bore no fruit, he was able to inspire Muslim intellectuals and public opinion leaders, sowing the seeds of revolt among them; his agitation resulted in the rebellion of the Egyptian army in 1882 against Khedive Tawfiq. The rebellion was, however, quickly suppressed by the British forces that intervened to keep Khedive Tawfiq in power.

The Islamic movement initiated and cultivated by Afghani was throughout his life an elitist movement unable to attract the support of the Egyptian masses. The failure of the Islamic movement to attract popular support during Afghani's time, and to a lesser extent during the time of al-Banna and Qutb, could be attributed to two interrelated factors. The first factor was the revolutionary nature of Afghani's message. He had led an all-out war against traditionalist ideas and thoughts, describing them as perverted and decadent, and blaming them for the Muslim inability to face modern challenges. He further blamed the ulama for the deteriorating conditions of the *ummah*, and called upon them to rethink and reevaluate a great deal of their doctrines. Immediately his call was met with strong opposition from the ulama who labeled him an "innovator." Traditionalist ulama who believed that Islamic thought had reached its full expansion and refinement long ago, saw Afghani's reformist ideas as a threat to the integrity of Islam. Second, Afghani had to deal with a community suffering from chronic illiteracy and fatalism and a long history of political quietism. Afghani's message, with its emphasis on political activism and scientific development, was, therefore, incomprehensible to the Egyptian masses.

It was not until the establishment of the Ikhwan by Hasan al-Banna in 1927 that the Islamic movement assumed a more popular stance, embarking on the support of the common individual. Al-Banna strongly believed that moral and intellectual reform must precede any meaningful sociopolitical change. Although al-Banna intended that the Ikhwan movement should be a prototype for an Islamic society, and should therefore engage itself in all aspects of social life including politics, he repeatedly emphasized that the Ikhwan must concentrate their efforts on social reform. Nevertheless, the Ikhwan were gradually driven (probably by their rapidly growing power) into the political arena, and became actively involved in Egyptian politics, thereby compromising their own strategy. Moreover, the contradiction between the declared strategy and practical activities of the Ikhwan was further complicated by the creation of the Special Organization, the paramilitary wing of the Ikhwan which was established to protect the formal organization but became instead a nightmare for the Ikhwan when it rebelled against the formal leadership and adopted its own agenda. The campaign of violence that was launched by the Special Organization put the Ikhwan face to face with the state. The state responded with an "iron fist" policy, first during the monarchist rule, and later during Nasser's, resulting in the almost complete dismantling of the Ikhwan movement.

The ideological framework developed by Qutb provided the movement with a powerful tool for analyzing modern society and a comprehensive strategy for dismantling the dominant political regime and replacing it with an Islamic one. Ironically, Qutb's sharp criticism and uncompromising approach were adopted by groups who, overlooking the solutions suggested by Qutb himself, employed classical solutions to address modern situations. The result was a variety of extremist groups who saw violence as the only effective method to bring out change.

In the one hundred years that elapsed since Afghani called for reform, the Islamic movement has grown and expanded markedly. The once elitist movement commands today the support of an increasing segment of Egyptian society. Yet the ultimate question which Afghani set out to tackle, later addressed by many writers including al-Banna and Qutb, remains today unresolved. The question of the nature of Islamic society and the relationship between society and the Shari'ah is still un-settled. The dispute between the reformist Afghani and traditionalist ulama regarding the characteristics of the ideal Islamic society continues to be a source of sharp division and schism among Islamists. Although traditionalists acknowledge today that the conditions of the Muslim community need profound change, they differ with the reformists about the nature of this change. Contemporary traditionalists perceive change in terms of renovating modern society so as to resemble the early Muslim society. Therefore, they demand that the early society be emulated in almost every detail. Reformists, on the other hand, though professing that the early Muslim society provides an excellent moral model, insist that the social and political practices of that society were but the outcome of the interaction between Islamic principles and historical circumstances. They conclude, therefore, that contemporary Muslims must use Islamic principles to shape their reality, rather than resuscitating historical situations.

The contemporary Islamic movement in Egypt today faces two major challenges. First, a political culture that fosters elitist politics. The average Egyptian citizen has been conditioned after almost ten centuries of quietism, to refrain from political involvement, and has been led to believe that political life is unpredictable, uncontrollable, and out of reach. Second, the dominance of traditionalist ideas and symbols have prevented the members of the Islamic movement and its followers from fully understanding and comprehending the ideas of the movement's reformist leaders. The future of the movement, therefore, could well be determined by its ability to cope and deal with these two great challenges.

III. Islamic Law and Human Rights

INTERLUDE III

Islamic Law and Human Rights

Islamic resurgence in Muslim societies is often associated with calls for strict application of Islamic law (Shari`ah). Although the notion of Islamic law, as demonstrated below, refers in its most essential meaning to the normative Islamic order, Shari`ah is very often associated with the application of *hudud* (Islamic punishments). The drive to apply Shari`ah *qua hudud* has received criticism from different quarters in both the Muslim and Western worlds. Islamic reformers in particular, are critical of applied a legal code developed to address the conditions of early Muslim societies of bygone eras to modern society that have evolved drastically different social, economic, and political conditions.

We examine, in part III, the notion of Islamic law and its relevance to contemporary Muslim society. We endeavor to distinguish between the universal and particular in Islamic law, and call for reforming the legal system in ways that help to retain the universal, and transcend the particular in historical Muslim experience. We focus particularly on the notion of human rights as an essential concept for ensuring that future legal systems in the Muslim world are sensitive to the rights and dignity of all, including those who do not profess Islam.

We then turn in chapter 8 to discuss Western criticism of Islamic approaches to human rights. I argue that focusing on the work of Muslim traditionalists and overlooking that of Muslim reformists can only distort actual developments in Muslim thought and society. I, further, argue that such distortions are the result of adopting an absolute universalist stance that encourages the imposition of Western values and lifestyle on Muslim society. To realize a truly universal human rights, I propose an alternative approach, based on a true and meaningful cross-cultural dialogue.

CHAPTER 6

Islamic Law (Shari`ah) and Society

Shari`ah has been the dominant moral and legal code of Muslim societies for the greater part of their history. During the early centuries of Islam, Shari`ah facilitated the social growth and development of Muslims, growth that culminated in the establishment of a vast empire and an outstanding civilization. By the close of the fifth century of Islam, however, Shari`ah began to lose its role as the guiding force that inspired Muslim creativity and ingenuity and that nurtured the growing spirit of the *ummah*. Consequently, the *ummah* entered a period of stagnation that gradually gave way to intellectual decline and social decadence. Regrettably, this painful trend continues to be more or less 'part of the individual consciousness and collective experience of Muslims.

We attempt, in this chapter, to trace the development of the principles of Islamic jurisprudence, and to assess the impact of Shari`ah on society. I argue that the law ceased to grow by the sixth century of Islam as a result of the development of classical legal theory; more specifically, law was put on hold, as it were, after the doctrine of the infallibility of *ijma`* (juristic consensus) was articulated. The rigid principles of classical theory, it is contended, have been primarily induced by the faulty epistemology employed by sixth-century jurists.

Shari`ah is a comprehensive system encompassing the whole field of human experience. It is not simply a legal system, but rather a composite system of law and morality. That is, Islamic law aspires to regulate all aspects of human activities, not only those that may entail legal consequences. Hence, all actions and relationships are evaluated in accordance with a scale of five moral standards.

According to Shari`ah, an act may be classified as obligatory (*wajib*), recommended (*mandub*), permissible (*mubah*), reprehensible (*makruh*), or prohibited (*haram*).[168] These five categories reflect the varying levels of moral demand placed on human acts by divine will. Acts that fall in the categories on the two opposite extremes are strictly demanded, whereas acts falling in the two categories around the neutral center of the scale are not as solemnly demanded, and hence their violation, though discouraged, is not condemned. To put it differently, while the individual is obligated morally to follow the commands of the first and last categories – i.e., the obligatory and prohibited – he is only encouraged to observe the commands of the second and fourth – i.e., the recommended and reprehensible.

It should be emphasized, however, that even the absolute commands of the law have essential moral, or more accurately religious, implications, and thus are not necessarily under state sanction. For instance, the pilgrimage to Makkah once in a lifetime is obligatory (*wajib*) for every Muslim who is physically and financially capable of performing this duty. Yet the state, according to Shari`ah, may not compel the individual to fulfill this personal obligation.

Notwithstanding the inextricable association between law and morality in Shari`ah, Muslim jurists conveniently differentiate between private and public morality – or, using Islamic-law vocabulary, *haqq Allah* (rights of God) and *huquq al-`ibad* (rights of humans) – and hold that only the latter may be subject to legal sanctions. Private morality includes purely religious activities pertaining directly to the spiritual relationship between a human being and God, labeled as `*ibadat* (services). Since `*ibadat*, or services, do not have, for the most part, any social consequences, the individual, it is argued, is answerable to God for fulfilling them, not to society. Public morality, on the other hand, encompasses those patterns of behavior that have social consequences, appropriately labeled *mu`amalat* (transactions). Because of the direct implications *mu`amalat* activities have on society's ability to maintain public peace and order, their regulation may be legally enforced by the state. The division of individual obligations and duties into categories of public and private is, nonetheless, more apparent than real; for, according to Islamic theory, all human activities, regardless of whether they are public or private, are subject to ethical judgment, because all human beings are ultimately accountable to God for their actions.

Law and morality, though interrelated, are perceived by most Western lawyers to be two distinct and separate spheres. Positive law theories predominant in Western society insist that law is only one of a number of social mechanisms – including religion, morality, education, etc., – employed in society to ensure individual conformity to social norms. This means that the ability of Western law to regulate social behavior is limited by, and contingent on the performance of other social institutions.

Only when the ideals and values promoted by other social institutions are compatible with those of the legal system can the law function effectively. Addressing the question of the impact of law on individual and social development, Iredell Jenkins argues that

> law is not an effective instrument for the formation of human character or the development of human potentialities. It has a very limited power to make men into acceptable social members or to help them become accomplished individuals. Furthermore, law can set minimum standards and define broad guidelines to assure that institutions do in fact provide the services and promote the purposes for which they acknowledge obligation and claim credit. Though law cannot secure the essential similarities that are necessary to a sound society, it can eliminate gross dissimilarity among individuals and groups, and it can prevent serious nonfeasance or misfeasance on the part of other institutions.[169]

In contrast, the impact of Islamic law on society is pervasive and far-reaching, for Shari`ah is an all-inclusive system combining both the legal and moral realms. Shari`ah has guided the development and performance of not only legal institutions, but also those of other institutions and agencies of society, including governmental, business, and educational institutions. This aspect of Islamic law can partially explain to us the success the law had in transforming heterogeneous and incongruent societies into one relatively homogeneous political community during the early centuries of Islam.

The Purpose of Shari`ah

According to Islamic theory, Shari`ah was revealed to provide a set of criteria so that right (*haqq*) may be distinguished from wrong *(batil)*. By adhering to the rules of law, the Muslims would develop a society superior in its moral as well as material quality to societies which fail to observe the revealed will of God. Shari`ah, as a comprehensive moral and legal system, aspires to regulate all aspects of human behavior to produce conformity with divine law. According to the *faqih* (Islamic jurists), adhering to the rules and principles of Shari`ah not only causes the individual to draw closer to God, but also facilitates the development of a just society in which the individual may be able to realize his or her potential, and whereby prosperity is ensured to all. In other words, while religion, as a set of values and beliefs, establishes the goals and ideals which society must strive to attain, Islamic law furnishes the code of conduct that should be observed by Muslims if they are to achieve the desired goals.

> Islamic Law (Shari`ah) is closely intertwined with religion, and both are considered expressions of God's will and justice, but

whereas the aim of religion is to define and determine goals (justice or others) the function of law is to indicate the path (the term Shari`ah indeed bears this meaning) by virtue of which God's justice and other goals are realized.[170]

The purpose of Shari`ah, therefore, is to provide the standards and criteria that would gain the ends prescribed by revelation. According to Islamic legal theory, justice, as the ultimate value that justifies the existence of law and as the ultimate criterion for the evaluation of social behavior, cannot be realized apart from the understanding of the purpose of human existence. Such understanding cannot be discovered by human reasoning, as natural law theory asserts. It must be acquired by direct exposure to divine will through revelation. Therefore, justice may only be fully realized when divine law is recognized and implemented by society.

Justice can be defined either as material or substantive (the goals and ideals that law intends to further), or as formal or procedural (the procedures and standards that must be observed to realize the ends of law). Substantive justice is the set of ideals that depict the best Islamic society, which in the end Shari`ah endeavors to achieve. Procedural justice is the standards and patterns of behavior that must be adhered to if a just society is ever to be realized.

The Development of Shari`ah

Classical legal theory was developed over the first five centuries of Islam. Initially, the Prophet was the sole legislator of the *ummah*. Community affairs were regulated by Qur'anic statements revealed in a piecemeal fashion to instruct Muslims regarding the appropriate patterns of behavior in relation to the various problems and questions that confronted the first community.

The early verses of the Qur'an, revealed in Makkah before the establishment of the Islamic city-state of Madinah, consisted of general statements concerning divine attributes, as well as man's mission and destiny. With the establishment of the first Islamic state in Madinah, the Qur'anic verses began to include injunctions and statements concerning the characteristics of a just society, along with sporadic legal enunciations. In addition to his principal mission as the bearer and verbalizer of revelation, the Prophet served as the head of the community and the interpreter of the Qur'an; he was always available both to clarify the intent of the Qur'anic verses and to respond to inquiries on issues and questions of which the Qur'an was either silent or ambiguous. The personal judgments made by the Prophet were later referred to as the Sunnah or Hadith, to distinguish them from the Qur'an.[171]

Initially the term *Sunnah* was used in reference to the practice of the Prophet and early Muslim *ummah* as they attempted to apply the injunctions of the Qur'an to daily life. As such the Sunnah was the living tradition of the community. The term Hadith, on the other hand, was used in connection with the utterances of the Prophet as they were circulated within the community and narrated by the Prophet's Companions to relate his practices and directives to other Muslims. Gradually, however, the whole of the Sunnah, the living tradition, was reflected in the Hadith, and the two terms became completely interchangeable by the fifth/eleventh century.[172]

With the death of the Prophet and the emergence of new circumstances and issues never before addressed by the Qur'an or the Sunnah, the question arose as to how the Shari`ah would subsequently be known. The answer was in the exercise of juristic speculation (*ijtihad*), a practice that had already been approved by the Prophet. However, a juristic opinion *(ra'y)* arrived at by the exercise of *ijtihad* could lead only to tentative conclusions or conjunctures *(zann)*. Such judgments were thus considered by jurists as subject to abrogation and refutation. But when juristic opinions arrived at through *ijtihad* were subjects of general agreement by the jurists *(fuqaha),* they were considered incontrovertible, and hence binding for the entire community. The juristic speculation of individual jurists and their consensus (*ijma`*) became, after the death of the Prophet, additional sources of Shari`ah, and new methods to define divine law.

Al-Shafi`i, an eminent classical jurist and the founder of one of the four major schools of law in the history of Islam,[173] presented in the second/seventh century the first discourse on the principles of Islamic jurisprudence *(usul al-fiqh),* which was later compiled by his students in a book entitled *Al-Risalah* (The Discourse). Following in the footsteps of his predecessors, al-Shafi`i recognized the four major principles of *usul al-fiqh*: the Qur'an, the Sunnah, *ijma`*, and *ijtihad*. He, however, redefined the last three principles.

Before al-Shafi`i presented his thesis in *Al-Risalah,* Muslim jurists by and large regarded the Sunnah, whether in the form of the living tradition of the community or the circulated narratives of the Hadith, as the practical application of the Qur'anic injunctions as they were understood by the Prophet and his Companions. As such, the Sunnah was used by jurists to gain insight into the meanings and practical application of Qur'anic principles. Furthermore, early jurists accepted a Hadith only when it was supported by the Islamic principles established by the Qur'an, and they did not hesitate to reject it when it conflicted with generally accepted rules.[174] However, al-Shafi`i insisted that the Hadith, being divinely inspired, could not be abrogated by the Qur'an, and thus the community was obliged to abide by its injunctions.[175]

As a result of al-Shafi'i's insistence on the intrinsic and independent authority of the Hadith, the Sunnah and Hadith were vested with superseding authority; for although the Qur'an continued, in theory, to be regarded as the primary source of law, the Hadith for all practical purposes was given predominance in formulating legal rulings. The Hadith was used not only to interpret the Qur'an, but also to limit its application and occasionally abrogate its injunctions.[176]

The third source of law in al-Shafi'i's legal theory was *ijma'*. To him, *ijma'* was not the consensus of the jurists but that of the community at large. Al-Shafi'i perceived two interrelated problems in the identification of *ijma'* with the consensus of the jurists. First, consensus of the jurists was used to perpetuate the living tradition of the various schools of law, preventing thereby the unification of Islamic law. Second, and probably the most crucial problem from the Shafi'i perspective, the consensus of jurists was used to reject the Hadith whenever the latter contradicted the prevailing doctrines of a particular school of law.'[177]

Indeed, al-Shafi'i was quite successful in making the Hadith an incontrovertible source of law, the second principal source after the Qur'an. Yet the triumph of al-Shafi'i's thesis did not come without opposition. It was strongly resisted even by eminent jurists and supporters of the Hadith. Ibn Qutayba, for instance, continued to hold that the Hadith could be rejected by the consensus of the jurists, thereby giving *ijma'* priority over the Hadith: 'We hold that *ijma'* is a surer vehicle of truth (or right) than the Hadith, for the latter is subject to forgetfulness, neglect, doubts, interpretations, and abrogation. . . . But *ijma'* is free from these contingencies."[178]

The final recognized source of law, according to al-Shafi'i, was *ijtihad*. Before al-Shafi'i, *ijtihad* was a comprehensive concept involving any method that employed reasoning for defining the divine law. Al-Shafi'i, however, confined *ijtihad* to the process of extending the application of established rules to new questions by analogy (*qiyas*)."[179] Analogical reasoning, in classical theory, required that the efficient cause (`illa) of the divine command be determined so that the application of the command may be extended to other objects sharing the same effect. For example, the jurists determined that the `illa for prohibiting the consumption of wine was its intoxicating effect. By analogy, the jurists decided, therefore, that any substance that possessed the same effect must also be prohibited, even though it may not have been explicitly forbidden by the letter of the Qur'an or Sunnah.

By limiting *ijtihad* to *qiyas*, al-Shafi'i hoped that he could render the former more systematic and, consequently, ensure the unity of law, while opposing the efforts of those who would be tempted to usurp the law for their own personal ends. *Qiyas*, nonetheless, continued to be considered by a significant number of jurists as only one of several methods through which the principle of *ijtihad* could be practiced. The followers of the Hanafi and Maliki schools of law, for instance, employed the principles of juristic preference *(istihsan)* and public good *(istislah)* respectively, regarding them as appropriate methods to derive the rules of Shari`ah. Apparently, the former method was employed by the Hanafi jurists to counteract the Shafi`i jurists' attempts to limit the concept of juristic speculation to the method of reasoning by analogy. *Istihsan* was an attempt to return to the freedom of *ra'y* that permitted jurists to make legal rulings without relying solely on analogy. For the more systematic jurists, however, rulings rendered through the application of *istihsan* were nothing more than arbitrary rulings or, as al-Shafi`i put it, *"innama al-istihsan taladhudh"* (*istihsan* is ruling by caprice).[180]

Istislah was another approach employed by Maliki, and to a lesser extent by Hanafi, jurists to escape the rigid form into which the Shari`ah was gradually cast by more conservative jurists (primarily the Shafi`i and Hanbali). The jurists who advocated the use of the *istislah* method argued that the principles of Shari`ah aimed at promoting the general interests of the community; therefore "public good" should guide legal decisions wherever revelation was silent with regard to the question under consideration.[181]

Classical Legal Theory

Despite the restrictions placed by al-Shafi`i and other scholars, Shari`ah continued to grow in terms of both its methodology and the body of new rules formulated in response to the concerns of a growing society. By the close of the fifth/eleventh century, however, the science of law began to decline, while the law itself was firmly cast into a rigid mold. It was during this advanced period of the history of Islamic legal thinking that the classical legal theory was formulated. But although the theory itself was the culmination of a long process of accumulation and growth, stretching over five centuries, its historical development was not reflected in the theory itself and was completely ignored by subsequent classical jurists.

Among the prime factors that contributed to the rigidity of law was the doctrine of the infallibility of *ijma`*. The principle of *ijma`* was defined first as the agreement of the early community, and was employed to substantiate the fundamental doctrines of the faith. With the establishment of the schools of law during the first two centuries, *ijma`* was redefined as the consensus of jurists on rulings originally established through *ijtihad*.

The principle of the consensus of jurists was first designed as a means to substantiate the speculative judgments of individual jurists, and hence, confer on them a higher degree of certainty and authority. Gradually, however, the theory of the infallibility of *ijma`* was advanced, thereby turning the early pragmatic authority of the legal rulings which enjoyed consensus of the jurists into theoretical absoluteness.

According to the theory of the infallibility of *ijma`*, a juristic consensus on an issue should be considered as the final step toward understanding the "truth" of that issue. The doctrine of the infallibility of *ijma`* was supported by a Hadith in which the Prophet was reported to have said: "My community shall never agree on an error?"[182] As a result of this new definition of *ijma`*, jurists were discouraged from reexamining decisions or judgments on which consensus had been reached, for such reexamination was, according to classical theory, pointless and unnecessary. Thus, it was only a matter of time before jurists came to the conclusion that "all essential questions had been thoroughly discussed and finally settled, and a consensus gradually established itself that from then on no one could have the necessary qualifications for independent reasoning in law."[183]

Henceforth, *ijtihad* ceased to be one of the functions of the jurist, let alone a source of law. For one thing, *ijtihad* was perceived to be senseless after Shari`ah was completed and the essential questions answered. But in addition, "the qualifications for *ijtihad* were made so immaculate and rigorous and were set so high that they were humanly impossible."[184] Gradually the principle of *ijtihad* was replaced by that of *taqlid* (imitation), whereby the jurist was supposed to master the official doctrine of his school and apply it to new situations. This meant that "the doctrine had to be derived not independently from the Qur'an, the Sunnah, and the consensus, but from the authoritative handbooks of the several schools."[185]

Clearly, the theory of the infallibility of *ijma`* was decisive in casting Islamic law into a rigid mold, for it mystified the relationship between the ideal and historical elements of law, that is, it confused law as a volatile and abstract ideal with the concrete rules derived from it and captured in the historical experience of a specific social organization.

The question arises here as to what extent can Shari`ah be regarded, as the classical theory insists, as the manifestation of the divine will? To answer this question we need first to distinguish the levels of meaning that separate the ideal from the existential in Islamic legal thought. In this connection the term Shari`ah or law may refer to any of the following four meanings:

First, law may be perceived as the eternal set of principles which reflect the divine will as it is related to the human situation; that is, those principles that relate to the purpose of human existence and the universal rules that must be observed by men to achieve that purpose.

Second, law could be regarded as the revelationary verbalization of the eternal principles in the form of a revealed word or message that discloses divine will to mankind. The Qur'an, the manifestation of divine will, consists of two categories of rules: universal rules (*ahkam kulliyah*) embodied in general Qur'anic statements, and particular rules *(ahkam far`iyah)* revealed in connection with specific instances, which hence may be considered as concrete applications of the universal rules.

Third, law may be viewed as the understanding of revelation as reflected in jurists' oral and written statements. The Qur'an was revealed over a 23-year period in piecemeal fashion in response to the various questions and problems facing the evolving Muslim community. In order to define divine will on new situations never before addressed by revelation, Muslim jurists had to develop a legal theory that spelled out the Shari`ah, and establish the methods of deriving and applying its rules. The jurists had to define the overall objectives of Shari`ah, and, using inductive reasoning, rediscover the fundamental principles underlying the formulation of the rules of Shari`ah. Classical jurists had also to develop the appropriate method that could be used to define the fundamental principles of Shari`ah and expand their application to new situations.

Finally, law could be seen as the positive rules derived from the theoretical principles of Shari`ah and used to regulate social and individual behavior. These rules are collected in major encyclopedic works, as well as in numerous handbooks used by the major schools of law. It is this very specific and concrete meaning of law which usually comes to mind when the term Shari`ah is pronounced.

Evidently, the classical legal theory failed to distinguish the general and abstract ideals of Shari`ah from the specific and concrete body of doctrine. That is, it confused the ideals embodied in the Qur'an and the practice of the early Muslim community with the ideologies developed later by jurists. In fact, this confusion did not occur at the early stages of the development of Shari`ah, but only at a later stage, after the four schools of law began to take shape during the third and fourth centuries, and finally with the formulation of the classical theory of law.

Earlier jurists, including the founders of the major schools of law, recognized the difference between the ideal and doctrinal elements of law, for they did not hesitate to reject previous legal theories and doctrines, replacing them with others. It was this distinction that ensured the dynamism of Shari`ah and its growth during the early centuries of Islam. By constructing new theories, and modifying the old legal theories, the connection between the ideal and existential was maintained and Shari`ah was thus flexible enough to respond to the concerns of a developing society. However, when the prevailing doctrine of the fifth century was ideal-ized, Shari`ah lost its flexibility, and the relationship between law and society was gradually severed. Henceforth, the efforts of the jurists were directed toward resisting any developments that would render social practices incompatible with the existing legal code, instead of modifying legal doctrines so that new social developments could be guided by Is-lamic ideals.

The four levels of meanings that separate the ideal from the existen-tial elements of law enable us to see the fatal epistemological error that the proponents of the classical legal theory commit when they insist on the infallibility of the principle of *ijma`*. The classical legal theory mis-takenly asserts that the ideals which the law aspires to realize have been captured, once and for all, in the legal doctrines expounded by early ju-rists, and that classical legal doctrines, substantiated by *ijma`*, have at-tained absolute universality. Implicit in this assertion is the assumption that as legal decisions move from the domain of the individual to that of the community, they give up their subjectivity and specificity. When they finally become the subject of juristic consensus, legal decisions acquire complete objectivity and universality.

Such a perception is manifestly faulty, for it could be true only if we ignore the historical evolution of the human experience. As long as the future state of society, be it in the material condition or social organiza-tion, is concealed and, uncertain, law must keep the way open for new possibilities and change. It should be emphasized here that the relation-ship between the third and fourth meanings of Shari`ah (i.e., law as inter-pretation and as positive rules) is dialectical, and must be kept that way if law is to be able to function more effectively. For in order for the ideal to have a positive effect, its universality and objectivity must become em-bodied in a specific and concrete doctrine. Only when the universal ideal is reduced into particular and local rules and institutions, can it begin to transform the human world. However, the embodiment of the ideal in a concrete rule or institution should always be regarded as tentative, and the possibility for future reevaluation or modification should likewise be kept open.[186]

The positive rules of Shari`ah as well as the legal doctrines that have been formulated by Muslim jurists are therefore tentative, because they have been formulated by fallible human beings situated in specific his-torical moments. *Ijma`* cannot confer universality or absoluteness on rules or decisions agreed upon by any particular generation. All that *ijma`* can do is to make the rules more objective for a specific community situ-ated in a specific time and space. The claim that the positive rules of Shari`ah (or more accurately the rules of *fiqh*) and divine will are identi-cal is erroneous and ill-founded, for it ignores the historical significance of the legal doctrine and the human agency that has been responsible for its development.

Islamic Law and Society

The development of the classical legal theory by the fifth/eleventh century marked the beginning of a long process in which law was gradually detached from society. Up to that point, the divergence between rules of law and social practices was confined to the political arena, as the development of political institutions, namely the establishment of hereditary rule, ceased, after the fourth successor (caliph) to the Prophet, to correspond to the principles laid down by constitutional theory. Despite the fact that the Islamic political system (caliphate) had become a hereditary system after the establishment of the Umayyad dynasty, it was never sanctioned or recognized by the *fuqaha'* as such. They maintained that the ruler (*imam*) could be either elected (*ikhtiyar*) or designated (*`ahd*) and that the selected head of the community should meet certain physical, moral, and intellectual requirements. Al-Mawardi (d. 450/1058), for instance, predicated these two modes of selection on the practice of the Muslim community during the rightly guided caliphate. He based the election of the imam on "the precedent of the choice of Abu Bakr (the first caliph) by election and that of `Umar (the second caliph) by nomination."[187] Al-Mawardi also required that the imam should receive confirmation (*bay`ah*) of the *ummah* or their representatives as it was practiced during the early caliphate, a practice that was modeled after the *bay`ah* of al-Aqaba, in which people expressed their allegiance to the Prophet and acknowledged his commission and leadership.[188]

To resolve the contradiction between the *de jure* requirements of involving the *ummah* or their representatives in the selection of the Imam and *de facto* hereditary rule, the *fuqaha'* divided the selection process into two stages: *ikhtiyar* and *bay`ah*. While most leading jurists and schools of law agreed that the imam may be nominated by one or two competent individuals, they differed as to what constitutes confirmation; though the widely accepted proposition was that it was the right of the community, through their local leaders (*ahl al-hall wa al-`aqd*) and ulama, to confirm the ruler.

The jurists' failure to have any impact on the actual procedure through which the ruler was selected is reflected in the idealistic nature of the classical constitutional theory; the theory is primarily concerned with defining substantive rights and duties, while failing to address the procedures needed for securing these rights and duties.

The doctrine of the caliphate did not offer any adequate means of identifying the persons empowered to choose and install the caliph, or, if necessary, depose him, nor did it indicate the process by which they should come to decisions. A corrupt ruler should be deposed if it does not invite anarchy, but the doctrine is silent on who is to decide this, or how.[189]

After the fifth century, however, law began to lose touch with reality, not only in the political realm, but also in the social and economic, or, using Islamic vocabulary, in the sphere of *mu`amalat*. Furthermore, with the idealization of the fifth-century legal code, the law became increasingly rigid, unable to respond to the growing needs of society. To mitigate the rigidity of law in subsequent centuries, many jurists employed legal devices (*hiyal shar`iyah*) through which "an act may seemingly be lawful in accordance with the literal meaning of the law, but could hardly be in conformity with the spirit or the general purposes of the law?"[190] Indeed, by the eighth century, law became primarily concerned with procedural and technical matters, while ignoring substantive questions. This meant that classical jurists in later centuries had virtually subordinated substantive justice to procedural justice.

Despite the efforts to make Shari`ah flexible through the use of legal devices, Shari`ah's ability to respond to social concerns continued to diminish, while the gap between the rules of law and social practices broadened.

This trend continued until the collapse of the traditional sociopolitical order by this century, which was the result of the European colonization of the Muslim world. The European invasion of Muslim lands was the blow that shook Muslim civilization. As a result, Muslim jurists and scholars were faced with the challenge of explaining how, in the scheme of things, the Western world, which after all did not have the privilege of being ruled by Shari`ah, was able to attain military and scientific superiority over the Muslim community. One of the early responses was advanced by Jamaluddin Afghani, who attributed Muslim decline to the deficient outlook promoted by classical legal theory and its proponents. It is not revelation, Afghani proclaimed, that should be held responsible for Muslim decadence, but the faulty interpretations of classical jurists. Afghani was alarmed by the jurists' obsession with procedural and technical matters to the neglect of substantive questions. He thus accused classical jurists of wasting time and energy on trivial matters, occupying their minds with minutiae and subtleties, instead of addressing important problems facing the Muslim community.[191] Like Afghani, Muhammad Abduh, a leading modern jurist, asserted that Shari`ah would affect prosperity only when its objectives were properly understood, and its principles correctly interpreted and implemented.

The Shari`ah is designed by God to bring worldly as well as spiritual success to man. Its social prescriptions are assumed to assure the best and most prosperous of earthly communities, provided that they are properly observed.[192]

Conclusion

Islamic legal theory asserts that law can only be established by an impartial legislator who has full knowledge of the purpose of human existence. By necessity, therefore, God must be the ultimate lawgiver of society. According to Islamic legal theory, Shari'ah is revealed to provide a set of criteria so that right may be distinguished from wrong. By adhering to the rules of law, Muslims are assured to develop a society superior in its moral as well as material quality to other societies that fail to observe revelation.

Because revelation ceased upon the death of the Prophet, the community lost its direct access to divine will. Hence the question arose as to how divine law was to be known. The answer was in the practice of *ijtihad*, whereby jurists resorted to the use of *ra'y* to discover the principles embodied in revelation and then extends their application to new situations never before addressed by revelation. Because of the speculative nature of independent reasoning, jurists introduced the principle of *ijma`* to confer a higher degree of certainty and authority on their judgments.

In the fifth century, the doctrine of the infallibility of *ijma`* was introduced, whereby rulings that were subject to juristic consensus were considered to be incontrovertible. Jurists concluded that essential questions had been thoroughly discussed, and were, therefore, settled once and for all. Henceforth, law (rules of *fiqh*) lost its earlier flexibility and was cast into a rigid mold from which it has not emerged. Jurists could no longer consult the original sources of law, but had to derive new rules from the fifth-century legal code, which was idealized and codified in the handbooks of the major schools of law.

Clearly, the rigidity of law has been the result of the faulty epistemology of the classical legal theory, and more specifically the doctrine of the infallibility of juristic consensus. For the theory fails to distinguish between the various levels of meaning of the law, namely, the difference between the abstract ideals of law, and the concrete body of rules and doctrines. In other words, the classical theory mistakenly asserts that the ideals that the law aspires to realize have been permanently captured in the legal doctrines expounded by early jurists. As such, the classical theory has certainly been instrumental in hindering the development of Muslim societies and bringing Islamic civilization to ruin. After the theory assumed prominence in legal circles, the efforts of the jurists were directed toward resisting any development that would render social practices incompatible with the existing legal code, instead of modifying legal doctrines so that new social development could be guided by Islamic ideals.

After the fifth century, classical legal theory became the dominant paradigm around which Islamic law evolved. The theory was handed down unchallenged from generation to generation until the turn of this century, when Muslims underwent a devastating defeat at the hands of European powers. The defeat was overwhelming, indeed, for it exposed Muslims – who were still convinced that they were on the top of the world – to a superior mode of civilization, thereby compelling them to reevaluate their assumptions. The Muslims' humiliating defeat by outside forces was the anomaly that violated the central premise of the classical theory, for it became quite apparent that Shari`ah had ceased to produce the superior society it once created and sustained.

CHAPTER 7

Human Rights and
Islamic Legal Reform

Is Islam compatible with human rights? This question has in recent years been the focus of attention of numerous human rights scholars, who have produced varying answers and advanced conflicting views. Any one who undertakes to study the literature generated in the process of answering the above question soon realizes that his or her task is exceedingly complex. For one finds that the foremost critics of traditional Shari`ah are united with its ardent advocates in denying any relationship between Islam and human rights. One also finds that the proponents of a human rights conception rooted in an Islamic worldview stand condemned by both modernist and traditionalist scholars: by the former because of their association with Islam, and by the latter because of their advocacy of human rights. In the midst of the contradiction and confusion that riddle the discourse on Islam and human rights, clarity and understanding are sacrificed.

At the core of the confusion lays a static and ahistorical approach that fails to distinguish the universal from its historical manifestation in particular forms, and refuses to relate the applications of the Islamic principles to their historical contexts and premodern sociopolitical conditions. Therefore, modern human rights scholars are quick to point out that historically, Muslims and non-Muslims were not treated equally under Islamic law, in complete disregard to the gulf that separates the nationalist structure of modern political organization and the communalist structure of premodern political societies. Likewise, Muslim traditionalists, driven by a similar static outlook, and oblivious to the drastic social and political changes that separate historical and contemporary Muslim societies, insist on embracing the rules expounded by early jurists, even when the application of these historical rules would negate the universal principles of Islam which gave them force in the first place.

While agreeing with the modern critics of historical Shari`ah that its application in modern society would lead to serious violation of human rights, I reject the contention that Islamic law has been oblivious to the notion of human rights. I argue that the failure of modern critics to discern a human rights tradition in Islam results from a static and ahistoric outlook that divorces the Shari`ah rules developed by classical scholars from the sociopolitical structure of early Muslim society.

I further contend that for a modern human rights tradition to take hold in modern Muslim society, it should be rooted in the moral/religious commitments of Muslims. This can be achieved not through an imposition of a human rights tradition evolved in an alien culture, but by appealing to the conception of human dignity embedded in the Qur'anic texts, and by employing the concept of reciprocity which lies at the core of the Qur'anic notion of justice.

I, therefore, conclude by showing that the application of the Islamic sources through a paradigm that incorporates the principles of human dignity and moral reciprocity into a modern society – characterized by cultural plurality and globalizing technology – is bound to evolve a human rights tradition capable of ensuring equal protections of the moral autonomy of both individuals and groups.

Historical Shari`ah and its Modern Critics

Shari`ah has been the subject of an elaborate and penetrating critique by human rights scholars. Modern scholars who have examined human rights schemes, advanced by contemporary Muslim authorities, have concluded that these schemes run far short of the protections provided by international human rights, enshrined in the Universal Declaration of Human Rights (UDHR). Thus, Mayer contends that contemporary endorsement of international human rights by Muslims is more apparent than real, because all human rights pronouncements by Muslim individuals and groups have been curtailed by qualifications rooted in Shari`ah.[193] The application of Shari`ah law would lead, she concludes, to serious breaches of international human rights. More specifically, the application of Islamic law would lead to the erosion of religious freedom and to discrimination against women and non-Muslims.[194]

Heiner Brelefeldt echoes the concerns of Mayer regarding historical Shari`ah's capacity to provide for human rights protections, particularly for women and non-Muslims. Examining areas of conflict between Shari`ah and human rights, he notes:

> Due to the timing of its development, it is hardly surprising that the classical Shari`ah differs from the modern idea of universal human rights. Although the Shari`ah puts a great deal of emphasis on the equality of all the faithful before God, it traditionally assumes un-

equal rights between men and women and between Muslims and members of other religious communities.[195]

Similar arguments are made by Rhoda Howard, who points out that traditional Shari`ah fails to provide for equal protections of the law for women and non-Muslims. "According to traditional interpretations," she writes, "Islam excludes entire categories of people, most notably women, slaves [sic], and non-Muslims, from equality under the law, although it does set out careful rules for their unequal protection."[196] Howard cautions, however, against any conclusion that would suggest that the classical legal system was unjust, and goes on to argue that "compared with Europe until barely a century and a half ago, Islamic societies might well be characterized as far more just in the modern sense of protecting human rights."[197] Still, Howard is quick to deny the possibility of developing a modern human rights tradition, rooted in Islamic worldview, insisting that "Islamic conception of justice is not one of human rights."[198]

Perhaps the most penetrating and systematic critique of traditional Shari`ah is provided by Abdullahi An-Na`im. In his *Toward an Islamic Reformation*, An-Na`im discusses specific examples of violation of religious freedom by Shari`ah rules, and cites instances of discrimination against women and non-Muslims in the historical legal system.[199] However, unlike the previous critics of Shari`ah, An-Na`im realizes that the possibility and importance of evolving a human rights tradition from within the Islamic normative system, and warns against any external imposition.[200] To do this, he calls for an Islamic reformation aimed at overcoming contradictions between international human rights and Shari`ah rules, and proposes a methodological approach based on what he calls "the evolutionary principle" introduced in the seventies by his late mentor, Mahmoud Muhammad Taha. According to this principle, the Makkan Qur'an embodies the eternal principles of the Islamic revelation which emphasize human solidarity and establish the principle of justice for all, regardless of religion, gender, or race. It is further argued that the Madinan Qur'an places the solidarity of male Muslims above all others, thereby giving rise to discrimination against women and non-Muslims. For this reason, An-Na`im contends, one finds contradictions between the Makkan and Madinan Qur'an.[201] While the Makkan Qur'an emphasizes freedom of religion and the peaceful coexistence among different religions, the Madinan Qur'an exerted Muslims to compel the unbelievers to accept Islam, and introduced measures that discriminate against women and against non-Muslims.[202] Rightly recognizing that classical jurists introduced the principle of *naskh* (abrogation) to discard early Qur'anic statements that appeared to contradict later statements, An-Na`im calls for the application of reverse *naskh*, i.e., the abrogation of the Madinan Qur'an whenever it contradicts the Makkan.[203] An-Na'im concludes by making a passionate plea that succinctly summarizes his approach:

> Unless the basis of modern Islamic law is shifted away from those texts of the Qur'an and Sunnah of the Madinah stage, which constituted the foundations of the construction of Shari'ah, there is no way of avoiding drastic and serious violation of universal standards of human rights. There is no way to abolish slavery as a legal institution and no way to eliminate all forms and shades of discrimination against women and non-Muslims as long as we remain bound by the framework of Shari'ah.[204]

An-Na'im's proposal seems on its face value to provide a quick fix to the contradictions between historical Shari'ah and international human rights. However, the "evolutionary principle," alluded to earlier, is not sustainable, I contend, as it can be easily faulted on both theoretical and practical grounds. First, since the Qur'an is considered by Muslims, as An-Na'im himself agrees, as a divine revelation, one has to accept the totality of the Qur'anic statements as a single discourse. Therefore, one is not justified in abrogating the Madinan verses altogether on the grounds that they address a particular historical society. Rather one has to eliminate the possibility of generalizing particular rules by demonstrating their particularity. Such a procedure would permit one to arrive at the same result without reverting to a wholesale rejection of one-third of the Qur'an. Second, negating the Madinan Qur'an would not be acceptable by the majority of Muslims, including those who agree with An-Na'im that there should be a fresh reading of the Islamic sources so as to effect a sweeping legal reform. For the Qur'anic statements revealed in Madinah do not only comment on family matters and relationships with non-Muslims, but also on such issues relating to fundamental Islamic practices as the performance of prayer, *zakat*, fasting, and *hajj*. Third, negating one-third of a book which the majority of Muslims consider to be incontrovertible is counterproductive, particularly when it can be shown that the contradictions between the Makkan and Madinan statements on women and non-Muslims are more apparent than real, resulting from faulty interpretations by classical scholars, as well as the application of atomistic methodologies of derivation.

A better and more effective approach to reforming historical Shari'ah is one that sets out from the very notion that constitutes the *raison d'être* for the articulation of human rights in Western tradition, viz. human dignity. Since the Qur'anic texts embody clear and developed notion of human dignity, restructuring Shari'ah rules – particularly those which relate to the public sphere – on the basis of the Qur'anic notion of human dignity would lead, I contend, to a situation in which the civil and political liberties of all citizens are protected – regardless of gender, ethnic, or religious distinctions. Further, setting out from the notion of human dignity to reform the Shari`ah has another advantage: It has the potential to nurture a liberal tradition without being limited to the tradition of individualistic liberalism, which many scholars consider to be Western specific. As will be shown in the next section, developing a human rights tradition on the basis of Islamic worldview and heritage extends the notion of moral autonomy, presupposed by human dignity, from the individual to the community.

Dignity, Reciprocity, and Universal Claims

The critics of Shari`ah have used UDHR as the standard through which Shari`ah is evaluated and faulted. Because UDHR is rooted in the political culture of Western society, and is informed by the philosophical outlook of Western liberalism, its application in other societies requires that the universal validity of its principles is made evident to other peoples, particularly those whose worldviews and historical experiences are different from that of the West. Realizing that the claim of universality cannot be established on theoretical grounds, most "international human rights" advocates advance practical and pragmatic reasons for establishing universality claims. Some emphasize the fact that peoples of different cultural and geographical backgrounds "share a common humanity, which means that they are equally deserving of rights and freedom."[205] Others point out that the UDHR has been framed by representatives of the various nations that constitute the United Nations (UN), and hence conclude that UDHR receives the support of various cultures and religious communities. Still others argue that human rights were developed in modern times to protect individuals from the encroachment of the modern nation-state. Because the nation-state is the basic political organization for all societies and cultures, the need for adopting international human rights to protect individual liberties is universal.[206]

The pragmatic arguments for the universality of human rights are problematic, because they either completely overlook the significant impact that cultural differentiation has on values and perceptions, or ignore the fact that agreements through the United Nations reflect, more often than not, political compromises by political elites, rather than normative consensus. Further, many of the ruling elites who pretend to speak on the behalf of the peoples of the developing world lack political legitimacy and public support, and have embraced ideological outlooks at odds with the surrounding cultures. In the absence of genuine democracy in the countries of the South, no one can ascertain whether, or to what extent, official policies reflect popular views and preferences.

Given the Western roots of international human rights, and the absence of any theoretical foundation or practical grounds for their universal claims, I propose that a more fundamental criteria should be used to develop a human rights tradition, rooted in Islamic values and ethos, and capable of protecting the rights, and promoting the interests of citizens, regardless of religious, gender, racial, or national distinctions. The fundamental criteria to which I am referring are the concept of *dignity* and the principle of *reciprocity.*

Human dignity is the reason for which international human rights have been delineated. The preamble of the UDHR begins by emphasizing this very point. In Western tradition, the concept of dignity has been best elaborated by Kant, who points out that human beings are moral agents, and should hence, always be treated as ends, and never as means. Conceiving every human being as an end means that he or she should always be treated as a subject, capable of identifying and pursuing his or her interests. This does not mean that one cannot use the services of others to achieve one's goals, but that the services they provide must be performed with their consent, and should be based on their full realization of the intents, significations, and consequences of their actions. Compelling people to act under the use or threat of force violates their dignity.

Likewise, the Qur'an describes the human person as a unique being among the creatures of God, endowed with rational capacity to understand the natural order, and to distinguish right from wrong; and elevated over the entire creation by a moral capacity to commit oneself to a specific moral vision, and the ability to translate ideas and values to physical and social forms. Life is presented as a trial in which people have the opportunity to make choices, and are individually responsible for the choices they make. Therefore, central to the notion of dignity in both Western and Islamic traditions, is the notion of moral autonomy (i.e., the freedom to make rational choices), and to accept the outcome of the rational choices one makes.

At the heart of the notion of dignity, though, is not a social license to do whatever one wishes, but a moral character that acts out of deep convictions, including the conviction that one ought to respect the moral choices of others, and the expectation that others should reciprocate and respect one's choices. That is, dignity lies in the profound sense of moral autonomy which enables the person to behave in accordance with his or her moral commitments and convictions, regardless of whether others agree with him or her, or approve of their choices. It is for this very reason that the behavior of those who are willing to give up their moral autonomy, in exchange for personal gratification, brings to mind the image of a shameless act deprived of dignity. While those who are ready to withstand adversities, even ridicule, rather than betray their moral commitments or submit to the arbitrary will of others make us appreciate human dignity.

Although the individual sense of dignity cannot be taken away, but can only be strengthened, by the use of arbitrary force to restrict moral autonomy, the belief in human equality, and the transcendental nature of moral responsibility require that the moral autonomy of the individual be protected by a system of rights from violation by others, particularly by a superior power, such as the state, or an organized social group. A person who refuses to compromise deeply held principles in exchange for a generous monetary reward, or in the face of a serious threat to one's safety, exemplifies human dignity at its best.

Yet moral autonomy associated with human dignity is not limited to the individual, but involves the moral autonomy of the group to which one belongs as well. Because the concretization of the moral choices one makes requires the cooperation of all individuals who share the same moral vision, the autonomy of individuals – and hence their dignity – hinges on the autonomy of the group to which they belong. It is here where the notion of individualism in the Western and Muslim historical experience diverge. In the tradition of Western individualism, the individual is seen as a member of a homogeneous community, and the freedom of the individual means that he or she has the right to enact their moral choices, as long as they do not violate the freedom of others.[207] However, in the tradition of Islamic legal and political thought, society is not seen as homogenous, but consisting of a plurality of moral communities, each of which has the freedom to actualize its own moral vision.[208]

Emphasizing the moral autonomy of groups is exceedingly important in a postmodern society that combines global orientation with moral and cultural fragmentation. The homogenous culture in which Western individualism was developed has already become something of the past. Cultural fragmentation and the coexistence of a multitude of moral communities is today the reality of societies that once enjoyed remarkable cultural homogeneity, such as the French and the German. Protecting human dignity in a heterogeneous society requires a markedly new approach whereby the moral autonomy of the individual is linked to that of the moral community to which he or she belongs.

While the notion of human dignity emphasizes the moral autonomy of individuals and groups, the extent of this autonomy can be specified by employing another principle, viz. the principle of reciprocity. The principle, central to all religious and secular ethics, has been appropriated from Christian ethics by modern Western scholars, and has been given a secular expression in Kant's categorical imperative: "Act only on that maxim through which you can at the same time will that it become a universal law."[209] Similarly, the principle of reciprocity lies at the core of the

Islamic concept of justice. The Qur'an is pervaded with injunctions that encourage the Muslims to reciprocate good for good and evil for evil.[210]

But reciprocity, as the most fundamental principle of justice, is often employed to denote mutual recognition by individual members of the community, and rarely a relationship among moral groups and communities. This applies to both modern and premodern scholars. It is evident that while classical Muslim jurists recognized the moral autonomy of non-Muslim religious communities, they did not attribute to them equal moral freedom, and hence failed to develop rules that they would accept if they happened to come under the hegemony of others. The same can be said about those Western scholars who are driven by a single-minded desire to export those human rights schemes to the rest of the world, and who have shown little interest in engaging non-Western points of view in any meaningful cross-cultural dialogue.

Having identified the criteria for evaluating historical Shari`ah, we can now turn to examine its pronouncements concerning the civil and political rights of individuals.

Classical Legal Theory: Three Fault Lines

We started our discussion by asking whether a political order based on Islamic ethos is capable of promoting human rights. We argued that critics of Islamic law have advanced the proposition that women and non-Muslims did not enjoy equal rights with Muslim men. However, the evidence presented by the critics of Shari`ah is inconclusive as to whether the fault lines that separate Muslims and non-Muslims, as well as men and women, stem from intrinsic features of the Islamic sources themselves, or whether they result from the failure to develop Shari`ah to cater to modern settings. This ambivalence may be attributed – at least partially – to the fact that Islamic sources and legal rules appear to combine statements that emphasize equality with other statements justifying religious and gender differentiation. It is, therefore, incumbent upon us, before we go on to study the possibilities of reform, to understand the reasons behind the contradictions cited by the critics, and to examine the nature of the methods and arguments used to justify and reconcile contradictions.

Human rights scholars have identified various Shari`ah rules which are in direct contradiction with international human rights. The Shari`ah rules incongruent with international human rights can be subsumed under three major headings: restrictions on freedom of religion, discrimination against women, and discrimination against non-Muslims. However, a close examination of the corpus of Shari`ah rules developed by early jurists reveals three important facts that eluded modern critics of Shari`ah. First, that Shari`ah rules concerning particular issues have changed over time, pursuant to changes in the social and political structures of Muslim society. Secondly, jurists have adopted varying positions regarding women's and non-Muslim rights. These positions were influenced by the cultural milieu of the jurist, and the jurisprudential school to which he belonged. Thirdly, while the systems of rights developed by classical Muslim jurists were far from being perfect, it is evident that classical jurists recognized the intrinsic dignity of non-Muslims and women, even when they failed to provide a complete and comprehensive list of rights for its protection.

Early jurists recognized that non-Muslims who have entered into a peace convenant with Muslims are entitled to full religious freedom, and equal protection of the law as far as their rights to personal safety and property are concerned. Thus Muhammad bin al-Hasan al-Shaybani states in unequivocal terms that when non-Muslims enter into a peace covenant with Muslims, "Muslims should not appropriate any of their [the non-Muslims] houses and land, nor should they intrude into any of their dwellings. Because they have become party to a covenant of peace, and because on the day of the [peace of] Khaybar, the Prophet's spokesman announced that none of the property of the covenanter is permitted to them [the Muslim]. Also because they [the non-Muslims] have accepted the peace covenant so as they may enjoy their properties and rights on par with Muslims."[211] Similarly, early Muslim jurists recognized the right of non-Muslims to self-determination, and awarded them full moral and legal autonomy in the villages and towns under their control. Therefore, al-Shaybani, the author of the most authoritative work on non-Muslim rights, insists that the Christians who have entered into a peace covenant (*dhimma*) – hence became *dhimmis* – have all the freedom to trade in wine and pork in their towns, even though such practice is considered immoral and illegal among Muslims.[212] However, *dhimmis* were prohibited to do the same in towns and villages controlled by Muslims.

Likewise, early Muslim jurists recognized the right of *dhimmis* to hold public office, including the office of a judge and minister. However, because judges had to refer to laws sanctioned by the religious traditions of the various religious communities, non-Muslim judges could not administer law in Muslim communities, nor were Muslim judges permitted to enforce Shari`ah on the *dhimmis*. There was no disagreement among the various schools of jurisprudence on the right of non-Muslims to be ruled according to their laws; they only differed in whether the positions held by non-Muslim magistrates were judicial in nature, and hence the magistrates could be called judges, or whether they were purely political, and therefore the magistrates were indeed political leaders.[213] Al-Mawardi, hence distinguished between two types of ministerial positions:

plenipotentiary minister (*wazir tafwid*) and *executive* minister (*wazir tanfiz*). The two positions differ in that the former acts independently from the caliph, while the latter has to act on the instructions of the caliph, and within the limitations set by him.[214] Therefore, early jurists permitted *dhimmis* to hold the office of the executive, but not the *plenipotentiary*, minister.[215]

Given the communal nature of the social and political organizations of premodern Muslim society – indeed most premodern societies for that matter – it would be erroneous to argue that *dhimmis* were considered second-class citizens, or that they were not treated with equal "concern and respect." Such a conclusion results from an ahistorical perception of society, whereby a premodern, communally-based society is evaluated using concepts – such as *citizen* or *equal protection of the law* – developed under conditions quite unlike those that existed in the historical Muslim society.

But while early Islamic law recognized the civil and political rights and liberties of non-Muslim *dhimmis*, Shari`ah rules underwent drastic revision, beginning with the eighth century of Islam. This was a time of great political turmoil throughout the Muslim world. It was during that time that the Mongols invaded Central and West Asia inflicting tremendous losses on various dynasties and kingdoms, and destroying the seat of the caliphate in Baghdad. This coincided with the crusaders' control of Palestine and the coast of Syria. In the West, the Muslim power in Spain was being gradually eroded. It was under such conditions of mistrust and suspicion that a set of provisions attributed to an agreement between the Caliph Omar and the Syrian Christians were publicized in a treatise written by Ibn al-Qayyim.[216] The origin of these provisions is dubious, but their intent is clear: to humiliate Christian *dhimmis* and to set them apart in dress code and appearance. Their impact, however, was limited, as the Ottomans, who replaced the Abbasids as the hegemonic power in the Muslim world, continued the early practice of granting legal and administrative autonomy to non-Muslim subjects.

When we turn to examine the attitude toward women in historical Shari`ah we find that the situation here is more perplexing. For, on the one hand, one can see clearly that Shari`ah considers women as autonomous persons with full legal capacity: they enjoy full control over their property; their consent is required for marriage and they have the right to initiate the process of divorce; they can initiate legal proceedings and can grant or receive the power of attorney; they can even assume public office and serve in the capacity of judges. But, on the other hand, one can also see that the historical prejudice against women in general has worked against them in the historical Muslim society, and that Muslim jurists managed to undermine their independent legal personality by a host of legal devices. However, it can be easily demonstrated that the desire to place limitations on the civil and political rights of Muslim women was not of the same intensity across legal schools. The most conservative stance came from the Hanbali, and, to a lesser degree, the Shafi`i schools. The Hanafi school displayed, on the other hand, a more liberal attitude toward women, allowing them more leverage in pursuing their civil rights.

While Shafi`i and Malik permit, for instance, the father to compel his daughter in matters of marriage, Abu Hanifa, al-Thawri, al-Awza'i, and the majority of early jurists insist that a girl has the final say in marriage matters.[217] Similarly, Shafi`i requires the consent of the guardian of a woman for the validation of marriage, whereas Abu Hanifa, al-Shu`bi, and al-Zuhri permits a woman to marry herself despite her family disapproval.[218] However, all legal schools recognize the women's right to terminate the marriage but only under conditions that vary from one school to another.[219] Likewise, there is disagreement among jurists as to whether women can assume public office; while Ibn Jarir al-Tabari places no limitations on women's right to assume the post of judge in all legal matters, al-Mawardi contends that women cannot be allowed to serve as judges under any circumstances. Abu Hanifa allows women to serve as judges but only in cases involving commercial deals.[220]

We may conclude that while historical Shari`ah recognized the capacity of non-Muslims and women to enjoy certain civil and political liberties, it managed, nonetheless, to curtail these liberties on social and rational grounds. The degree of limitation on the exercise of civil and political rights also varied across historical periods and legal schools. And hence, while our observations give us reasons for optimism about the capacity of Islamic values and ideals to promote human rights, they point to the inability of the classical legal system to promote human rights in modern times, and to the urgent need for undertaking legal reform of traditional Islamic law.

The Imperative of Rational Mediation of Islamic Sources

Shari`ah law was historically developed by Muslim jurists by applying human reasoning to revealed texts with the aim to develop a normative system capable of regulating individual actions and social interactions. Early jurists relied primarily on the Qur'an and the practices of the Prophet to elaborate the rules of Shari`ah, and referred to the process through which Shari`ah rules were elaborated by the term *ijtihad*. Recognizing the imperative of rational mediation for understanding the rules of Shari`ah, early jurists exerted a great deal of time and energy to define the grammar of interpreting the divine texts and energy to define the grammar of interpreting the divine texts and the logic of reasoning about their implications. The differences in methodological approaches led to the differentiation of the various schools of jurisprudence. Because the Qur'anic texts were given in a concrete form, whereby the Qur'an commented on the actions and interactions of the early Muslim community, and directed early Muslims in concrete situations, the jurists applied *qiyas* to expand the application of the Qur'anic precepts to new cases. The *qiyas* technique, widely accepted by the schools of jurisprudence, requires the jurists to identify the efficient reason ('*illa*) of a specific Qur'anic statement, and to use this reason as the basis for extending the application of the Qur'anic precept to new cases. For example, early jurists extended the prohibition of wine to all intoxicating substance on the grounds that intoxication was the reason for the Qur'anic prohibition of wine. Early jurists also utilized the statements and actions of the Prophet and his Companions as a means to arrive at a better understanding of the revealed texts. The practices of the Prophet and his Companions became known as the Sunnah and were captured in the hadith narrations. Early jurists did not feel that the Sunnah has an authority independent from the Qur'an, and hence did not hesitate to reject a hadith narration whenever it was in a clear contradiction with a Qur'anic statement.[221]

As we saw in the previous chapter, *ijtihad* took a decisive turn when Muhammad bin Idris al-Shafi`i declared that the Sunnah was an inviolable source of law on par with the Qur'an, and insisted that it enjoyed an independent authority.[222] Shafi`i confined *ijtihad* to *qiyas*, declaring all other legal reasoning to be arbitrary.[223] The restrictions on *ijtihad* were further extended by Ahmad bin Hanbal, who insisted that legal analogy has to be used only as a last resort. He, therefore, required that even a weak hadith has to be given priority over legal analogy.[224] The other two major schools of jurisprudence of the Sunni branch of Islam,[225] the Hanafi and Maliki, were able to escape the severe restrictions on *ijtihad* imposed by Shafi`i and Hanbali schools by employing the techniques of *istihsan* and *istislah* respectively. *Istihsan* meant that the jurist was not bound by the apparent reason of a particular rule, but could utilize other reasons of Shari`ah whenever deemed more relevant. *Istislah*, on the other hand, allowed the jurist to base the rules of Shari`ah on public interests and utility, rather than confining them to `*illa*.

The desire of Hanafi and Maliki jurists to overcome the literalist approach that equates *ijtihad* with *qiyas* (à la Shafi`i), or with linguistic explication of the Qur'an by reference to hadith (à la Hanbali), has inspired them to develop methods aimed at prioritizing Shari`ah rules and principles. Methods such as *al-qaw'id al-fiqhiyyah* (juristic rules) or *al-maqasid al-shari`iyyah* (Shari`ah purposes) aim at the systematization of the Shari`ah rules by eliminating internal contradiction, and constitute what is referred to today as the *maqasid* approach.

By its emphasis on meaning, reasoning, and purposes the *maqasid* approach provides a powerful tool for reforming historical Shari`ah, because it rejects the literal reading of statements apart from their rationale, and insists that this rationale cannot contradict basic Islamic values. The definitive exposition of this approach can be found in the work of the Andalusian jurist Ibrahim bin Ishaq al-Shatibi, *Al-Muwafaqat*. The *maqasid* approach expounded by Shatibi can be summarized in the following points: (1) Shari`ah rules purport to promote human interests; (2) Shari`ah consists of a hierarchy of rules, whereby the particular rules (*ahkam juz'iyyah*) are subsumed under universal laws (*qawanin kulliyyah*); (3) General rules must be modified to accommodate – whenever possible – particular rules; (4) Particular rules that contradict general rules should be rejected or ignored; (5) The various rules and laws of Shari`ah aim at advancing five general purposes: the protection of religion, life, reason, property, and progeny.

In the remainder of this paper, I will undertake a fresh interpretation of the Islamic sources on the moral positions women and non-Muslims enjoy, and the rights and obligations assigned to them. I propose to employ a methodology rooted in the *maqasid* approach, and based on the following five principles:

- *Principle 1*: Rights and obligations cannot be established on the basis of individual statements of the Qur'an and Sunnah, but have to accord with the totality of relevant statements. Therefore, a jurist is required, according to this principle, to consult all relevant texts *before rendering a specific ruling.*

- *Principle 2*: The multiplicity of Qur'anic rules must be reduced into a coherent set of universal principles. The universal principles should be used to ensure the systematic application of Shari`ah in modern context. Such systematization should prevent an application of a specific (*khass*) rule in violation of a general (`*amm*), or a particular (*juz'i*) in violation of a universal (*kulli*).

- *Principle 3*: Because the generalization of a rule presupposes that the reason for its enactment is clear, no rule should be generalized unless its reason has been explicated. This principle requires that Qur'anic rules relating to social actions and interactions should be understood fully, and systematized with other rules. If this requirement is met, the literalist application of Shari`ah would be eliminated.

- *Principle 4*: Because the universalization of a principle requires that the conditions of its application be identical, regardless of time and space, no principle can be declared universal if the particularity of the context for which it was intended is evident. This principle complements *Principle 3* by requiring the jurist to examine the extent to which a specific statement or rule is directly connected with the sociopolitical context in which it was revealed.

- *Principle 5*: Qur'anic statements take priority over Prophetic ones. Hence, in the case of conflict and real contradiction, Qur'anic precepts override Prophetic ones.[226]
- Utilizing the methodological framework outlined above, I turn now to examine the extent to which religious restrictions on religious freedom and the rights of women and non-Muslims are rooted in the attitudes and practices of historical Muslim communities, and how far these restrictions can be attributed to revealed texts.

Freedom of Conviction

There is ample evidence in the Qur'an, both the Makkan and Madinan, that individuals should be able to accept or reject a particular faith on the basis of personal conviction, and that no amount of external pressure or compulsion should be permitted: "No compulsion in religion: truth stands out clear from error" (2:256), and "If it had been the Lord's will, they would have believed–All who are on earth! Will you then compel mankind, against their will, to believe!" (10:99). By emphasizing people's right to freely follow their conviction, the Qur'an reiterates a long standing position, which it traces back to one of the earliest known Prophets, Noah.[227]

Not only does the Qur'an recognize the individual's right to freedom of conviction, but it also recognizes his/her moral freedom to act on the basis of their conviction.[228] The principle that the larger community has no right to interfere in one's choices of faith and conviction can be seen further in the fact that the Qur'an emphasizes that the individual is accountable for the moral choices he or she makes in this life to their Creator alone.[229]

Yet despite the Qur'anic emphasis on the freedom of conviction and moral autonomy, most classical jurists contend that a person who renounces Islam or converts to another religion commits a crime of *ridda* (apostasy) punishable by death. However, because the Qur'an supported religious freedom,[230] classical jurists advocated the death penalty for *ridda* (renouncing Islam) based on two hadith texts and the precedent of the Muslims fighting against Arab apostates under the leadership of Abu Bakr, the first caliph. Although this evidence is shaky and does not stand under close scrutiny, the two hadith texts reported in *Sahih Bukhari* state:

"Kill whoever changes his religion" and "Three acts permit the taking of a person's life: a soul for a soul, the adultery of a married man, and renouncing religion while severing ties with the community."

Now both hadith statements cannot stand as credible evidence because they contravene numerous Qur'anic evidence. According to the *Maqasid* approach, a hadith can limit the application of a general Qur'anic statement, but can never negate it.[231] Besides, the hadith even contradicts the practices of the Prophet who reportedly pardoned Muslims who committed *ridda*. One well-known example is that of Abdullah bin Sa`d who was pardoned after Osman bin Affan pleaded on his behalf. Ibn Hisham narrated in his *Sirah* that the Prophet pardoned the people of Quraysh after Muslims entered Makkah victorious in the eighth year of the Islamic calendar. The Prophet excluded few individuals from this general pardon, whom he ordered to be killed if captured, including Abdullah bin Sa`d. Abdullah was one of the few persons appointed by the Prophet to write the revealed texts. After spending a while with the Muslims in Madinah, he renounced Islam and returned to the religion of Quraysh. He was brought to the court of the Prophet by Osman, who appealed for his pardon. He was pardoned even though he was still, as the narration indicates, in a state of *ridda* and was yet to reembrace Islam.[232] If *ridda* was indeed a *hadd* (sing. of *hudud*), neither Osman would be able to plead for him, nor would the Prophet pardon him in violation of the Islamic law. Therefore, I am inclined to the increasingly popular view among contemporary scholars, that *ridda* does not involve a moral act of conversion, but a military act of rebellion, whose calming justifies the use of force and the return of fire.[233]

To make things worse, classical jurists extended the death penalty to cases of misinterpretation of divine texts, or negligence of religious practices. Thus, classical jurists insisted that a Muslim who negates or neglects prayer could be executed if he does not repent within three days. Although the vast majority of classical jurists maintained that it was not necessary for a Muslim to openly renounce Islam to be subject to the death penalty, it was sufficient, however, for him to say or do something contrary to Islam to be executed. Although jurists called neglecting religious duties or contravening orthodox interpretations *zandaqa* (heresy) rather than *ridda*, they treated both equally in their severity.[234] Interestingly, heresy punishment is not based on any Qur'anic or Prophetic texts, but on a faulty theory of right.

Jurists divided the widely accepted *theory of right* into three types:[235] (1) Rights of God (*Huquq* Allah): These consist of all obligations that one has to discharge simply because they are divine commands, even when the human interests or utilities in undertaking them are not apparent, such as prayers, fasting, *hajj*, etc.; (2) Rights shared by God and His servants (*Huquq Allah wa al-'Ibad*): These include acts that are obligatory because they are demanded by God, but they are also intended to protect the public, such as *hudud* law, *jihad*, *zakat*, etc., and (3) Rights of God's servants (*Huquq al-'Ibad*): These are rights intended to protect individual interests, such as fulfilling promises, paying back debts, honoring contracts. Still, people are accountable for their fulfillment to God.

As can be seen, the *theory of right* devised by late classical jurists – around the eighth century of Islam – emphasizes that people are ultimately answerable to God in all their dealings. However, by using the term rights of God to underscore the moral duty of the individual, and his/her accountability before God, classical jurists obscured the fact that rights are invoked to support legal claims and to enforce the interests of the right-holder. Because the Qur'an makes it abundantly clear that obeying the divine revelation does not advance the interests of God, but only those of the human being, the phrase "rights of God" signifies only the moral obligations of the believers toward God, and by no means should they be taken as a justification of legal claims.[236] It follows that the rights of God which are exclusively personal should be considered as moral obligations for which people are only answerable to God in the life to come. As such, accepting or rejecting a specific interpretation or a particular religious doctrine, and observing or neglecting fundamental religious practices, including prayer or *hajj*, should have no legal implications whatsoever. A legal theory in congruence with the Qur'anic framework should distinguish between moral and legal obligations, and confine the latter to public law that promote public interests (constitutional, criminal, etc.) and private law that advances private interests (trade, family, personal, etc.).

Unless the above legal reform is undertaken, there is no way to ensure that *takfir* (charging one with disbelief) and *zandaqa* claims would not become a political weapon in the hands of political groups to be used as a means to eliminate rivals and opponents. Indeed there is ample evidence to show that *zandaqa* and *takfir* have been used by the political authorities during the Umayyad and Abbasid dynasties to persecute political dissidents.[237]

Religious Equality and Moral Autonomy

We have already seen that the record of historical Shari'ah concerning the human rights of non-Muslims is mixed. On the one hand, the Shari'ah recognized the rights of non-Muslims to enjoy equal protection of the law as far as their life, property, and personal security are concerned. Non-Muslims also enjoyed the rights to freedom of conviction, and the right for self-determination as far as their legal and administrative conditions were involved. On the other hand, classical jurists imposed a number of restrictions on non-Muslims in the area of dress code, display of religious symbols, the construction of churches in predominantly Muslim districts, the use of mounts and carrying of weapons, etc.[238] I have already suggested that the restrictions imposed on non-Muslims do not stem from Qur'anic standards, but rather security concerns during the political turmoil associated with the Mongol and crusade invasions. Therefore, the apparent indifference on the part of Shari`ah toward the civil and political rights of non-Muslims stems not from any insensitivities attributable to classical jurists, but rather to the literalist approach of contemporary traditionalist jurists. Indeed, the literalist and imitative approach of Islamic traditionalism has been the main obstacle in the way toward evolving a human rights tradition rooted in Islamic sources.

The first thing that strikes us when we study the Qur'anic texts is that the Qur'an neither confines faith and salvation to those who accept the Islamic revelation, nor deny faith and salvation to other religions.[239] Indeed the Qur'an does not limit the attribution of faith and salvation to the People of the Book (Jews and Christians) but extend it to believers of other faiths.[240]

Nor does the Qur'an consider all those who accepted Islam as true believers. For some have accepted the new religion as a general mode of life but failed to internalize its worldview and ethical mission:

> The desert Arabs say, "We believe." Say, "Ye have no faith; but you (only) say, 'We have submitted our wills to God,' for not yet has faith entered your hearts. But if you obey God and His messenger, he will not belittle aught of your deeds: for God is oft-forgiving, most merciful." (49:14)

Others conformed to Islamic teachings only in appearance, but continued to harbor suspicion and doubts, even ill-will toward Islam and its adherents and advocates.[241] It follows that believers and disbelievers can belong to all religions.

Because believers and disbelievers cannot be distinguished on religious lines, as they run across all religions, the Qur'an urges Muslims to seek a political order based on peaceful cooperation and mutual respect, and warns them against placing religious solidarity over covenanted rights and the principles of justice.[242]

Equipped with the above set of principles, the Prophet managed to establish in Madinah a multireligious political community, based on a set of universal principles that constituted the Pact of Madinah (*Sahifat al-Madinah*).[243] The various rules enunciated in the Pact were aimed at maintaining peace and cooperation, protecting the life and property of the inhabitants of Madinah, fighting aggression and injustice regardless of tribal or religious affiliations, and ensuring freedom of religion and movement. It is remarkable that the Madinah Pact placed the rules of justice over and above religious solidarity, and affirmed the rights of the victim of aggression and injustice to rectitude regardless of their tribal or religious affiliation, or that of the culprit.

However, it is not sufficient today for Muslim jurists to recognize the moral autonomy of non-Muslim communities, as the classical jurists did. The Qur'anic concept of justice requires that they employ the principle of reciprocity in delineating the overall legal structure to govern the religiously and morally pluralistic societies of today. That is, contemporary Muslims should avoid invading the moral space of other communities in as much as they would dread the imposition of alien moral or legal rules in their moral space.

Women's Rights: Public Equality and Family Privacy

When approaching Islamic sources to shed light on women's rights' issues, a clear distinction emerges between the rights of women in the public sphere, and their rights in the area of family law. For while Islamic sources differentiate men's and women's responsibilities within the family, all limitations on women's rights imposed by classical scholars in the public sphere were based on either faulty interpretations of Islamic texts, or practical limitations associated with the social and political structures of historical society.

The Qur'an is unequivocal in assigning equal responsibilities for men and women for maintaining public order: "The believers, men and women, are protectors one of another; they enjoin the right (*ma'ruf*) and forbid the intolerable (*munkar*); they observe regular prayers, practice regular charity, and obey God and His Messenger" (9:71). Since men and women are entrusted with the same public responsibility to enjoin the right and forbid the intolerable, one should expect that both would enjoy equal political rights. Yet it is obvious that classical jurists deny women political equality with men. The question, therefore, arises as to what is the basis of the classical position? Jurists who deny women the right to public office base their arguments on one Qur'anic and one prophetic statement. The Qur'anic statement reads: "Men are the protectors (*qawwamun*) of women, because God has given the one more (strength) than the other, and because men support women from their means" (4:34). The word *qawwamun* which connotes "support" and "protection" has come to signify authority as well. The fact that *qawwamun* also signifies authority is not difficult to see as the remainder of the above Qur'anic statement empowers men with the right to discipline women guilty of mischief. But can the above verse be used to deny women access to public office? The answer is an emphatic no. For the authority implied by *qawwamun* and the obedience it entails is relevant – even under classical interpretation – within the confines of the family. It is clear that the Qur'an does not intend to give authority to every single man over every single woman. Nor do those who extend the implication of this verse to the public sphere expect that any single woman in society should obey any single man, known to her or not. If this is the case, no one can invoke the notion of *qawwamun* to deny women access to public office.

The other textual evidence used by classical jurists, which continues to be held by contemporary traditionalist jurists, is in the form of a hadith text that states: "They shall never succeed those who entrust their affairs to a woman."[244] Reportedly the statement is a comment made by the Prophet upon hearing the news of the accession of Buran, the daughter of King Anusherawan, to the Persian throne after the passing away of her father. I wish to argue here that there are sufficient reasons to show that the above hadith does not stand up to close scrutiny, and cannot, hence, be allowed to undermine the principle of moral and political equality between the sexes, which is firmly established in the Qur'anic texts. (1) The hadith statement is not given in the form of a directive, but an opinion that has to be understood in its historical and cultural context. That is, the hadith has to be interpreted in the context of a historical society where women were not active participants in political life, and in the context of a political culture that places the hereditary rule over the principle of merit in deciding political succession. (2) The hadith is a single statement that has no support in the most authoritative Islamic source – i.e., the Qur'an. (3) The hadith stands in a direct contradiction with the principle of moral and political equality of the sexes, a principle established by numerous Qur'anic verses. (4) Finally, the hadith, being a singular narration (*khabar ahad*), is of a lesser degree of certainty than the Qur'anic narration (*khabar mutawatar*), and hence cannot overrule principles established in the Qur'an.

We have to conclude, therefore, that the Islamic sources support the right of women to have full access to public office, and to enjoy complete equality with men in public life. Our discussion of the notion of *qawwamun*, which provides men with a degree of authority over women, must be confined to the realm of family life. It is in the family, and in the family alone, that all of the practices cited by the critics of Shari'ah as instances of gender inequality can be found, namely polygamy, unequal inheritance, and interreligious marriages.[245] Defenders of these inequalities among contemporary Muslim intellectuals have cited various biological, psychological, and functional bases to justify inequalities within a framework of complementary family roles. Western critics, on the other hand, dismiss gender role arguments as outdated and irrelevant, and insist that for women to live a life of dignity, society must declare the two sexes absolutely equal, and reject any legal rule that sanctions differentiation among the sexes.

While I do recognize the complexity of the issues involved in the debate on gender equality and gender roles, and the need for undertaking further research to examine the socio-historical meaning of biological differences between the sexes, and the sociopolitical significance of psychological differences – if any – between genders, I think that the debate is neither relevant nor helpful for the purpose of elaborating human rights. It is obvious that the findings of all empirical studies on the issue of sexual differences have been disputed on ideological grounds and have been interpreted in support of competing normative positions. There is nothing to suggest that human beings would ever subordinate their moral beliefs to empirical knowledge – at least not in an historically relevant timeframe. I propose, instead, that for the purpose of advancing equitable rights for all, we should focus our attention on how to ensure that marriage constitutes a consensual relationship that contribute equally to advancing the interests of the various parties involved. This, I suggest, can be achieved within a legal framework by: (1) providing men and women with equal rights to enter into the relationship on their own terms, and to leave whenever they decide the relationship has become exploitative or dissatisfying, and (2) empowering women so as to ensure that they can negotiate the conditions of their marriage from a point of strength, and to ensure that they receive the legal support needed to help them exit a relationship if it becomes undignifying.

The point being stressed here is that marriage should be viewed as a voluntary and contractual relationship, entered into with the aim of founding a family. In keeping within the framework of human rights, our efforts should focus on liberating the individual, morally and legally, from the impositions of arbitrary wills, rather than imposing a specific moral vision or legal code on him or her. Mature men and women should be able to negotiate the terms of their relationship freely without imposition from outside. Because, more often than not, families are organized in keeping with specific religious traditions of recognized moral autonomy, it is wrong for a person who belongs to one moral community to impose his or her moral vision on others.

The above point can be illustrated by looking into few concrete examples. Forcing a woman to stay in a marriage against her will violates her right to moral autonomy and hence contravenes her civil liberties, even if this was done in keeping with a specific religious tradition, such as Catholicism. By the same token, a woman should not be forced to stay in a marriage that brings no satisfaction or happiness for the sake of keeping with Catholic morality and religion. Similarly, a woman who elects to maintain her marriage even after she became aware of her husband's intention to take a second wife, permitted under Shari`ah, must be allowed to do so. The law should provide her with the option to opt for a dignified exit under reasonable conditions. But it would be sheer arrogance for a person belonging to another moral or religious view to insist that their moral values or religious practices should prevail over her voluntarily made choice.

Even when one truly believes that the moral system to which he or she belongs is superior to others, and that others, by following different moralities, are not being treated to the full respect they deserve, one's moral system should not be imposed on others through legal means. For human dignity, which human rights intend to protect, requires that the person be first persuaded to the superiority of this or that moral system, so as to allow him/her the choice to be the agent through which the legal system is reformed. Human rights advocates should ensure the free flow of information, and a political environment conducive to freedom of speech and action.

Due to the importance of the family to human society, all religions stress certain attitudes and values to keep it intact, and to extend its protection to the fragile souls who were brought to life within its confines. Human rights scholars should not direct their efforts to undermine religious attitudes and values, but should focus on the conditions that allow free and equal entrance and exist to the two genders. This would mean that while Muslim women may keep in line with their religious conviction and refuse to marry non-Muslim men, those who elect to violate the religious code should have the legal freedom to do so. By abandoning the requirements of marriage within her faith, a Muslim woman is vulnerable to moral condemnation by her family and religious community, and may suffer civil consequences, but should not be subject to the state's punitive retribution. The Islamic state, we should remember, is conceptually and practically multi-confessional, and is, therefore, constitutionally committed to the moral autonomy of individuals within and across religions.

The Islamic state may not enforce all requirements of Shari`ah, particularly when the enforcement of such requirements (marriage conditions in this case) violates a higher principle of greater relevance to state action, namely freedom of religion. As we saw earlier, in violating the moral requirements of Shari`ah, people are answerable to their Creator, not to the state.

Conclusion

Our examination of the Qur'anic discourse reveals to us the significance it places on the moral autonomy of human beings. While the

Qur'an urges people to adopt high moral standards, it makes it quite clear that people are ultimately accountable to their Creator for their moral failings. The Qur'an further stresses that while it is not always possible for people to stay on a high moral plane, they should strive to the best of their ability to do so. Those who have been more fortunate to lead a moral life should strive, with tolerance and sympathy, to persuade others to adopt their vision of a good life, but they should never go to the extent of imposing their morality on others. It was such an attitude which allowed early Muslims to embrace diverse cultural groups, and to cooperate and peacefully coexist with a plurality of religious communities.

The tolerant attitude and pluralistic outlook was later diluted, giving rise to a more intrusive approach in which the lines separating the moral from the legal became blurred. The traditionalist stance was further compounded by undermining the principle of moral equality between men and women advanced in the Qur'anic texts. This was done by giving more weight to particular pronouncements, while ignoring universal principles and general purposes. Gradually, therefore, the moral autonomy of individuals and groups was severely compromised. Interestingly, though, in their zeal to assert Islamic morality through legal enforcement, the traditional jurists unwittingly undermined the moral fabric of society. This is because moral character does not develop under conditions of rigid restrictions on free speech and action. By definition, a moral choice presupposes that the individual has also the choice of acting immorally, or in accordance with standards that does not rise to the level of moral action. Take this choice away, morality cannot be distinguished from hypocrisy and duplicity.

There is a dire need today for Muslims to undertake a legal reform so as to restore the principle of moral autonomy to both individuals and cultural groups. By so doing, Muslims would have a greater opportunity to rid their communities from oppression, corruption, and hypocrisy. They would have also the chance to join hands with an increasing number of individuals and groups belonging to the various religious communities of the world to fight global injustice and oppression. The UDHR, should be viewed as a common thread that can bind the efforts of people belonging to diverse moral communities the world over. As I tried to show in this paper, supporting international human rights does not mean that one has to accept the various interpretations assigned to them. While the dominant interpretations of the various articles of UDHR reflect the moral inclination of Western individualism, the universal principles themselves are compatible with Islamic values and ethos. Indeed, the rejection of UDHR on the grounds that it does not fit neatly into a specific moral code derived from Islamic sources is not only a theoretical mistake, but a strategic blunder as well. Whereas the rejection of UDHR is likely to deprive the Muslims from achieving greater political liberation, a strong commitment to its principles would undoubtedly allow them to enter the global debate, and give them the opportunity to bring their values and ethos to bear positively on the future development of human rights discourse.

CHAPTER 8

Human Rights and
Cross-Cultural Dialogue

Cross-cultural dialogue is a recurring theme in international human rights literature. Some human rights scholars underscore the need for a cross-cultural discourse for transmitting human rights concerns and practices to non-Western societies, while others dismiss the call for engaging non-Western cultures in a dialogue as counterproductive, since it can only lead to compromising the universality of human rights.[246]

The purpose of this chapter is to point out inconsistencies in the work of some leading human rights scholars, involved in assessing human rights trends in the Middle East, who advocate a cross-cultural approach to understanding human rights in non-Western cultures. I argue that a close examination of what is referred to as a cross-cultural dialogue reveals unmistakable elements of hegemonic discourse. It is quite evident that many human rights scholars specializing in the study of Islam and the Middle East are not engaged in a two-way communication with Islamic reformers to help attain a better understanding of the context and direction of Islamic reform, but rather are engaged in a hegemonic discourse whose effect has been the overshadowing of a reformist discourse rooted in an Islamic worldview.

I stress, however, that the distorted picture that comes out of this hegemonic discourse does not stem out of any malicious intent to mislead, but rather is due to conceptual and methodological reasons. Methodologically, the approach to studying human rights situations in the Middle East is ahistorical and static, failing to detect actual developments in discourse and practice, and unable hence, to reveal the vigorous cultural reform currently underway in the Muslim world. Conceptually, the distortion in the picture of the human rights debate in the Middle East is due to the fact that observations are filtered through an absolute-universalistic outlook, oblivious to the importance of the notions of culture, cultural variation, and cultural dynamism on understanding human rights situations.

I further contend that while Islamic reform has a long way to go before it can ensure individual liberty and equality for all, it has been moving slowly but consistently toward a vision of an open, egalitarian, and tolerant society, and that it has already embraced international human rights as the defining principles of its vision of future society. I conclude by identifying the preconditions for a genuine cross-cultural dialogue, and cautioning against attempts to subvert human rights by employing human rights as a tool to justify the imposition of external values and choices, rather than an instrument for fighting coercion and imposition.

The Making of a Hegemonic Discourse

The value of scholarship derives from its ability to bring meaning and enlightenment to the lives of people, and to sharpen their understanding of the complex world in which they live. All scholars realize that in order to bring about clear understanding, and to explain actions and events in the complex world of humanity, this world must be reduced to a manageable set of concepts. However, for a complex world to be reduced without distortions, scholars must take special care to maintain balance among the various elements and components that constitute it. The failure to maintain balance, say by failing to reflect the size and significance of the various forces locked in an intellectual or political struggle, is bound to bring about misunderstanding rather than understanding, and to create an ugly image out of the most beautiful object of understanding. Distortion is thus the most fatal act a scholar can commit.

The importance of human rights lies in the instrumental role they play to protect the weak against the powerful, and to liberate the oppressed from their oppressors. It is widely accepted by human rights scholars that the right to free speech is not needed to protect those who celebrate the praise of the established power, but rather to make room for dissenting views and opinions. It is therefore embarrassing, even disheartening, to see human rights scholars siding with oppressive regimes against their oppressed subjects by ignoring the actual abuses of the former, while condemning the latter on the grounds of an imaginary legal system they supposedly intend to resuscitate as soon as they shake off their yokes, and obtain commanding power.

Now, combine the above two scenarios in the discourse of human rights scholars who are, wittingly or unwittingly, involved in distorting reality and using human rights to justify cultural imperialism and penetration, and you end up with a potentially devastating discourse entitled "Islam and human rights." To be fair to the participants in this discourse, the debate over the compatibility of Islam with human rights is still far from reaching the state of affairs described above, and it is not difficult to see that there are few hopeful signs, which, if pursued seriously, could shift the direction of the current debate toward more fruitful and promising ends. Among the promising signs is the notion of cross-cultural dialogue on human rights, and the notion of human rights based on international morality. But unless such notions are pursued seriously, it is only a matter of time before we arrive at the dreadful scenario described above, whereby scholarship and human rights become instruments for subjugation and control, and the hope of a more caring world in which might is truly restrained by right is completely dashed.

Indeed, even at this relatively early stage of the discourse on Islam and human rights, one can see that a *strategic formation* of an essentially hegemonic discourse is already in the making. Central to any hegemonic discourse – or strategic discursive formation – is the recasting of the subject of the study (in this case the attitudes and values of the adherents of Islam) in such a manner that the strategic interests of the hegemonic culture are advanced vis-à-vis other cultures. That is to say, the main effect of the formation of a hegemonic discourse is not understanding the "other," but justifying actions that aim at its subjugation or elimination. The image of the "other" culture is presented in such a negative way that the discourse recipients are convinced that it is utterly useless to listen to the discussion, or engage it in any meaningful dialogue.[247] As I argue below, the negative presentation of the "other" does not necessarily stem from a malicious intent to distort the facts. Rather, distortion is often the outcome of the strategic positioning of the scholar in a particular culture, which makes him/her more susceptible to the particular interests and historical experiences of the social group to which he/she belongs, and the tendency to evaluate other cultures and groups though notions and theories derived from these particular experiences and interests.

While there is no shortage of academic works that display a clear pattern of hegemonic discourse, I have made a careful decision to exclude the works of scholars who have openly advanced prejudicial arguments,[248] and to focus my analysis on examples taken from the writings of moderate scholars who have presented relatively more balanced views on the subject. One such example can be found in Ann E. Mayer's highly acclaimed work on Islam and human rights. The main thesis in her work is that contemporary Islamic human rights schemes borrow their substance from international human rights, but use Shari`ah to limit human rights applications. She argues that since historical Shari`ah discriminates against women and non-Muslims, limiting human rights by Shari`ah rules is tantamount to canceling out the protections they intend to ensure.

To demonstrate her thesis, Mayer examines four documents (the Iranian Constitution, the Universal Islamic Declaration of Human Rights, al-Azhar's model constitution of an Islamic state, and the Cairo Declaration on Human Rights) and two works by Muslim traditionalists (Mawdudi and Tabanda). Mayer discusses in detail the views of Muslim traditionalists, and shows that they have wholeheartedly accepted historical Shari`ah, opposing any efforts to reinterpret Islamic sources in ways that would lead to recognizing the right of all people – regardless of their religious, gender, or ethnic distinctions – to equal freedom. She rightly concludes that Islamic human rights schemes are effectively undermined when read through the eyes of traditionalist spokesmen of Islam. By relying extensively on the traditionalist interpretations of Shari`ah, Mayer is, therefore, able to make a persuasive case to support her thesis. Her persuasiveness is attained, however, at the expense of sacrificing clarity, and omitting crucial facts. One such crucial fact missing in Mayer's work is the intense debate currently underway between Islamic reformers and traditionalists on the relevance of premodern Shari`ah to modern Islamic society. Indeed, Mayer herself realizes, in the context of criticizing the use of Shari`ah for defining the scope of individual freedom in the Iranian Constitution, the slippery nature of her arguments, and poses an important question that goes into the heart of her contention:

> Could it not be the case, one might ask, that the Islamic qualifications on rights might be narrower than the ones permitted under international law, that these clauses could be interpreted to mean that the government would have to produce much stronger justifications for curbing human rights than it would under secular criteria? That is, one might say that the assumption that broad Islamic qualifications on rights imply the erosion of rights protection is only that – an assumption.[249]

Mayer immediately dismisses the doubts raised in the above question, insisting that "[a]lthough in the abstract this question might seem justified, there are indications that warrant the assumption that these qualifications are designed to dilute rights."[250] She goes on to cite three grounds for her contention: (1) that the Iranian government excludes "[l]iberal Muslims with strong commitments to human rights, like Mehdi Bazargan and Muslim clerks like Taleghani, who believe that Islam protects individual rights and freedoms …"[251] (2) that Middle Eastern governments in general are "hostile to claims on behalf of individual liberties and the rights of the citizens,"[252] and (3) that there is "no developed tradition of Islamic human rights protections."[253]

Yet it is not difficult to show, on a closer examination, that the grounds cited by Mayer are fragile, and do not warrant her assumption. Thus the first point she advances supports the contention I raised earlier that she is relying on traditionalist interpretations of Shari`ah while obscuring the role of Islamic reformers in bringing about profound sociopolitical change to Muslim society. For Mehdi Bazargan is himself a leading figure in the Islamic reform movement that contributed to the demise of the authoritarian regime of the Shah. He was a member of the committee that drafted the Iranian Constitution, and the first prime minister in post-revolution Iran. He continued to work toward the creation of an open, egalitarian, and tolerant Islamic society after he was pushed to the opposition by the traditionalist policies of the Ayatollahs until his death. His efforts, and those of other Islamic reformers, gave rise to a vibrant reform movement, opposing the conservative regime in Iran. The movement has recently succeeded in dislodging the conservatives from the executive branch, bring more moderate government under Khatami.

Similarly, to argue that Middle Eastern governments are "hostile to claims on behalf of individual liberties" is to miss the point. For one needs only to remember that these regimes embrace the ideologies of developmentalism – in their both nationalist and socialist forms – which justify forced assimilation and cultural imposition, the very ideologies that gave rise to Islamic reform movements. These governments are, by and large, avowedly antagonistic to Islamic reform, and have rejected in the past all attempts to base social development on Islamic values or ethos. The recent efforts on the part of some Muslim governments to incorporate certain elements of historical Shari`ah into the law are aimed at gaining the support of traditionalist jurists in their struggle against Islamic reformers.

Finally, Mayer's contention that there is "no developed tradition of Islamic human rights protections" is perplexing, and illustrative of a legalistic approach that lacks sensitivity to cultural dynamism. For while it is true that historical Shari`ah does not support a full-fledged system of human rights protection in modern society, Islamic reformers have been actively engaged, since Afghani and Abduh, in efforts to reform traditional Shari`ah, as it is shown below. Still, it is inaccurate to suggest that one cannot find principles, laws, and doctrines that can provide strong foundation for Islamic human rights tradition. Indeed, as early as the second century of Islam (eighth century) Muslim jurists have recognized the rights of non-Muslims to equal protection of the law as far as their personal safety and property are concerned, as well as their right to full religious freedom. Thus Muhammad bin Hassan al-Shaybani, the author of the most authoritative classical work on non-Muslim rights, states in unequivocal terms that when Muslims enter into a peace covenant with non-Muslims, "Muslims should not appropriate any of their [the non-Muslims] houses and land, nor should they intrude into any of their dwellings. Because they [have become] party to a covenant of peace, and because on the day of the [peace of] Khaybar, the Prophet's spokesman announced that none of the property of the covenanters is permitted to them [Muslims]. Also because they [non-Muslims] have accepted the peace covenant so as they may enjoy their properties and rights on par with Muslims."[254] Similarly, al-Shaybani concedes that Christians who have entered into a peace covenant with Muslims have the right to practice their religion and maintain their Churches, and are entitled to trade freely in wine and pork in their own towns, even though trade in, and consumption of, the two items is prohibited to Muslims under Shari`ah rules.[255]

Evidently, Mayer's assumption that Shari`ah rules are bound to effect excessive restrictions on Islamic human rights schemes rests solely on reading these schemes through the eyes of the traditionalists, while keeping the views of reform-minded Muslim scholars and activists in the background. Indeed, leaving crucial facts and evidence out, while conveniently focusing on radical and traditionalist elements of Islamic resurgence are characteristic of those human rights scholars who have been quick to dismiss the profound Islamic reform currently underway in Muslim societies, and to overlook its anti-traditionalist stance and liberal tendencies and ethos.

Similarly, scholars engaged in hegemonic discourse often water down the negative impact of the self-serving foreign policies of major Western powers on cultural reform, and on the maturation of human rights traditions. Thus Bassam Tibi dismisses the selective application of human rights by Western powers as irrelevant to the debate on human rights practices in the Middle East, and rejects the complaint of non-Western critics against selective application as mere polemics.[256] He goes further to denounce non-Western opposition to Western hegemony as unwarranted resistance "disguised as a claim to cultural authenticity."[257] Tibi does not stop even once to ask: whence comes this hostility? Nor does he seem interested in finding out whether the non-West is resisting the principles of human rights themselves, or only Western interpretations of the mode and scope of their application. In fact Tibi seems to be completely oblivious to the possibility that non-Western hostility might have to do with the support Western powers lend to oppressive non-Western regimes, ruled by hated dictators. The hegemonic nature of the intellectual discourse in which Tibi is engaged is so pervasive that it turns out that even the notion of "cross-cultural consensus" he vigorously advocates does not involve a dialogue among autonomous cultures engaged in rational persuasion, but a coercive discourse that takes the form of a monologue through which non-Western cultures are expected to learn the manners and habits of a presumably morally superior West.[258]

The Purpose of Human Rights:
From Autonomy to Paternalism

Can international human rights, which borrow their moral and intellectual strength from natural rights tradition – a tradition that places great emphasis on human dignity and individual autonomy – be used as an instrument to patronize and control other cultures? The answer to this question can be found in an article written by a human rights scholar and Middle East specialist, under the title "An Essay on Islamic Cultural Relativism in the Discourse of Human Rights."[259] The article begins by pointing out certain oppressive practices of the Iranian Islamist regime, and rightly identifies as the source of these practices the regime's failure to recognize the incompatibility of nation-state structures with the historically based Islamic legal system. However, the author turns, in the second part of his article, to direct his moral indignation of the Iranian regime at the practice of *hijab* (Islamic dress) by Muslim women. Rejecting the assertion by Muslim women that their voluntarily adoption of the *hijab* signifies a self-expression of their idea of Islamic decency, and an "affirmation of female autonomy and subjectivity," Afshari insists that the assertion is:

> illusory, more a symptom of a deeply rooted sociocultural malady than a sign of female autonomy. It is illusory because the precondition that necessitates the adoption of the *hijab* is set by the patriarchal reinvigoration of control and dominance, a new *bay`a* (oath of allegiance) to male autonomy and subjectivity. It is illusory because the wearer's notions of propriety and modesty have internalized the androcentric norms of the culture.[260]

The above argument is unmistakably paternalistic, even presumptuous, as it, in effect, accuses Muslim women of false consciousness. Because Muslim women have internalized the "androcentric norms of the culture," Afshari contends, their assertion of moral autonomy is an empty claim. He further goes on to claim that in addition to being subconsciously misguided, Muslim women have another reason for wearing *hijab*, viz. to avoid "those sanctioned practices that permit harassment of women in public, forcing them to comply with repressive norms and rewarding them by according them a marked difference in the ways men treat women in public."[261] The problem of this second argument is not that it has not been substantiated by facts, but that it is totally contrary to actual practices in most Muslim societies that have experienced Islamic resurgence. Afshari seems completely oblivious to the fact that in countries, such as Syria in the early eighties, and Turkey today, the harassment is indeed practiced against those who wear *hijab*, rather than those who choose otherwise.[262]

Afshari's appeal to human rights as the grounds to condemn those who voluntarily assert their moral autonomy is troubling, not only because of its peculiar logic, but more so because it draws its strength from the strategic positioning of its author within a hegemonic culture, and from the strategic formation of a hegemonic discourse on which the author's arguments feed. Indeed, Afshari is clear as to the intellectual source that gives him the philosophical grounds to deny to Muslims any claims to cultural authenticity. The philosophical grounds, he tells us, is furnished by Rhoda Howard's conception of human dignity.[263] The question arises, therefore, as to what conception of human rights and human dignity that drives someone to boldly deny to Muslims the capacity of experiencing cultural authenticity, and to use international human rights to prevent Muslim peoples from enjoying their moral autonomy?

Howard has consistently defined dignity in such a way so as to denote submission to "society values, customs, and norms."[264] Thus Howard's conception of dignity – reads community's respect of the individual – stands at odds with the notion of human rights, and is no more the grounds for its justification. As she puts it: "Dignity frequently means acceptance of social rules and norms: human rights implies challenge to precisely those norms. Dignity is often associated with social constraint, whereas human rights are associated with autonomy and freedom."[265] According to the above conception, human rights are not an expression of human dignity, but its negation. No more does dignity rest on the subjective feeling of self-respect and moral autonomy that motivate a person to demand that others respect his/her moral choices, but has become completely dependent on the acknowledgement and respect of others.

Howard's conception of human dignity, which places it at odds with the notion of universal rights, strikes us as being disingenuous. For the very notion of individual rights, advanced first by natural rights scholars, is derived from the notion of human dignity. Kant thus argues that human beings may claim dignity because they are the origin of all values. Unlike the objects of the natural world that serve as means, and hence, have a relative value (or price), human beings are ends in themselves and have "an intrinsic value – that is, dignity."[266] Human dignity derives from the fact that the human being is a "rational being who obeys no law other than that which he [or she] at the same time enact himself [or herself]."[267] The rational volition that individuals possess, which imputes relative values to all objects, and enacts universal laws to guide action, is the source of dignity that the moral person may claim. Human rights thus represent mutual recognition among rational, and morally autonomous, human beings, and affirm the capacity each of them has for moral self-determination.

Because human dignity denotes the moral autonomy of the individual, it can be best observed not under favorable social circumstances, when the individual's moral choices are agreeable to the established power, but rather under adverse conditions, when the individual chooses to stick to his/her moral choices even at the peril of invoking the wrath of the power that be. A person who refuses to change his testimony against corrupt authorities despite a serious threat to his/her life, or a promise of substantial monetary reward, acts with dignity because he/she chooses to act pursuant to moral principles and universal laws, rather than succumbing to the arbitrary will of others, or agreeing to sell themselves to the highest bidder. To say that human dignity "is often associated with social constraint," as Howard says, is to miss the point. The *respect* society shows to those who abide by its moral code signifies *reciprocity* rather than dignity. That is, people tend to reciprocate by respecting those who show respect to their moral choices, and by showing contempt to those who disregard and violate their moral code. Of course different moral systems demand different levels of conformity, and tolerate varying degrees of dissent.

In homogenous societies — such as a tribe or a religious community — the moral autonomy of the individual is subsumed in the moral autonomy of the group to which he/she belongs, and hence his/her dignity lies in observing the tribal or communal norms, and their refusal to deviate from them under pressure of an arbitrary will of a powerful individual or group. Here, reciprocity lies in ensuring the uniformity of action, and in treating with respect those who respect the established norms, and with disdain those who ignore and violate common morality. However, as soon as we move from a homogenous to heterogeneous societies, where different moral communities live side by side, it becomes obvious that moral differences have to be normalized and incorporated into the normative system that govern the heterogeneous whole. Under such circumstances individual autonomy cannot be obtained unless the moral autonomy of the group to which one belongs is ensured. Under heterogeneous conditions, which are the conditions of postmodern society, human rights should aim at protecting the moral autonomy of weaker moral groups against the possibility of forced moral penetration by powerful groups. Similarly, reciprocity requires that each moral group recognize that the other groups are entitled to the same moral autonomy they wish to enjoy, and that they should not insist on imposing their own moral principles, even when they truly believe that these principles are universally valid, as they would naturally dread that such imposition be directed against them. The danger of Afshari's argument that Muslim women who voluntarily choose to express their notion of Islamic modesty are guilty of having unconsciously succumbed to "the andocentric norms of the culture" is that it can be easily turned against the self-expression of women of any culture, including Western culture.

It should not be difficult, then, to see why the arguments of those who fail to recognize the autonomy of non-Western moral communities, and who insist on using international human rights to impose their moral vision on others run contrary to the spirit, if not the letter, of international human rights, enshrined in the UDHR.[268] If human rights are meant to protect the human dignity and moral autonomy of individuals, one cannot appeal to human rights to force Muslim women to abandon their voluntarily adopted *hijab* under the pretext of false consciousness, as Afshari does.[269] I am sure that the Turkish generals and secular fundamentalists would be glad to adopt the argument of false consciousness to justify their authoritarian and anti-democratic decree to prevent Muslim women from adopting their dress style in accordance with their religious conviction, a decree that is tantamount to religious persecution.

While it is quite legitimate for individuals to advocate their moral views so as to persuade others of their value and their enriching effects on social life, it is contrary to dignity and justice for one moral point of view to justify its legal enforcement on the grounds of moral superiority. In the absence of a universally acceptable moral authority, moral superiority can only be established by moral persuasion. Such persuasion can take place through cross-cultural dialogue.

Cultural Dynamism and the
Logic of Islamic Reform

The recent interest in studying the compatibility of Islam with human rights came as a result of the increasing reassertiveness of Islamic beliefs and values in Muslim societies in the last three decades, a phenomenon widely studied under the rubrics of Islamic resurgence, Islamic revivalism, or Islamic fundamentalism. The reawakening of religious consciousness in Muslim societies has been most visible in the political sphere, and has led to the increasing demand by Islamist groups throughout the Muslim world for the reconstruction of the political and legal systems so as to bring them into accord with the rules of Shari`ah.

But while the various groups and individuals advocating the return of Islam as a source of public norms are united in advancing this common goal, they are disparately divided in their varying visions as to what constitutes an Islamic public order. The diversity in orientations and visions of Islamic advocates complicates the task of scholars and writers interested in examining the phenomenon of Islamic resurgence and assessing its social impacts and political ramifications. Faced with the overwhelming complexity of Islamic reassertiveness, some scholars chose to ignore the differences that separate various Islamic groups, opting for a simplistic approach in which the more radical views are taken as representative of Islamic resurgence. This approach is more popular among international relations specialists because, it seems to coincide with the worst-scenario analysis favored by national security analysts.[270] The problem with this approach, though, is not only that it reinforces prejudices and distorts realities, but it also prevents the development of effective foreign policy and undermines the ability of American policy makers to influence developments in the Muslim world.

The majority of scholars devoted to studying Islam and the Muslim world have managed, however, to convey the complexity of Islamic resurgence by grouping the variety of views and positions into a number of major trends. A wide range of terms has been used by various authors. The classification list includes such terms as traditionalists, radicals, fundamentalists, modernists, moderates, liberals, etc.[271] Still, the picture which emerges out of an honest and faithful efforts to depict reality at a specific historical moment can be as misleading and deceptive as the picture of an acrobat taken a few moments after hitting a springboard. The acrobat appears forever suspended in the air. A person unfamiliar with the gravity force, says a citizen of an eternal spaceship, would fail to realize that what he observes is a rare moment in the life of human beings; even a person familiar with the law of gravity would be at loss to determine whether the framed acrobat is moving upward or downward. Determining the dynamism and direction of cultural reform in Muslim society, and the positioning of Islamic forces in the course of societal change, is essential for understanding whether an Islamic political and legal reform is compatible with human rights.

Unfortunately, most of what has been written by human rights scholars on Islam's compatibility with human rights overlooks the question of cultural dynamism and reform direction. Thus we find that an insightful and penetrating work as Mayer's *Islam and Human Rights* succeeds only in revealing the tension over the issues of political reform and human rights, but not its direction. Her conclusion, therefore, appears ambivalent, if not perplexing. "[T]he diluted rights in Islamic human rights schemes examined here," she argues, "should not be ascribed to peculiar features of Islam or its inherent incompatibility with human rights."[272] Islam seems to be the source of both liberation and restriction, of both reformation and stagnation. The question thus arises as to where Islam stands in the context of cultural change.

To begin with, we should recognize that the drive for Islamic reform has intensified as a result of the realization by Muslim intellectuals that developmentalism ideologies, advocated by Muslim ruling elites, have not led to any meaningful political or social progress in Muslim societies, but have instead resulted in the entrenchment in power of a self-serving ruling class whose main goal is to maintain a lavish lifestyle. In post-colonial Muslim societies, ruling elites have worked hard for, and succeeded in, creating for themselves and their cronies islands of plenty in the midst of oceans of poverty. Many Muslim intellectuals, alienated by the high-handed strategies of developmentalism, became convinced that the only viable political and legal reform is one rooted in the moral commitments of the Muslim community.

Since its inception in the middle of the nineteenth century, Islamic reform movement has rejected the traditionalist interpretations of Islam, and embarked on an ambitious reform project, aiming at relating Islamic beliefs and values to modern life.[273] The works of Afghani, Abduh, and Rida — the founders of what has been termed the reform school – present us with an unmistakably egalitarian and liberal discourse, emphasizing openness and tolerance. Early reformists rejected the anti-intellectual approach of traditionalist jurists, and advocated a rational and critical reading of the works of classical Muslims. They rejected, for instance, the restrictive role assigned by traditionalist jurists to women, emphasizing the importance of women's education and social participation. Indeed, as early as the 1930s, Muhammed Rashid Rida not only did advocate the right of women to education and social participation, but also their right to political participation.[274] Similarly, al-Kawakibi attributed the cultural decline of Muslim society to the denial of women to their right to education, and stressed the importance of their public involvement for their ability to provide proper guidance and sound upbringing for children.[275]

While reformist scholars were, and continue even today to be, outnumbered by their traditionalist counterparts, they have exerted a profound and far-reaching influence on contemporary society. Their impact can be seen in the increasingly more open views adopted by leading figures within the traditionalist schools. Several influential and widely respected jurists within traditionalist circles are on record in supporting democracy, human rights, including the right of women to compete equally with men for public office.[276] The views they express today, and teach in public, and in Shari`ah departments of traditional Islamic colleges, would have been sufficient for them to be branded as heretics just a century ago. Leading scholars of the Azhar University, such as Muhammad Abu Zahra, Mahmoud Shaltoot, Muhammad al-Ghazali, and Yusuf al-Qardawi, have been emphasizing equality between men and women, and between Muslims and non-Muslims.

The views of reformers continue to mature in the direction of recognizing human dignity and reciprocity in society. Most recently, Fahmi Huwaydi, a leading journalist in the Arab World and respected Muslim reformist, addressed the question of equality between Muslims and non-Muslims in a book entitled *Muwatinun La Dhimmiyun* (Citizens Not

Dhimmis). Huwaydi rejected the *dhimmi* classification of non-Muslims as a historically relevant concept, and demonstrated, by referring to Islamic sources, that non-Muslims in a Muslim political order enjoy full citizenship rights on par with Muslims.[277] The views advanced by Huwaydi are supported by the views of the founder and leader of the main Islamic opposition in Tunisia who stresses that non-Muslims enjoy equal citizenship with the Muslim majority.[278] Al-Ghanoushi also advocates the right of women to participate on equal footing with men in public life. "There is nothing in Islam," he writes, "that justifies the exclusion of half of the Muslim society from participating and acting in the public sphere. In fact, to do this is to do injustice to Islam and its community in the first place, and to women [afterward]."[279] Similar arguments for gender equality can be seen in the writings of leading Shi`i jurists including Murtada Mutahiri, Muhammad Khatami, and Muhammad Mahdi Shamsuddin.[280]

Given the continuous expansion and maturation of Islamic reformist views, focusing on the views of the traditionalists, or on "middle-ground positions" is bound to distort the reality of cultural reform in the Muslim society, and obscure the direction and dynamism of social change. To doubt the potential of Islamic reform — despite the overwhelming evidence of gradual change of views toward a more liberal and egalitarian position advocated by reformists — because of the shortcomings of current reality is tantamount to doubting the liberating ethos of the declaration of independence at the time of its promulgation because the American society did not include women and blacks in the notion of "the people." It took almost two centuries, and a lot of struggle on the part of countless individuals who strongly believed in human dignity, to bring this ethos to bear on the reality of social practices.

Again, despite the breathtaking cultural changes that took place in the twentieth-century Muslim societies, we still find scholars who want to convince us that there is such a thing as a never-changing "Islamic culture." Thus, Tibi is able to make sweeping generalizations on Islam and Muslim cultures. He writes:

> If Muslims are to embrace international human rights law standards full-heartedly, they need to achieve cultural-religious reforms in Islam—not as faith but as a cultural and legal system. In fact, Islam is a distinct cultural system in which the collective, not the individual, lies at the center of the respective worldview. The concept of human rights, as Mayer rightfully stresses, is "individualistic" in the sense "that it generally expresses claims of a part against the whole." The part pointed out by Mayer is the individual who lives in a civil society and the whole is the state as an overall political structure. Islam makes no such distinction. In Islamic doctrine, the individual is considered a limb of a collectivity, which is the *umma*/community of believers. Furthermore, rights are entitlements and are different from duties. In Islam,

Muslims, as believers, have duties/*fara'id* vis-à-vis the community/*umma*, but no individual rights in the sense of entitlements.[281]

We are told in one breath that (1) Muslims are in need for cultural-religious reform, (2) Islam is not a set of values and beliefs that—like other religions—gives rise to various cultural forms, but a "distinct cultural system," and (3) Muslims have only duties toward the community, but "no individual rights in the sense of entitlements."

Tibi is not the first to argue that the emphasis in Islam is on duty rather than rights. Donnelly advances similar arguments when he contends that, "Muslims are regularly and forcefully enjoined to treat their fellow men with respect and dignity, but the basis for these injunctions are divine commands that establish only duties, not human rights."[282] Yet these assertions only reflect the lack of awareness, and possibility access, to the hundreds of voluminous works in Islamic law that elaborate various rights, and judicial procedures for protecting those rights, in the historical Muslim society. Suffice it here to give one example from the work of the classical Muslim jurist al-Mawardi (d. 450/1086). Recognizing people's right to form their own views, and to disagree with the prevailing views and dominant social and political beliefs, he stresses that "if a group of Muslims rebelled by disagreeing with the views of the community, and forged their own ideology, they are to be left alone and should not be fought, and the rules of justice should be applied to them in accordance with their rights and obligations."[283] Further, Muslims were always able to resort to the numerous courts of law established to enforce the rules of law in the areas of family, commercial, and criminal laws. They were also able to appeal to a high court, the court of *mazalim,* whenever they were not satisfied with ordinary courts rulings, or their rights were violated by governors or public officials.[284]

Tibi's statement that "Muslims ... have duties ... but not rights in the sense of entitlement" is a true description of contemporary Muslim society, but not "Islamic culture" throughout Muslim history. Contemporary Muslims do not enjoy rights not because these rights are not on the books, but very often because they are ruled by authoritarian regimes and police states that have very little respect to the idea of the rule of law. The "Islamic culture" in which the individual is lost in the crowd of collectivity is that of authoritarian Muslim regimes who have entered into an unholy alliance with contemporary Islamic traditionalists against Muslim reformers. Authoritarian Muslim rulers have found it more convenient to cooperate with traditionalist jurists, whose agenda does not include such items as political participation, or constitutional and legal reforms, in their fight against reform ideas and their advocates.

Universalism and the
Imperative of Cultural Mediation

I have argued so far against a static and ahistorical approach to understanding the Islamic position on international human rights adopted by many human rights scholars critical of views held by Islamic traditionalists. I have maintained that such an approach inevitably distorts reality, since it fails to uncover the dynamism and direction of cultural reform currently underway in Muslim society. My contention is not that Muslim cultures have already achieved the desired political and legal reforms, or that they have already brought about effective protection of individual rights and social justice. Far from it; I rather contend that Islamic reform has been a positive force in liberating Muslim consciousness from both the crushing and oppressive ideologies of developmentalism, and the limiting practices of Islamic traditionalism. I turn in this section to explore the relationship between moral universalism and cultural relativism, and to underscore the need for, even the imperative of, cultural mediation of any meaningful legal reform. The argument in this section paves the way for introducing, in the subsequent section, a slightly modified approach to cross-cultural dialogue.

Since the adoption of the Universal Declaration of Human Rights in 1948 by the UN General Assembly, and the subsequent empowerment of the UN Human Rights Commission to monitor and ensure compliance of state members in 1976, the question of the universality of international human rights has been hotly debated. Two main positions can be clearly distinguished: absolute universalism and absolute relativism. The former holds that culture is irrelevant to the moral validity of human rights, while the latter insists that culture is the only source of moral validity.[285] Both positions fail to capture the full scope of the intercourse between culture and universal values, and both have been used to advance self-serving interests.

Absolute (or radical) cultural relativism cannot be theoretically maintained, given the fact that one can hardly find today a society that still maintains a homogenous culture. Besides, considering the dynamic nature of culture no community can claim that the cultural tradition it espouses is either eternally static, or is not involved in a process of cultural exchange with outside cultures. Absolute cultural relativism is often advanced by authoritarian regimes to shut off external criticism of the excessive use of power to silencing internal opposition. Absolute moral universalism, on the other hand, is oblivious to the fact that moral values and legal systems are the outcome of the rationalization of a specific charismatic vision or worldview.[286] Practically, radical universalism could be turned into an instrument in the hands of hegemonic cultures, and could be used for imposing the morality of one culture on another, as Donnelly explains:

> The dangers of the moral imperialism implied by radical universalism hardly need be emphasized. Radical universalism is subject to other moral objections as well. Moral rules, including human rights, function within a moral community. Radical universalism requires a rigid hierarchical ordering of the multiple moral communities to which individuals and groups belong. In order to preserve complete universality for human rights, the radical universalist must give absolute priority to the demands of the cosmopolitan moral community over all other ("lower") moral communities.[287]

The radicalism of the two positions discussed above can be avoided by recognizing that for legal reform to succeed, it must coincide with cultural reform. That is, one must recognize that culture is the only mediating milieu for restructuring individual and social consciousness so as to make them receptive to, and supportive of, international human rights. Yet even when cultural reform results in acknowledging the universal validity of human rights, a reasonable degree of cultural relativism must be allowed so the universal principles are interpreted from within the specific sociopolitical context of society, and are brought to bear on the particular circumstances of the various communities.[288] An absolute universalism that ignores the essential role played by culture for the moral development of the individual suffers from "normative blindness" and is detrimental to both the dominant cosmopolitan culture, and the indigenous cultures it intends to reform. The devastating effects of the experimentations undertaken in Australia, Canada, and the United States to assimilate the aborigines illustrate the impossibility of achieving moral development apart from the cultural tradition to which an individual belongs. They also illustrate the arrogance of the developmentalist outlook that equates moral superiority with economic and technological advancement.

The devastating consequences of the "normative blindness" of absolute universalism advocated by numerous human rights scholars is not limited to non-Western traditions, but extend to the tradition of modernity itself. That is, by attempting to globalize Western modernism in the name of international human rights, the West runs the risk of preventing, or at least delaying, the development of alternative cultural forms which could enrich the culture of modernity itself, and help it overcome some of the acute problems it currently confronts, including the problem of "normative blindness." It seems, though, that for the latter problem to be overcome, a major reform in the dominant Western schools of jurisprudence is needed. As Richard Falk notes, neither in positivist nor in naturalist jurisprudence "does culture enter into the deliberative process of interpreting the meaning, justifying the applicability, and working for the implementation of human rights."[289]

A cultural reform aimed at liberating the individual from traditionalist interpretations of Islam is already underway, as noted earlier. Reformers are appealing to the values and ethos embodied in the Islamic sources to restore the moral autonomy of the individual, and to develop an egalitarian political culture. The reform is, therefore, Islamic in nature and intent, and cannot be otherwise. All reform movements that have brought about profound cultural reform have been religious. The essentially secularist and individualistic modern West owes its genesis, as Weber reminded us in his *Protestant Ethic*, to the Religious Reformation that took place in the Occident at the dawn of the modern West. The Orient should be allowed to undertake its own reformation, which would inevitably result in the reorientation and rationalization of the religious values and beliefs of the people of the orient, and must hence, take the form of a Confucian, Hindu, or Islamic Reformation.

Islam is a religion which has historically given rise to a variety of cultural forms. Like all divine revelations, it emphasizes individual responsibility, and admonishes its followers to adhere to its moral code even if that would dismay the larger society to which they belong. While it values social cooperation, it by no means places the collective above the individual. Historically, Islam has given rise to unmistakably individualistic forms of philosophical, literary, and artistic expressions. It has in the past inspired individual creativity that can be seen in the work of eminent figures, such as al-Farabi, Ibn Rushd (Averroes), Ibn Sina (Avicenna), and Ibn Khadun, to cite just a few names well known for their contribution to Western scholarship. What is described as collective orientation of the "Islamic Culture" is a relatively new phenomenon in Muslim society, resulting from the rational and moral decline of Muslims in the last two centuries, and effected by the ascendancy in the post-colonial era of authoritarian regimes, demanding total individual conformity in the name of developmentalist ideologies.

Despite a heightened interest in the notion of cross-cultural dialogue, there are very few Western scholars who are engaged in a real dialogue with the advocates of Islamic reform. There are many reasons for this, including the legalistic orientation of the two dominant schools of legal jurisprudence in the West, and the defensive and apologetic approach of Islamic traditionalism. But a true and meaningful dialogue is a must if human rights scholars, who are strategically based in the West, were to have positive influence on the growth and maturation of human rights reform in Muslim societies. It might be worthwhile to quote in this regard the insightful words made by Leonard Binder little over a decade ago:

It may nevertheless be questioned whether any sort of exchange between Western scholarship and the current Islamic movement is actually taking place, since the development specialists seem to be talking to one another while the leading exponents of the Islamic revival have decided to break off the dialogue. In point of fact, the dialogue has not yet been broken off, and most of the present work is devoted to an analysis and critique of some of the more interesting texts in which this cultural conversation is still being pursued. This is not a completely open and reciprocal form of discursive interaction, if only because Western intellectuals read very little of what Muslim intellectuals write. Still, insofar as these [Muslim] thinkers explore Western ideas and confront them with the hegemonic forms of Muslim thought, they carry out the dialogue in their own works. I believe that the further strengthening of Islamic liberalism and the possibility for the emergence of liberal regimes in the Middle East is directly linked to the invigoration and wider diffusion of this dialogue.[290]

The words of Binder are as true today as they were little over a decade ago when he uttered them. Still, it might not be too late for the advocates of Western universalism to abandon their radical universalist position, which has ironically strengthened the radical relativist position taken by Muslim traditionalists, and to embark on a meaningful dialogue with Muslim reformers. However, for a meaningful cross-cultural dialogue to take place, a number of conditions must be observed; the elaboration of these conditions is the main concern of the next section.

Preconditions of a True Cross-Cultural Dialogue

Proponents of absolute universalism premise their arguments on either of the following two presuppositions: (1) that the notion of culture – i.e., a normative system supported by a set of values and beliefs commonly accepted by a group of people – is irrelevant to the debate on the meaning and desirability of human rights, or (2) that human rights are compatible with a set of moral values commonly shared by all cultures. I argue in this section that the first premise is erroneous, and contend that for the common values to be universally valid, a non-hegemonic cross-cultural dialogue must take place among representatives of various moral communities.

Scholars who deny the relevance of culture to the human rights debate usually favor a unilinear view of history that equates moral with technical superiority. According to this view, human cultures form a continuum in which primitive cultures represent one extreme while modern culture represents the other. Primitive cultures are seen to be lacking not only in technology, but in morality as well. Primitive cultures are described as barbaric and savage, while modern culture is seen as refined and civilized. History, from a unilinear viewpoint, is nothing but the movement from the primitive to the modern which forms the end of history.[291] The logical conclusion of the conception of history as modernization is that modern culture is the measure of all cultures. The problem with this conception, though, is that it fails to account for important historical events. The unilinear conception of history fails, for instance, to explain why the European culture was more vibrant and developed—politically, philosophically, and artistically—during the Roman civilization than in medieval times. From the modernization perspective, culture is not relevant to the debate on human rights because there is nothing for modern culture to learn from other cultures. Modern culture should set the standards for both moral and technical action, and then pass them on to less developed cultures.

This is in essence, the conclusion of a leading advocate of radical universalism in a chapter published as part of an edited book entitled *Human Rights in Cross-Cultural Perspectives: A Quest for Consensus.* Taking exception to the idea of a cross-cultural consensus on human rights, Howard writes:

> In this chapter I have argued against the enterprise of surveying world cultures and religions in order to establish consensus on human rights that would answer charges that such are a Western creation.

> To look for an anthropologically based consensus on the content of human rights is to miss the point. There may be aspects of agreement worth noting among what many societies take to be fundamental to a life of dignity and what the modern notion of human rights includes as its content. The concept of human rights is not universal in origin, however; and it cannot be located in most societies.[292]

Granted that an elaborate set of rights, purporting to protect the individual against an excessive or arbitrary use of power by the state, was first articulated by the modern West, one should not dismiss cross-cultural consensus as irrelevant. For even if we were to assume that the West could learn nothing from non-Western cultures, a cross-cultural dialogue would still be needed to understand the implications of applying a set of extremely abstract rights in various sociopolitical milieus. Such an understanding should help expand the margin of tolerance for cultural differences, and the appreciation of the complexity of cultural reform and the need to allow this process to run its natural course.[293]

Other proponents of absolute universalism concede that human rights are a cultural concept, and acknowledge the need for a cross-cultural basis for the claim of universal validity. One interesting proposal has been advanced by Bassam Tibi in the form of international morality to be "shared by all civilizations."[294] Noting Huntington's warning against an impending "clash of civilizations," Tibi underscores the vitality of international morality for binding the various "civilizations" in a peaceful pact. He rightly points out that "human rights cannot be established internationally on the basis of overall universalism but rather on such cross-cultural foundations for a universal morality."[295] He further emphasizes the importance of "unbiased cultural dialogue and intercultural communication," freed from the limiting concerns of foreign policy and national interests.[296] It turns out, however, that the cross-cultural dialogue he envisaged does not involve a true cross-cultural exchange, but rather a one-sided intellectual exercise that aims at addressing the question of "what ought to be done to make Muslims speak the language of human rights in their own tongue?"[297]

It is obvious that an absolute universalistic stance is incompatible with "unbiased cultural dialogue," even when the proponents of such a stance truly desire this dialogue. A coercive discourse in which the proponents of one of the contending points of view feel justified by strategically dictating their own morality to others cannot be called a cross-cultural dialogue, but rather a hegemonic discourse. A true and meaningful dialogue requires that the parties involved be truly interested in understanding the opposing views, and are involved in "a completely open and reciprocal form of discursive interaction."[298] The transition from a hegemonic discourse to a cross-cultural dialogue requires, therefore, more than the manipulation of linguistic usage. The transition requires change in attitude and approach, from one that relies on power relationship to one that depends on rational interaction, or, to use Habermasian categories, a transition from a strategic speech act whose aim is to advance the interests of the powerful actor, to communicative speech act, whose goal is to influence the actions of others by appealing to their rational sense.[299] Put more precisely, for the transition from a hegemonic discourse, denoting a strategic interaction, to a true cross-cultural dialogue, signifying a communicative interaction, to take place, three preconditions must be met: (1) the universalism of human rights must be established objectively, (2) the moral autonomy of the various national and cultural communities that form the world community must be recognized and respected, and (3) the self-righteous claim by any cultural group of the superiority of its moral system must be rejected.

Arguments for the universality of human rights invoke, more often than not, the subjective rather than the objective dimension of universalism. Subjective universalism is monological because it takes "the form of a hypothetical process of argumentation occurring in the individual mind."[300] Subjective universalization process follows the pattern set by Kant in the form of the Categorical Imperative: "Act only on that maxim through which you can at the same time will that it should become a universal law."[301] From a Kantian point of view, a rule can be universal if it passes the test of the *reciprocity principle*, viz. if the person who adopts the rule as a maxim for his/her action is willing to be treated by others according to the same rule. The principle of universalization as formulated by Kant is a subjective principle that can have a universal validity only insofar as others share the same moral subjectivity with the moral actor. Put differently, the Kantian principle of universalization, which takes the form of a subjective process of generalization, can work only in a homogenous culture in which people share common intersubjectivity. However, as soon as one moves into a world characterized by cultural pluralism, say a world which resembles the international society, a different principle of universalization would be needed. Here, a new version of the Categorical Imperative, such as the one formulated by Thomas McCarthy, would be more relevant:

> Rather than ascribing as valid to all others any maxim that I can will to be a universal law, I must submit my maxim to all others for purposes of discursively testing its claim to universality. The emphasis shifts from what each can will without contradiction to be a general law, to what all can will in agreement to be a universal norm.[302]

McCarthy's reformulation of Kant's Categorical Imperative, inspired by Habermas's Communicative Action, reflects an implicit realization of the increasing cultural fragmentation of modern consciousness. If the stipulation of explicit agreement for the fulfillment of communicative action is relevant to cultures that share common intersubjectivity, it is more urgent in a cross-cultural dialogue. Needless to say, agreements and disagreements in the context of rational dialogue require rational justification, and not simply the assertion of preference and choice.

A cross-cultural dialogue has two aims. First, it helps reduce apprehension, which may result from excessive speculation and extrapolation from one culture to another, and clarify cross-cultural misreading and misunderstanding. Second, it enriches internal debates in a particular culture by communicating different experiences, and the critical insights of outsiders. The value of a Tocqueville's critical insight into democracy in America, or a Schacht's critical analysis of Islamic law cannot be overstated. However, for a true dialogue to take place and to be maintained with a reasonable degree of objectivity, the interlocutors should recognize the moral autonomy of other cultural groups. This means that the solidarity of external groups with the substantive views of one of the internal groups locked in moral and political struggle should not be allowed to take priority over the principle of justice.

Human Rights, Cultural Reform, and Political Participation

For human rights principles to take hold in the social and political practices of a political community, these principles must be rooted in the cultural outlook and moral commitments of its members. In societies where human rights violations are rampant, such violations may partially be attributed to the lack of cultural sensitivities and commitments, and partially to authoritarian regimes which have little or no respect to human rights. In these societies enforcement of human rights requires a vibrant cultural reform and vigorous political struggle. It follows that human rights, cultural reform, and political participation are locked forever in a three-sided dialectical relationship.[303] Each of the constituting components of the above relationship does influence, and is, in turn, influenced by, the others. This process has been working slowly but surely in Western societies since the Protestant Reformation took place few centuries ago. The democratization process should go hand in hand with cultural reform and increased sensitivity to human rights.

As I argued earlier, a similar process has been going on in Muslim societies for little over a century now. However, the reformation process in Muslim societies has been complicated by both direct and indirect influences of the outside world. Intervention of Western powers in the internal affairs of Muslim countries, whether in the form of colonialism and direct military intervention, or in the form of unlimited support to authoritarian regimes, has disturbed the historical process of cultural reform and political liberalization and democratization. During the Cold War, military dictators received tremendous financial and military support allowing them to become completely independent from the influence of internal politics and popular support. And as long as these regimes cooperated to advance the national interests of their respective patrons they could act with impurity against their people. The human rights of the people were considered secondary to the interests of superpowers. They were invoked only insofar as they could be used to advance the national interests of the power that be.

In the Muslim world, cultural reformation is facing stiff resistance from authoritarian regimes, intent on suppressing the egalitarian and liberating ethos of reform movements. The suppression of freedom of expression and association by authoritarian regimes in the Muslim world is responsible, not only for the stifling of cultural debate essential for reform, but also for the rise of Islamic radicalism. It is not uncommon for radicals to point to the selective application of human rights – popularized as double standards – to justify their rejection and to foster public cynicism.

International human rights are articulated as a means for protecting individual dignity against an arbitrary power, and to allow a distinct minority to exercise self-determination. Any attempt by external powers to bring about legal change contrary to the moral values of a people through the agency of an authoritarian regime in the name of human rights amounts to a coercive act of moral imperialism, and would make mockery of the very notion of human rights. Human Rights scholars who are concerned about cultural practices which are in contradiction of human rights should engage indigenous cultures through an open dialogue to both effect change and understand the source of limitations. It should also, and perhaps in the first place, focus on exposing efforts by external powers to maintain authoritarian regimes so long as the latter are willing to protect their "national interest," even when the support extended to anti-democratic regimes amounts to inflicting great pain and suffering on countless human beings crushed under the abusive schemes of their rules.

IV.   Islam in a Global Cultural Order

Islam in a Global Order

In the previous chapters, we focused on internal tensions within Middle Eastern society and their impact on sociopolitical transformations. We argued that the tensions are fundamentally linked to the interfusion of Islamic tradition and Western modernity, which take the form of political struggle between Islamic and secularist movements. In Part IV, we examined the tension on the global level by focusing on the interplay between Islam and the West.

It is evident that the Islam-West interplay is too complicated and multifaceted to be neatly reduced into the broad categories of "Islam" and "West." Both Islam and the West are far more diverse to be reduced to two monolithic categories. Besides, the interaction between the two is not purely political or strategic, but takes a variety of forms, including cultural, intellectual, and religious interactions.

Still, focusing on the interaction of Islam and the West should help us enhance our understanding, on the one hand, of the dynamism of internal conflicts and changes, and, on the other hand, shed light on recent developments in world politics in which Islam has increasingly become an intricate element of global tensions.

In trying to shed light on a complex interaction between Islam and the West, I focus particularly on what has been termed the "hegemonic discourse," as well as on US foreign policy. Despite important differences between the US and other Western countries in their postures and actions toward international issues, the lone superpower status of the United States has made its intentions and actions on the world stage the most decisive in setting the direction of world politics. European states have all rallied behind the US on major foreign policy issues, particularly those relating to political Islam and Islamic resurgence.

In examining the Islam-West interactions, two points stand out. First, the West's stance toward political Islam is influenced more by ideological leanings and less by actual development on the ground. Second, US foreign policy has been gradually moving from one concerned with developing international order rooted in international law and in the desire to strengthen democratic forces around the world, to one obsessed with economically and geopolitically defined national interests. Such a shift in focus is bound, if it is allowed to proceed further, to undermine international law, and to polarize and, hence, destabilize the international order.

CHAPTER 9

Islam and the West: Resurgence and Ambivalence

The collapse of the Soviet Union in 1989 marked the beginning of a new era in world politics, an era invariably labeled as the "New World Order" or "the Post-Soviet Order." The New World Order has been perceived by many in the West as a peaceful order in which the rules of international law prevail, and the principles of right and justice are implemented by the collective action of the world community, represented by the United Nations organization and its numerous organs. In the Middle East, however, the overall perception is quite the opposite. Middle Eastern critics argue that the Soviet Union's demise has emboldened the West, and led to more aggressive and intrusive US actions toward the region.

The purpose of this chapter is twofold. First, it examines the nature of the global order that emerged after the Soviet Union's demise, and explores the extent to which the claim of an order based on law and justice is in force. Second, the chapter proposes a number of measures needed to counteract the negative effects of the new global regime, and to utilize the opportunities it has opened up.

I begin by examining the intellectual and popular discourse on Islam in the West, and exploring the basic tenets that guide US foreign policy toward Islam and the Middle East. I argue that US foreign policy has been gradually shifting from one based on the deeply held American values of freedom, self-determination, and human rights, to one in which the freedom and human rights of others are subordinated to America's national interests. I, further, contend that the principles of current US foreign policy are plagued with inconsistencies, selectivity, and short-sightedness that is bound to hurt America and American interests in the long run. Therefore, I advocate a return to a foreign policy informed by

American values to ensure that US stamina and power is not consumed in building Pax-Americana. To avoid becoming an empire, I conclude, US economic and geopolitical interests must not be placed over and above the right of other nations to live a life of freedom and dignity.

World Order: Continuity and Change

The present world order may be traced back to the Peace of West-phalia of 1648, which marked the end of political unity based on shared beliefs and moral commitments. With the demise of transcendental and hence transnational unity, the nation-state became the basic unit in the European state system, and national interest became the paramount value guiding the actions of Western political leaders. However, the nation-state system did not become entrenched and commonly recognized among Europeans until World War I. By the end of the First World War, the League of Nations was established as the first global organization. Yet, rather than facilitating cooperation among nations to prevent aggression, the League soon became an instrument of the Great Powers. It was manipulated by colonial powers, most notably Britain, France and Japan, and was used to legitimize expansion and aggression. The League gave Britain and France formal mandate over much of the Middle East, and gave Japan a similar mandate over former German colonies in Southeast Asia.[304]

The expansion of Western powers to Africa and Asia throughout the nineteenth and early twentieth centuries was a crucial step toward the globalization of European cultures. The colonial era allowed the West to recreate the non-Western world in its own image. Consequently, the European nation-state system was globalized, and nation-states proliferated. World War II put an end to the League of Nations and the international regime it created, but gave birth to another international organization, the United Nations.

The United Nations was established in April 1945 by fifty states, led by the victors of the Second World War: The United States, Britain, France, the Soviet Union, and the Republic of China. The membership in the United Nations continued to grow over the years as more colonies achieved independence. The establishment of the United Nations and its continual expansion marked not only the globalization of the European nation-state system but also the emergence of an international regime governed by the permanent members of the Security Council.

The establishment of the United Nations was, undoubtedly, an important landmark in the globalization of the liberal capitalist model that evolved for centuries in the West. Nevertheless, the globalization of liberal capitalism was not complete, for the Western model of international order was challenged by a rival order propounded by the socialist world, under the leadership of the Soviet Union. Initially, the socialist movement envisaged a world order based on common commitments and shared interests, thereby rejecting nationalist exclusivity and exploitative practices in the name of national interests. However, the socialist movement failed to provide a workable and just model capable of actualizing its universalistic claims. Soon the socialist vision was corrupted by Soviet practices, and by the excessive use of force and compulsion to achieve socialist objectives.

The ideological differences and conflicting interests of the Soviet Union on the one hand, and the United States and its European allies on the other, prevented either of the two rivals from achieving full domination of world politics. However, with the demise of the socialist bloc and the breakup of the Soviet Union, the system of bipolarity came to an end, and the last obstacle in the face of Western globalism and hegemony was removed. Today, the United States and its European allies stand triumphantly at the helm of a centrally regulated and controlled international order.

In short, throughout all the turmoil and changes in world politics over the last three centuries, one thing persisted: the drive to establish a global order based on Western ideals and values. Today, the West seems to have achieved its century-old dream of a unified international regime. With the exception of a few pockets of resistance here and, there, the world appears to have accepted the political, economic, and social forms generated in the womb of Western culture. The resistance to the new world order seems to come from social and political groups in the Muslim world that insist on adopting a model of sociopolitical organization informed by Islam and Islamic values. Apparently, Islam has emerged in the Muslim world as an alternative framework for resisting Western domination. We examined, in the last few chapters, the nature of the Islamic resurgence, and the internal dynamism that govern the struggle for reform in Muslim societies. We concentrate, in the remainder of this chapter, on the Western response to Islamic resurgence, particularly in the realm of intellectual and popular discourse, and the realm of political action and foreign policy.

It is important, though, to point out that the realms of discourse and policy are only structurally separate, but the two maintain a reciprocal relationship. The significance of the actions undertaken by media reporters and foreign policy actors lies in the fact that they reinforce one another, leading to constant and continuous escalation in the confrontation between Islam and the West. That is, by supporting military dictators in the Muslim world, policymakers create conditions conducive to political radicalism, as the suppressive measures of the state push certain opposition groups to violence. On the other hand, by concentrating on radical groups, and presenting them as the representatives *par excellence* of con-

temporary Islamic resurgence, media reporters reinforce the fears of policymakers and encourage them to stick to their hard line.

Contemplating Islam: Apprehension and Anxiety

The Middle East is a multiethnic and multireligious society, but is
one that is ultimately defined in Islamic terms. For a short while around
the Middle of the twentieth century, Western scholars and statesmen
thought that modern transformations of Middle Eastern society had already transcended Islam, and relegated Islamic ethos to the annals of
history. Most recently, Western analysts went to the other extreme, turning Islam into a geopolitical threat, and counseling that the United States
undertakes a containment strategy toward Islamic states and movements.
The theme of Islamic threat continues to be controversial in academic
and policy-making circles, and is far from receiving a unanimous acceptance, as many scholars of repute have persuasively rejected this contention.[305] Still, the "Islamic threat" theme has powerful advocates, who
have so far prevailed, as we will see below, in current US foreign policy
debate.

Current Western interest in Islam dates back to the mid-seventies,
when increasing segments of Muslim society began to pursue with vigor
the ideal of establishing an Islamic society and state. The powerful resurgence of Islamic ideas and practices was felt at all levels of society and
took various forms, including intellectual and political.

This development came as a surprise to many Western scholars and
policy makers, who declared, in the late 1950s, the triumph of Western
liberalism and the demise of Islam in the Muslim world. For instance,
Daniel Lerner, made the following assessment of the place of Islam in the
Middle Eastern society in his highly acclaimed work, *The Passing of
Traditional Society*:

> Whether from East or West, modernization poses the same basic
> challenge – the infusion of "a rationalist and positivist spirit" against
> which scholars seem agreed, "Islam is absolutely defenseless." The
> phasing and modality of the process have changed, however, in the
> past decade. Where Europeanization once penetrated only the upper
> level of Middle East society, affecting mainly leisure-class fashions,
> modernization today diffuses among a wider population and touches
> public institutions as well as private aspirations with its disquieting
> "positivist spirit."[306]

By the late 1980s, Western perception of Islam took a drastically different form. With the spread of Islamic reassertiveness eastward and
westward, within and beyond the Muslim society – a phenomenon often
referred to as Islamic resurgence – many eminent scholars in the West
began to view Islam not as a dying creed of purely historical significance,

but as a formidable force and potential threat to the global hegemony of the United States. In his widely read book, *The End of History and the Last Man*, Francis Fukuyama has the following to say about Islam:

> It is true that Islam constitutes a systematic and coherent ideology, just like liberalism and communism, with its own code of morality and doctrine of political and social justice. The appeal of Islam is potentially universal, reaching out to all men as men, and not just to members of a particular ethnic or national group. And Islam has indeed defeated liberal democracy in many parts of the Islamic world, posing a grave threat to liberal practices even in countries where it has not achieved political power directly. The end of the cold war in Europe was followed immediately by a challenge to the West from Iraq, in which Islam was arguably a factor.[307]

Similar sentiments were expressed by Zbigniew Brzezinski, former national security advisor during the Carter administration. In *Out of Control*, a book published right after the demise of the Soviet Union, Brzezinski sounds more alarming, as he warns against an Islamic expansion to Central Asia, taking advantage, as he puts it, of the power vacuum created by the collapse of the Soviet Empire:

> Since nature abhors vacuum, it is already evident that outside powers, particularly the neighboring Islamic states, are likely to try to fill the geopolitical void created in Central Asia by the collapse of the Russian imperial sway. Turkey, Iran, and Pakistan have already been jockeying in order to extend their influence, while the more distant Saudi Arabia has been financing a major effort to revitalize the region's Moslem cultural and religious heritage. Islam is thus pushing northward, reversing the geopolitical momentum of the last two centuries.[308]

While Brezenzinski does not dismiss the capacity of Islam to effect sociopolitical transformations of global proportions, he rightly points out to the current limitations of contemporary Islamic reassertiveness, reflected in the absence of a concrete model for translating Islamic ideals into social reality.

Perhaps the most alarming forecast of the future relationship between Islam and the West comes from an advocate of developmentalism, who was suddenly transformed in the early 1990s into a prophet of doom. Samuel Huntington, a leading Harvard scholar, raised the specter of civilizational war between Western civilization on the one hand, and Islamic and Confucian civilizations on the other.[309] To handle the Confucian-Islamic threat, Huntington proposed, the West should strive to:

> limit the expansion of the military strength of Confucian and Islamic states; to moderate the reduction of Western military capabilities and maintain military superiority in East and Southwest Asia; to exploit differences and conflicts among Confucian and Islamic states; to

support in other civilizations groups sympathetic to Western values and interests; to strengthen international institutions that reflect and legitimate Western interests and values and to promote the involvement of non-Western states in those institutions.[310]

The increasingly antogonistic tone toward Islam and the Middle East does not stop at the level of debate and discourse, but is frequently translated into actions and policies that profoundly affect the life of Middle Easterners. We, therefore, turn in the next two sections to examine US foreign policy, understand its tenets and principles, and to review US foreign policy toward Islam and the Middle East.

US Foreign Policy and its Principles

US foreign policy is often characterized by American leaders and foreign policy analysts as one of benevolence and good will toward foreign countries. American actions toward other nations are frequently expressed in such terms as the provision of foreign aide, the promotion of human rights, and the defense and strengthening of democratic rule. America's self-perception of the way it projects its enormous power has been succinctly described by Lawrence H. Summers, who served as deputy secretary of treasury in the Clinton administration, when he called the United States "the first nonimperialist superpower."[311]

Indeed, American leaders have always been careful to distance US policies and actions from those associated with empires and empire building. A nation that came to existence by rejecting imperialistic policies and fighting imperialist armies under the banner of freedom and democracy, the United States has never been comfortable to send its troops to control other nations. And despite its short flirtations with colonial adventures in the Philippines, the United States has managed to stay away from ruling other counties directly.

Still, the United States' projection of power in Latin America, Africa, Asia, and the Middle East is often subsumed by popular movements in those regions under the rubric of imperialism or neo-colonialism. In fact, the charge of imperialism was made against US foreign policy by one of its brilliant children. John Dewey, a great American philosopher and sociologist of international repute, accused American political leaders in an article published in 1927 in *The Republic*, under the title "Imperialism is Easy," of this very embarrassing stigma. Dewey was aware of the dichotomy of action and intention in American foreign policy, and, therefore, stressed that "[i]mperialism is a result, not a purpose or plan."[312] He went on to argue that American actions toward Mexico have all the features of imperialism, even when the American government acts to protect the freedom of movement and private property of ordinary

American businesses. He, thus, concluded that imperialism "can be prevented only by regulating the conditions out of which it proceeds."[313]

In 1996, The Heritage Foundation (HF) produced a voluminous document entitled *Restoring American Leadership: US Foreign Policy and Defense Blueprint.* The 1996 Blueprint was an expanded version of an earlier blueprint the Foundation published in 1992 under the title *Making the World Safe for America.* The document complained of the lack of clear direction in US foreign policy, and called for a "clear, principled, and consistent leadership."[314]

The new direction advocated by The Heritage Foundation, epitomized in the phrase "making the world safe for America," is a far-cry from the early direction US foreign policy took a little over a century ago under the able leadership of Woodrow Wilson. In the declaration of war speech before a joint session of the Congress in 1917, Wilson made it abundantly clear that the projection of American power beyond US bonders was intended to make the world "safe for democracy."[315] A year later, on the eve of the defeat of the Central Powers in 1918, Wilson introduced a program of fourteen points he called the "program of the world's peace."[316] All fourteen points stressed the need to promote world peace by guaranteeing nations, small and large, their political and economic independence and the right to develop their own national institutions.[317] Point fourteen introduced the then novel ideas of "international organization" and "international law" that represented America's commitment to the rule of law and its contribution to world peace. "A general association of nations," Wilson proclaimed, "must be formed under specific covenants for the purpose of affording mutual guarantees of political independence and territorial integrity of great and small states alike."[318]

Wilson's failed bid for reelection, and the Congress's hostility toward the idea of the League of Nations, deprived the newly founded League from Wilson's commitment to the principles of self-determination and democracy, and the League was transformed by the two established European powers of Britain and France into an instrument to be used for furthering their imperialist ambitions in the Middle East. For this purpose the League devised the peculiar institution of the "mandate." Britain and France were given "mandates" to practically have direct rule over the gulf municipalities, Iraq, Jordan, Lebanon, Palestine, and Syria.

The League of Nations, and its mandated colonialism, was among the casualties of World War II, but the idea of world peace promoted by an international organization and international law was resuscitated by Harry Truman. In 1945, Truman announced twelve points, which he described as the "fundamentals of American foreign policy." The twelfth point introduced the United Nations organization as the new instrument for promoting world peace. "We are convinced," he stated, "that the preservation of peace between nations requires a United Nations Organization comprised of all peace-loving nations of the world who are willing jointly to use force if necessary to insure peace."[319]

The other eleven points Truman announced stressed America's commitment to freedom and self-government. The first point made it quite clear that the Untied States does not, and will not, seek territorial expansion or self-advantage. "We seek," Truman declared, "not territorial expansion or self advantage. We have no plans for aggression against any other state, large or small. We have no objective which need clash with the peaceful aims of any other nation."[320]

Ambivalence between Interests and Ideals

Over the five decades since Truman made his declaration of the fundamentals of US foreign policy, the principles continued to shift from ones based on freedom and self-government, to principles concerned mainly with US economic and geopolitical interests.

The shift is, fortunately, neither complete nor clear. American leaders mindful of the public abhorring of imperialist objectives have always coached the aim of military adventures in a language that stress democracy and human rights. The sad reality, though, is that concerns for human rights have been aligned with US national interests to the point where the overwhelming perception today is that the US government uses human rights as an instrument for advancing national interests.

The Heritage Foundation blueprint, indeed, brings clarity to US foreign policy by making explicit what has been silently practiced and implicitly upheld by successive US administrations, beginning with Nixon's. The blueprint urges US leaders to champion liberty around the world. "By nurturing this dream of liberty for others," the Heritage Foundation contends, "the United States is grounding its foreign policy in a universal idea that is good for both America and the World."[321]

The commitment to liberty advocated by the foundation is, however, conditioned by another principle: the principle of selective engagement. The foundation insists that while the US "must be deeply engaged in international affairs to protect its freedom and security," it should do that by adopting "a strategy of selective engagement that would enable America to apply military power only when vital or important interests are threatened ..."[322] Among the vital interests listed in the foundation's blueprint that justify the use of military power are "trade protectionism, trade wars, and trade blocs."[323]

To ensure that American leaders have great flexibility in selecting the issues and regions that require US engagement, the document rejects any solemn commitment to the international structures and the United

Nations. The foundation counsels that the US must be free "from the constraints imposed by excessive multilateralism," because "too much reliance on global institutions like the UN impinges on American sovereignty and weakens the leadership role America must play to protect freedom around the world."[324]

In sum, US foreign policy as envisaged by the Heritage Foundation, and as has been practiced in effect for sometime now, is based on three cardinal principles:

1. US should promote freedom and democracy in other regions of the world, since this is the only defensible moral grounds on which the projection of US military power can be justified.

2. US moral concerns for freedom and democracy must be curtailed by the national interests of the United States, which fundamentally take the form of economic and geopolitical US concerns.

3. To harmonize principles 1 and 2, the US must adopt the principle of selective engagement, which aligns US morality to economic concerns, and hence, subordinate the former to the latter.

The foreign policy described by the Heritage Foundation's blueprint is a policy that subordinates the universal principles of right and justice to the national interests of the United States, and reduces the United Nations and its resolutions to a convenient instrument to be invoked only when it serves US interests. While the document and the strategy it advocates is quite disturbing, it is more disturbing to note that it, indeed, describes the tenets of US foreign policy since the Nixon administration.

Since our discussion is linked directly to Islam and the Middle East, I will endeavor in the next two sections to illustrate that US foreign policy has been informed by the very principles outlined above long before the Heritage Foundation issued its blueprint. I argue that these principles are in the long run a recipe for disaster, as they have impacted negatively on the lives of many nations, and are likely to create more devastation in the years to come, thereby producing more antagonistic attitudes toward the Untied States, and gradually transforming the later into a world empire.

US Policy Toward the Middle East

American leaders often reiterate America's commitment to freedom, democracy, and human rights, but the sad fact is that in many parts of the world, and particularly in the Middle East, America is associated not with freedom and democracy but with suppressive and autocratic regimes. For the last fifty years, successive United States governments have stood behind self-appointed leaders, providing them with financial and military support, as well as security and political advice. Far from being the guardian of freedom and democracy, the United States is often seen as the power behind military regimes and brutal dictators.

The United States involvement in Iran is a case in point. The United States Central Intelligence Agency (CIA) was directly involved in engineering the *coup d'état* that removed the democratically elected government of Mohammed Mosaddeq, and installed the Shah regime in Iran in 1954. Despite his abuse of his people's civil liberties, and his extensive use of state security forces to suppress critics and opposition forces, the Shah continued to receive the blessings of American leaders. President Carter, who insisted that the United States foreign policy must be based on America's commitment to human rights, praised the Shah during a visit shortly before the latter was ousted by the Islamic revolution. The United States later took an active part in arming Saddam Hussein in a bid to topple the revolutionary government in Tehran. To ensure the cooperation of the Iraqi military government, the Reagan administration kept silent when Saddam used chemical weapons against Iranians as well as against the Kurdish opposition in Northern Iraq. It was only when the belligerent Saddam turned his newly acquired military strength against the oil rich Gulf countries that he was declared a renegade.

The blunders of United States foreign policy in the Middle East have not ended with the Gulf war. Rather than finishing Saddam, the US-led coalition decided to keep him in power and to impose an economic embargo on Iraq. The American decision brought about a human disaster of great magnitude. For over a decade, the people of the Middle East, and many humanitarian workers and human rights activists, watched in horror as hundreds of thousands of ill-stricken and malnourished Iraqi civilians perished.[325]

America's commitments to freedom and democracy have hardly had any bearings on the United States' foreign policy toward Iraq and Iran. At times, US public officials seem oblivious to the humanitarian plights of Middle Eastern people, let alone their issues on human rights and dignity. In a "60 Minutes" segment aired by CBS on May 12, 1996 under the title "Punishing Saddam," Madeleine Albright, who was then US ambassador to the UN, displayed such a moment of utter contempt and disregard to the human conditions of Middle Eastern society. During her interview, CBS Reporter Leslie Stahl posed the following question: "We have heard that a half million children have died [as a result of the economic sanctions imposed on Iraq]. I mean, that's more children than [those who] died in Hiroshima. And – and you know, is the price worth it?" Albright responded by saying: "I think this is a very hard choice, but the price – we think the price is worth it." Albright has never had to answer for her cruel stance, but was instead confirmed six months later by Congress as the US secretary of state. No wonder that the United States is perceived by the Iraqis and Iranians as a technologically advanced military power, unrestrained by moral obligations in the pursuit of its own self-interest.

The failure of successive United States administrations to project clear and sustained interests in freedom and democracy can be seen in the United States position vis-à-vis the Israeli-Palestinian conflict. For decades, Arabs and Muslims watched the Israeli government expand its territories at the expense of its Arab neighbors. Israel was allowed to occupy the West Bank and Gaza, the Golan Heights, and South Lebanon with the tacit approval and blessings, and occasionally with the open support, of the United States government, in spite of successive UN resolutions and clear violation of International law.

> Over the past year, Middle Easterners watched countless pictures of Israeli soldiers shooting at rock-throwing Palestinian kids, of US-made Apache, designed to destroy tanks, used for assassinating Palestinian activists, and US-made tanks and rocket launchers used to suppress the Palestinian *Intifada*.

> The failure on the part of policy-makers to confront the inconsistencies of US foreign policy, and thus to acknowledge its malevolent consequences on other nations, continues to antagonize increasing segments of Middle Eastern peoples, and is threatening to polarize Muslim and Western countries, thereby rolling back early achievements of US foreign policy. Indeed, the Middle East provides us with a clear case study of the negative consequences of the tenets of the US foreign policy in force since the Nixon administration.[326]

US Policy Toward Terrorism

Terrorism is a plight that must be fought. No amount of anger and discontent can justify the targeting of non-combatant civilians with the brutality we all witnessed on September 11, 2001. The level of destruction inflicted on civilians, the brutality with which the terrorist attacks were executed, and the fact that the terrorist design is undertaken by extensive deliberation and determination sent shock waves throughout the world, and brought condemnation from foes and friends alike. Targeting thousands of unarmed civilians, using civilian airliners carrying civilian passengers, and bringing down two of the most spectacular buildings on the whole planet, in a drama that was played on live TV in front of millions of viewers, made the attacks even more sinister and apocalyptic.

But terrorism cannot be fought by mystifying it or by ignoring its root causes. The first step for developing a sound strategy to effectively combat terrorism is to examine the conditions that give rise to the anger, frustration, and desperation that fuel all terrorist acts. To focus on individuals and organizations that employ terror, while ignoring the socio-political circumstances that give rise to acts of desperation, can potentially strengthen the arms of the terrorists. A devastating force unleashed against elusive groups can exacerbate the very conditions that gave rise to resentment, frustration, and anger.

America is admired throughout the world for a political system characterized by freedom, democracy, and the rule of law. But America is resented in many parts of the world for, ironically, its willingness to support authoritarian and corrupt regimes as long as they advance America's economic and strategic interests. Those who are using terror against America are the product of political repression. They are the products of Middle Eastern regimes befriended by the United States, but have little respect for freedom and democracy. It is indeed a sad but true reality that many prefer to ignore: Free and democratic America has been nurturing repression aboard. To acknowledge this fact is the first step in dealing with the roots of terrorism.

Equally important is that we pursue a methodical and persistent approach to terrorism. Terrorism must be clearly defined, and systematically confronted. If terrorism is defined as the use of violence against unarmed civilians, then we have to ensure that all individuals and organizations that fit this description, regardless of their positioning and loyalty, are identified as such. The United States government has not been consistent in identifying terrorist acts. The United States government did not recognize the Russian brutal attacks against Chechnya, and its use of disproportionate force to flatten the Chechen capital for what it is, and for what it represents.

Similarly, The Israeli incursion into Lebanon, and Israel's shelling of Beirut and other civilian targets, resulting in thousands of civilian deaths, did not receive the moral condemnation it deserves. Israel continues to use excessive military force to suppress an essentially civilian uprising against its occupation of the West Bank and Gaza. The Bush administration has so far given Israel a free hand to bully the Palestinians and to violate the terms of its Oslo commitments.

Israel's bombardments of defenseless civilians, demolition of homes, blockades of villages, destruction of farms, confiscation of land, and indiscriminate killing of unarmed civilians are blatant violations of international law. Israel uses US weapons to inflict and perpetuate these appalling conditions on the Palestinians. We have seen recently how receptive the Israelis are to any firm position taken by the American government. The US is the only government that has the capacity to put an end to Israeli excesses and lift the nightmare of Israeli occupation of the Palestinian people.

Even though the actions of Israel drew strong criticism and condemnation from every human rights organization of note, including Human Rights Watch and Amnesty International, the UN High Commissioner for Human Rights, and the UN Security Council, US government has done nothing to pressure Israel to put an end to its excesses, but instead used its veto power to deflect any criticism by the Security Council of Israel's policy toward the Palestinians. The United States invoked its veto power thirty four times in the last three decades to block Security Council resolutions condemning Israeli aggression or criticizing Israeli actions against civilians.[327] The latest US veto took place on March 27, 2001 against a Security Council resolution calling for UN observers in the West Bank and Gaza.[328]

Evidently, terrorism is fueled by the actions of exclusivist regimes that privilege some and deny basic rights to others. It is fueled by rogue governments that use state security agencies and excessive force to silence critics and political opposition. To be effective in fighting terrorism we must dry the swamps of abuse and injustice that bred radicalism all over the world.

US Policy Toward Political Islam

The United States government has adopted an unambiguous and clear stance vis-à-vis Islam and its adherents, but its stance toward individuals and groups motivated by Islamic ideals is often ambivalent, and at times manifestly antagonistic. The American official position distinguishes between, on the one hand, Islam as the religion that claims over a billion followers, and, on the other, a radical Islam prone to violence and intolerance toward cultural and religious diversity.[329] This position has already been tested in the wake of September 11 terrorist attacks on New York and Washington DC. Faced with a violent backlash against Islamic symbols and centers in the US (or symbols and centers erroneously identified as Islamic), President Bush sent a clear message and stern warning to bigots who took advantage of the tragic incident to target Muslims.

However, the distinction between normal and radical Islam is far from being clear when it comes to political action inspired by Islamic values and symbols. In its most definitive use, "radical Islam" has been employed in reference to Islamic groups that use violent means in pursuit of political ends. As such September 11 attacks by apparently Islamically motivated groups fit neatly into this category. Yet the Clinton and Bush administrations have also used the term to describe Islamic resistance movements in Lebanon (Hizbollah), as well as the West Bank and Gaza (Hamas and Islamic Jihad). These organizations have been condemned as terrorist, even though all three have been involved in national liberation struggles against a violent and unsparing occupational force. The US has not so far given a precise definition of terrorism, and has avoided using the term to describe state-sponsored violence against civilians, such as the tactics of Israel's brutal occupation in Lebanon and the occupied territories.

Still, the United States has shown disturbing ambivalence toward all political groups that employ Islamic symbols, and who are engaged in Islamlically-oriented reform efforts. Successive US administrations have invariably displayed degrees of antagonism toward Islamic reform movements. From Iran to Sudan, and from Algeria to Turkey, the US government has been less than forthcoming in supporting efforts aiming at confronting authoritarian regimes, and fighting corruption, whenever those efforts were led by Islamic parties or movements.

To be fair to the American official position, the anxiety toward political Islam is not limited to the United States, as European Union countries and institutions have displayed similar sensitivities. The anxiety is, evidently, caused by the apparent clash between Islam and secularism in the Middle East, which brings images of the struggle between modern secularism and the ancient regime of Europe. In the Middle East, however, those images are illusionary and misleading, for here more often than not secularism disguises dogmatic, elitist, and autocratic trends, while Islamic ethos have inspired the drive toward a more open and democratic society.

The struggle between the Islamic parties and the Junta-controlled government of Turkey is a case in point. The US continues to align itself with, and overlooks the excesses of, the Turkish military-backed regime. The Turkish generals have interfered in the political process, forcing the democratically elected Prime Minister Necmettin Erbakan from office in 1998 because of his Islamic leanings; persecuted Turkish citizens because of their religious beliefs and preferences, firing many of them from the army and bureaucracy; banned Turkish women who chose to wear a headscarf from government offices, universities, and schools; and outlawed the teaching of the Qur'an to children below 12 years of age. Yet despite these blatant human rights violations, the United States chose to look the other way, refusing to use its considerable influence to curtail the excesses of its military allies.

The Refah Party, whom the Turkish Junta has accused of threatening the secularist foundation of the Turkish republic, hardly fits even the broadest definition of radical Islam. The Refah Party has shown an extraordinary commitment to democracy, and has exhibited a remarkable self-restraint in the face of provocation, intimidations, and outright repressive tactics by the presumably secular and democratic elites. The Party has been dissolved five times over the last thirty years, only to emerge every time stronger and with broader popular support. Refah was banned in early 1998, its property confiscated, and its top leadership banned from practicing politics for five years.

Commanding the largest number of seats in the parliament, Refah was dissolved under the pretext that it threatens the secular character of the Turkish Republic. The Turkish courts were unable to implicate the Refah Party in any violation of the law, and the Party was faulted for not persecuting Turkish women who chose to wear a headscarf to school and work. The party emerged few months later under the name of Fadila. The Fadila Party was once again outlawed in June 2001, and was charged "with inciting protests against a headscarf ban in universities and orchestrating a failed bid by one of its legislators in 1999 to take oath in parliament wearing a headscarf."[330]

Commenting on the Junta's efforts to save the Turkish Republic from Islamists, Nilufer Gole, a respected Turkish sociologist, underscored the paradox of Turkish secularism. "What I find a pity is," she explained, "that in the name of secularism, we go back to authoritarianism. This is a very vicious circle in Turkish politics which is very similar to other Muslim contexts which experienced modernity and secularism."[331]

Given the fact that the United States has for long supported the wrong parties in the Middle East, one may conclude that US foreign policy toward Islam is influenced by powerful groups and vocal individuals, whose views are anchored more in ideology and self-serving dogmas, and less in actual reality and real developments on the ground.[332]

Rethinking US Foreign Policy

The United States foreign policy that aligns American support behind tyrants and dictators, and against the legitimate aspirations of popular movements pursuing national independence or democratic rule, is informed by notions and principles advanced by political realists. That is, they are informed by the nationalist political culture of nineteenth-century Europe. The political realist approach to international politics insists that national leaders have one paramount obligation, namely to advance the national-interests of their nations, often defined in economic or geopolitical terms. Political realists justify this position by pointing out that in the absence of international law that can be enforced by a central authority, nations are justified in enforcing their own interests. To do otherwise, political realists stress, is to give unprincipled foreign powers the opportunity to grow unchecked.

The pursuit of self-defined national interests led Europe to two devastating world wars. This, however, did not put an end to political realism, even after the United States introduced a new approach to international relations based on international organizations and international law, as many of its advocates found in the Cold War atmosphere a basis for reproducing a bit more sophisticated argument to place national interests over the demand of right and justice.

The United States is the sole superpower today, and has the opportunity to restructure world politics so as to ensure that the principles of right and justice that guide the internal politics of the United States are brought to bear on international relations. That is, international politics should no more be based on the notion of might makes right. The American people have long rejected such a notion in national politics and fought a war of independence, and later a civil war, to ensure that those who have been endowed by their Creator with equal freedoms and dignity are treated as such. Indeed, the United States and the American people are uniquely situated to expand the values of freedom, equality, and rule of law from the national to the international domain. Not only is the United States an unrivaled superpower, but Americans constitute a microcosm of world population. America is a multiethnic and multireligious society whose ethnic and religious groups represent the major ethnic and religious communities that form the modern world. Africans, Anglo-Saxons, Arabs, Chinese, Indians, Japanese, Irish, Koreans, Latinos, and Slavs live peacefully in America, and work together in pursuit of their individual and collective dreams, and confess and practice different religions freely, including Judaism, Christianity, and Islam, along with a host of other religions.

To avoid turning the US into an empire that tramples on the legitimate rights of other peoples, good intentions and humane sentiments are not sufficient. What is important, we should recall Dewey's wise observations, is to ensure that the conditions that define US relations with other nations do not lend themselves to imperialistic actions and aims. "Imperialism," Dewey observed, "can only be prevented by regulating the conditions out of which it proceeds."

The only way to avoid becoming an empire is for the United States to submit fully to the rules of international laws, and to insist that economic and geopolitical interests do not surpass in importance the right of other nations to live a life of freedom and dignity.

Global Peace and American Leadership

The notion of a global order based on a set of universal principles, governing interaction among political communities in order to prevent aggression and protect human dignity, must be welcomed and supported by all, particularly those who can exert greater influence in bringing about a just international order. The people of the Middle East have a high stack in the realization of just global order, but many of their intellectuals have expressed misgivings and concerns about the current global order. These misgivings and concerns are not directed at the call for a universal application of international law, but rather at the lack of it. Middle Eastern intellectuals have been critical of the lack of political commitment to international law by the world's only superpower. They point out that the United States has been willing to support international law only when it does not conflict with its national interests, or when supporting it helps advance US interests. Thus, the West supported democracy in Eastern Europe and Russia because the triumph of the forces of democracy there meant the demise of an old rival and adversary, yet it stands behind military dictatorship in the Middle East because doing so is deemed to be in the national interest of Western states.

The September 11 tragedy magnified Mideast-US tensions and put the world in general, and the United States in particular, on a crossroad. We have the choice of marching forward toward global peace, rooted in rules of equitable law, and fairly administered to all, the strong and the weak, the far and the near, or to immerse ourselves in empire building in which the strong conquer and dominate the weak.

The United States is in a unique position – culturally, economically, and politically – to lead the world in either direction. And given this choice, I am confident that Americans would choose global peace over world empire. But for America to make the right choice, political leaders, as well as the leaders of public opinion, have to play a pivotal role in helping the public make the right move by choosing American values over America's narrow and short-term interests. It is true that lending support to corrupt governments makes it a bit easier, in the short run, for the United States to influence the foreign and domestic policies of these governments. In the long run, however, a foreign policy oblivious to moral standards is bound to corrupt American politics. Indeed, the terrorist attacks on New York and Washington DC have already compromised the precious freedom America cherishes in the form of an anti-terrorism legislation that exchanges freedom and due process for a false sense of security.

The Covenant of Madinah

The covenant of Madinah (Sahifat al-Madinah) was written under the direction of the Prophet of Islam, and served as the charter for the first Muslim polity, upon the immigration of the Prophet and his assumption of the highest political authority in the newly founded city-state of Madinah.

In the name of God, the compassionate, the merciful. This is a covenant given by Muhammad to the believers and the Muslims of Quraysh, Yathrib, and those who followed, joined, and fought with them. They constitute one *ummah* to the exclusion of all others. As was their custom, the Muhajirun from Quraysh are bound together and shall ransom their prisoners in kindness and justice as believers do. Following their own custom, Banu `Awf are bound together as they have been before. Every clan shall ransom its prisoners with the kindness and justice common among believers. [The text here repeats the same prescription concerning every clan of the Banu al-Harith, Banu Sa`idah, Banu Jusham, Banu al-Najjar, Banu `Amr ibn `Awf, and Banu al-Nabit].

The believers shall leave none of their members in destitution without giving him in kindness what he needs by way of ransom or bloodwit. No believer shall take as an ally a freedman of another Muslim without the permission of his previous master. All pious believers shall rise as one man against whosoever rebels or seeks to commit injustice, aggression, sin, or spread mutual enmity between the believers, even though he may be one of their sons. No believer shall slay a believer; neither shall he assist an unbeliever against a believer. Just as God's bond is one and indivisible, all believers shall stand behind the commitment of the least of them. All believers are bonded one to another to the exclusion of other men. Any Jew who follows us is entitled to our assistance and the same rights as any one of us, without injustice or partisanship.

This covenant is one and indivisible. No believer shall enter into a separate peace without all the believers whenever there is fighting in the cause of God, but will do so only on the basis of equality and justice to all others. In every military expedition we undertake our members shall be accompanied by others committed to the same objective. All believers shall avenge the blood of one another whenever any one of them falls fighting in the cause of God. The pious believers follow the best and most upright guidance. No unbeliever shall be allowed to place under his protection against the interest of a believer, any wealth or person belonging to Quryash. Whoever is convicted of killing a believer deliberately but without righteous cause, shall be liable to the relatives of the killed. Until the latter are satisfied, the killer shall be subject to retaliation by each and every believer. The killer shall have no rights whatever until this right of the believer is satisfied.

Whoever has entered into this covenant and believed in God and in the last day shall never protect or give shelter to a convict or criminal; whoever does so shall be cursed by God and upon him shall the divine wrath fall on the Day of Judgment. Neither repentance nor ransom shall be acceptable from him. No object of contention among you may not be referred to God and to Muhammad – may God's peace and blessing be upon him – for judgment. As the Jews fight on the side of the believers, they shall spend of their wealth on equal par with the believers.

The Jews have their religion and the Muslims theirs. Both enjoy the security of their own populace and clients except the unjust and the criminal among them. The unjust or the criminal destroys only himself and his family. The Jews of Banu Njjar, Banu al-Harith, Banu Sa`iddah, Banu Jusham, Banu al-Aws, Banu Tha`labah, Jafnah, and Banu al-Shutaybah – to all the same rights and privileges apply as to the Jews of Banu Aws. The clients of the tribe of Tha`labah enjoy the same rights and duties as the members of the tribe themselves. Likewise, the clients of the Jews as the Jews themselves. None of the foregoing shall go out to war except with the permission of Muhammad – may God's peace and blessing be upon him – though none may be prevented from taking revenge for a wound inflicted upon him. Whoever murders anyone will have murdered himself and the members of his family, unless it be the case of a man suffering a wrong, for God will accept his action.

The Jews shall bear their public expenses and so will the Muslims. Each shall assist the other against any violater of this covenant. Their relationship shall be one of mutual advice and consultation, and mutual assistance and charity rather than harm and aggression. However, no man is liable to a crime committed by his ally. Assistance is due to the party suffering an injustice, not to the one perpetrating it. Since the Jews fight on the side of the believers they shall spend their wealth on a par with them.

The town of Yathrib shall constitute a sanctuary for the parties of this covenant. Their neighbors shall be treated as themselves as long as they perpetrate no crime and commit no harm. No woman may be taken under protection without the consent of her family. Whatever difference or dispute between the parties to this covenant remains unsolved shall be referred to God and to Muhammad, the prophet of God – may God's peace and blessing be upon him. God is the guarantor of the piety and goodness that is embodied in this covenant. Neither the Quraysh nor their allies shall be given any protection.

The people of this covenant shall come to the assistance of one another against whoever attacks Yathrib. If they are called to cease hostilities and to enter into a peace, they shall be bound to do so in the interest of peace. If, on the other hand, they call upon the Muslims to cease hostilities and to enter into a peace, they shall be bound to do so in the interest of peace. If, on the other hand, they call upon the Muslims to cease hostilities and to enter into a peace, the Muslims shall be bound to do so and maintain the peace except when the war is against their religion. To every smaller group belongs the share which is their due as members of the larger group which is party to this covenant. The Jews of al-Aws, as well as their clients, are entitled to the same rights as this covenant has granted to its parties together with the goodness and charity of the latter. Charity and goodness are clearly distinguishable from crime and injury, and there is no responsibility except for one's own deeds. God is the guarantor of the truth and good will of this covenant. This covenant shall constitute no protection for the unjust or criminal. Whoever goes out to fight as well as whoever stays at home shall be safe and secure in this city unless he has perpetrated an injustice or committed a crime. God grants His protection to whoever acts in piety, charity, and goodness.

Universal Declaration of
Human Rights

On December 10, 1948 the General Assembly of the United Nations adopted and proclaimed the Universal Declaration of Human Rights (UDHR) the full text of which appears in the following pages. Following this historic act the Assembly called upon all member countries to publicize the text of the Declaration and "to cause it to be disseminated, displayed, read and expounded principally in schools and other educational institutions, without distinction based on the political status of countries or territories."

PREAMBLE

WHEREAS recognition of the inherent dignity and of the equal and inalienable rights of all members of the human family is the foundation of freedom, justice and peace in the world,

WHEREAS disregard and contempt for human rights have resulted in barbarous acts which have outraged the conscience of mankind, and the advent of a world in which human beings shall enjoy freedom of speech and belief and freedom from fear and want has been proclaimed as the highest aspiration of the common people,

WHEREAS it is essential, if man is not to be compelled to have recourse, as a last resort, to rebellion against tyranny and oppression, that human rights should be protected by the rule of law,

WHEREAS it is essential to promote the development of friendly relations between nations,

WHEREAS the peoples of the United Nations have in the Charter reaffirmed their faith in fundamental human rights, in the dignity and worth of the human person and in the equal rights of men and women and have determined to promote social progress and better standards of life in larger freedom,

WHEREAS Member States have pledged themselves to achieve, in cooperation with the United Nations, the promotion of universal respect for and observance of human rights and fundamental freedoms,

WHEREAS a common understanding of these rights and freedoms is of the greatest importance for the full realization of this pledge,

Now, Therefore **THE GENERAL ASSEMBLY** proclaims **THIS UNIVERSAL DECLARATION OF HUMAN RIGHTS** as a common standard of achievement for all peoples and all nations, to the end that every individual and every organ of society, keeping this Declaration constantly in mind, shall strive by teaching and education to promote respect for these rights and freedoms and by progressive measures, national and international, to secure their universal and effective recognition and observance, both among the peoples of Member States themselves and among the peoples of territories under their jurisdiction.

Article 1.

All human beings are born free and equal in dignity and rights. They are endowed with reason and conscience and should act toward one another in a spirit of brotherhood.

Article 2.

Everyone is entitled to all the rights and freedoms set forth in this Declaration, without distinction of any kind, such as race, colour, sex, language, religion, political or other opinion, national or social origin, property, birth or other status. Furthermore, no distinction shall be made on the basis of the political, jurisdictional or international status of the country or territory to which a person belongs, whether it be independent, trust, non-self-governing or under any other limitation of sovereignty.

Article 3.

Everyone has the right to life, liberty and security of person.

Article 4.

No one shall be held in slavery or servitude; slavery and the slave trade shall be prohibited in all their forms.

Article 5.

No one shall be subjected to torture or to cruel, inhuman or degrading treatment or punishment.

Article 6.

Everyone has the right to recognition everywhere as a person before the law.

Article 7.

All are equal before the law and are entitled without any discrimination to equal protection of the law. All are entitled to equal protection against any discrimination in violation of this Declaration and against any incitement to such discrimination.

Article 8.

Everyone has the right to an effective remedy by the competent national tribunals for acts violating the fundamental rights granted him by the constitution or by law.

Article 9.

No one shall be subjected to arbitrary arrest, detention or exile.

Article 10.

Everyone is entitled in full equality to a fair and public hearing by an independent and impartial tribunal, in the determination of his rights and obligations and of any criminal charge against him.

Article 11.

(1) Everyone charged with a penal offence has the right to be presumed innocent until proved guilty according to law in a public trial at which he has had all the guarantees necessary for his defence.

(2) No one shall be held guilty of any penal offence on account of any act or omission which did not constitute a penal offence, under national or international law, at the time when it was committed. Nor shall a heavier penalty be imposed than the one that was applicable at the time the penal offence was committed.

Article 12.

No one shall be subjected to arbitrary interference with his privacy, family, home or correspondence, nor to attacks upon his honour and reputation. Everyone has the right to the protection of the law against such interference or attacks.

Article 13.

(1) Everyone has the right to freedom of movement and residence within the borders of each state.

(2) Everyone has the right to leave any country, including his own, and to return to his country.

Article 14.

(1) Everyone has the right to seek and to enjoy in other countries asylum from persecution.

(2) This right may not be invoked in the case of prosecutions genuinely arising from non-political crimes or from acts contrary to the purposes and principles of the United Nations.

Article 15.

(1) Everyone has the right to a nationality.

(2) No one shall be arbitrarily deprived of his nationality nor denied the right to change his nationality.

Article 16.

(1) Men and women of full age, without any limitation due to race, nationality or religion, have the right to marry and to found a family. They are entitled to equal rights as to marriage, during marriage and at its dissolution.

(2) Marriage shall be entered into only with the free and full consent of the intending spouses.

(3) The family is the natural and fundamental group unit of society and is entitled to protection by society and the State.

Article 17.

(1) Everyone has the right to own property alone as well as in association with others.

(2) No one shall be arbitrarily deprived of his property.

Article 18.

Everyone has the right to freedom of thought, conscience and religion; this right includes freedom to change his religion or belief, and freedom, either alone or in community with others and in public or private, to manifest his religion or belief in teaching, practice, worship and observance.

Article 19.

Everyone has the right to freedom of opinion and expression; this right includes freedom to hold opinions without interference and to seek, receive and impart information and ideas through any media and regardless of frontiers.

Article 20.

(1) Everyone has the right to freedom of peaceful assembly and association.

(2) No one may be compelled to belong to an association.

Article 21.

(1) Everyone has the right to take part in the government of his country, directly or through freely chosen representatives.

(2) Everyone has the right of equal access to public service in his country.

(3) The will of the people shall be the basis of the authority of government; this will shall be expressed in periodic and genuine elections which shall be by universal and equal suffrage and shall be held by secret vote or by equivalent free voting procedures.

Article 22.

Everyone, as a member of society, has the right to social security and is entitled to realization, through national effort and international cooperation and in accordance with the organization and resources of each State, of the economic, social and cultural rights indispensable for his dignity and the free development of his personality.

Article 23.

(1) Everyone has the right to work, to free choice of employment, to just and favourable conditions of work and to protection against unemployment.

(2) Everyone, without any discrimination, has the right to equal pay for equal work.

(3) Everyone who works has the right to just and favourable remuneration ensuring for himself and his family an existence worthy of human dignity, and supplemented, if necessary, by other means of social protection.

(4) Everyone has the right to form and to join trade unions for the protection of his interests.

Article 24.

Everyone has the right to rest and leisure, including reasonable limitation of working hours and periodic holidays with pay.

Article 25.

(1) Everyone has the right to a standard of living adequate for the health and well-being of himself and of his family, including food, clothing, housing and medical care and necessary social services, and the right to security in the event of unemployment, sickness, disability, widowhood, old age or other lack of livelihood in circumstances beyond his control.

(2) Motherhood and childhood are entitled to special care and assistance. All children, whether born in or out of wedlock, shall enjoy the same social protection.

Article 26.

(1) Everyone has the right to education. Education shall be free, at least in the elementary and fundamental stages. Elementary education shall be compulsory. Technical and professional education shall be made generally available and higher education shall be equally accessible to all on the basis of merit.

(2) Education shall be directed to the full development of the human personality and to the strengthening of respect for human rights and fundamental freedoms. It shall promote understanding, tolerance and friendship among all nations, racial or religious groups, and shall further the activities of the United Nations for the maintenance of peace.

(3) Parents have a prior right to choose the kind of education that shall be given to their children.

Article 27.

(1) Everyone has the right freely to participate in the cultural life of the community, to enjoy the arts and to share in scientific advancement and its benefits.

(2) Everyone has the right to the protection of the moral and material interests resulting from any scientific, literary or artistic production of which he is the author.

Article 28.

Everyone is entitled to a social and international order in which the rights and freedoms set forth in this Declaration can be fully realized.

Article 29.

(1) Everyone has duties to the community in which alone the free and full development of his personality is possible.

(2) In the exercise of his rights and freedoms, everyone shall be subject only to such limitations as are determined by law solely for the purpose of securing due recognition and respect for the rights and freedoms of others and of meeting the just requirements of morality, public order and the general welfare in a democratic society.

(3) These rights and freedoms may in no case be exercised contrary to the purposes and principles of the United Nations.

Article 30.

Nothing in this Declaration may be interpreted as implying for any State, group or person any right to engage in any activity or to perform any act aimed at the destruction of any of the rights and freedoms set forth herein.

Adopted and proclaimed by General Assembly resolution 217 A (III) of 10 December 1948.

Universal Islamic Declaration
of Human Rights

21 Dhul Qaidah 1401 / 19 September 1981

This is a declaration for mankind, a guidance and instruction to those who fear God. (Al-Qur'an, Al-`Imran 3:138)

Foreword

Islam gave to mankind an ideal code of human rights fourteen centuries ago. These rights aim at conferring honour and dignity on mankind and eliminating exploitation, oppression and injustice.

Human rights in Islam are firmly rooted in the belief that God, and God alone, is the Law Giver and the Source of all human rights. Due to their divine origin, no ruler, government, assembly or authority can curtail or violate in any way the human rights conferred by God, nor can they be surrendered.

Human rights in Islam are an integral part of the overall Islamic order and it is obligatory on all Muslim governments and organs of society to implement them in letter and in spirit within the framework of that order.

It is unfortunate that human rights are being trampled upon with impunity in many countries of the world, including some Muslim countries. Such violations are a matter of serious concern and are arousing the conscience of more and more people throughout the world.

I sincerely hope that this *Declaration of Human Rights* will give a powerful impetus to the Muslim peoples to stand firm and defend resolutely and courageously the rights conferred on them by God.

This *Declaration of Human Rights* is the second fundamental document proclaimed by the Islamic Council to mark the beginning of the 15th Century of the Islamic era, the first being the *Universal Islamic Declaration* announced at the International Conference on The Prophet Muhammad (peace and blessings be upon him) and his Message, held in London from 12 to 15 April 1980.

The *Universal Islamic Declaration of Human Rights* is based on the Qur'an and the Sunnah and has been compiled by eminent Muslim scholars, jurists and representatives of Islamic movements and thought. May God reward them all for their efforts and guide us along the right path.

Paris 21 Dhul Qaidah 1401   Salem Azzam
19th September 1981   *Secretary General*

O men! Behold, We have created you all out of a male and a female, and have made you into nations and tribes, so that you might come to know one another. Verily, the noblest of you in the sight of God is the one who is most deeply conscious of Him. Behold, God is all-knowing, all aware. (Al-Qur'an, Al-Hujurat 49:13)

Preamble

WHEREAS the age-old human aspiration for a just world order wherein people could live, develop and prosper in an environment free from fear, oppression, exploitation and deprivation, remains largely unfulfilled;

WHEREAS the Divine Mercy unto mankind reflected in its having been endowed with super-abundant economic sustenance is being wasted, or unfairly or unjustly witheld from the inhabitants of the earth;

WHEREAS Allah (God) has given mankind through His revelations in the Holy Qur'an and the Sunnah of His Blessed Prophet Muhammad an abiding legal and moral framework within which to establish and regulate human institutions and relationships;

WHEREAS the human rights decreed by the Divine Law aim at conferring dignity and honour on mankind and are designed to eliminate oppression and injustice;

WHEREAS by virtue of their Divine source and sanction these rights can neither be curtailed, abrogated or disregarded by authorities, assemblies or other institutions, nor can they be surrendered or alienated;

Therefore we, as Muslims, who believe

(a) in God, the Beneficent and Merciful, the Creator, the Sustainer, the Sovereign, the sole Guide of mankind and the Source of all Law;

(b) in the Vicegerency (*Khilafah*) of man who has been created to fulfill the Will of God on earth;

(c) in the wisdom of Divine guidance brought by the Prophets, whose mission found its culmination in the final Divine message that was conveyed by the Prophet Muhammad (Peace be upon him) to all mankind;

(d) that rationality by itself without the light of revelation from God can neither be a sure guide in the affairs of mankind nor provide spiritual nourishment to the human soul, and, knowing that the teachings of Islam represent the quintessence of Divine guidance in its final and perfect form, feel duty-bound to remind man of the high status and dignity bestowed on him by God;

(e) in inviting all mankind to the message of Islam;

(f) that by the terms of our primeval covenant with God our duties and obligations have priority over our rights, and that each one of us is under a bounden duty to spread the teachings of Islam by word, deed, and indeed in all gentle ways, and to make them effective not only in our individual lives but also in the society around us;

(g) in our obligation to establish an Islamic order:

(i) wherein all human beings shall be equal and none shall enjoy a privilege or suffer a disadvantage or discrimination by reason of race, colour, sex, origin or language;

(ii) wherein all human beings are born free;

(iii) wherein slavery and forced labour are abhorred;

(iv) wherein conditions shall be established such that the institution of family shall be preserved, protected and honoured as the basis of all social life;

(v) wherein the rulers and the ruled alike are subject to, and equal before, the Law;

(vi) wherein obedience shall be rendered only to those commands that are in consonance with the Law;

(vii) wherein all worldly power shall be considered as a sacred trust, to be exercised within the limits prescribed by the Law and in a manner approved by it, and with due regard for the priorities fixed by it;

(viii) wherein all economic resources shall be treated as Divine blessings bestowed upon mankind, to be enjoyed by all in accordance with the rules and the values set out in the Qur'an and the Sunnah;

(ix) wherein all public affairs shall be determined and conducted, and the authority to administer them shall be exercised after mutual consultation *(Shura)* between the believers qualified to contribute to a decision which would accord well with the Law and the public good;

(x) wherein everyone shall undertake obligations proportionate to his capacity and shall be held responsible pro rata for his deeds;

(xi) wherein everyone shall, in case of an infringement of his rights, be assured of appropriate remedial measures in accordance with the Law;

(xii) wherein no one shall be deprived of the rights assured to him by the Law except by its authority and to the extent permitted by it;

(xiii) wherein every individual shall have the right to bring legal action against anyone who commits a crime against society as a whole or against any of its members;

(xiv) wherein every effort shall be made to

(a) secure unto mankind deliverance from every type of exploitation, injustice and oppression,

(b) ensure to everyone security, dignity and liberty in terms set out and by methods approved and within the limits set by the Law;

Do hereby, as servants of Allah and as members of the Universal Brotherhood of Islam, at the beginning of the Fifteenth Century of the Islamic Era, affirm our commitment to uphold the following inviolable and inalienable human rights that we consider are enjoined by Islam.

I. Right to Life

(a) Human life is sacred and inviolable and every effort shall be made to protect it. In particular no one shall be exposed to injury or death, except under the authority of the Law.

(b) Just as in life, so also after death, the sanctity of a person's body shall be inviolable. It is the obligation of believers to see that a deceased person's body is handled with due solemnity.

II. Right to Freedom

(a) Man is born free. No inroads shall be made on his right to liberty except under the authority and in due process of the Law.

(b) Every individual and every people has the inalienable right to freedom in all its forms – physical, cultural, economic and political – and shall be entitled to struggle by all available means against any infringement or abrogation of this right; and every oppressed individual or people has a legitimate claim to the support of other individuals and/or peoples in such a struggle.

III. Right to Equality and Prohibition Against Impermissible Discrimination

(a) All persons are equal before the Law and are entitled to equal opportunities and protection of the Law.

(b) All persons shall be entitled to equal wage for equal work.

(c) No person shall be denied the opportunity to work or be discriminated against in any manner or exposed to greater physical risk by reason of religious belief, colour, race, origin, sex or language.

IV. Right to Justice

(a) Every person has the right to be treated in accordance with the Law, and only in accordance with the Law.

(b) Every person has not only the right but also the obligation to protest against injustice; to recourse to remedies provided by the Law in respect of any unwarranted personal injury or loss; to self-defence against any charges that are preferred against him and to obtain fair adjudication before an independent judicial tribunal in any dispute with public authorities or any other person.

(c) It is the right and duty of every person to defend the rights of any other person and the community in general *(Hisbah)*.

(d) No person shall be discriminated against while seeking to defend private and public rights.

(e) It is the right and duty of every Muslim to refuse to obey any command which is contrary to the Law, no matter by whom it may be issued.

V. Right to Fair Trial

(a) No person shall be adjudged guilty of an offence and made liable to punishment except after proof of his guilt before an independent judicial tribunal.

(b) No person shall be adjudged guilty except after a fair trial and after reasonable opportunity for defence has been provided to him.

(c) Punishment shall be awarded in accordance with the Law, in proportion to the seriousness of the offence and with due consideration of the circumstances under which it was committed.

(d) No act shall be considered a crime unless it is stipulated as such in the clear wording of the Law.

(e) Every individual is responsible for his actions. Responsibility for a crime cannot be vicariously extended to other members of his family or group, who are not otherwise directly or indirectly involved in the commission of the crime in question.

VI. Right to Protection Against Abuse of Power

Every person has the right to protection against harassment by official agencies. He is not liable to account for himself except for making a defence to the charges made against him or where he is found in a situation wherein a question regarding suspicion of his involvement in a crime could be *reasonably* raised

VII. Right to Protection Against Torture

No person shall be subjected to torture in mind or body, or degraded, or threatened with injury either to himself or to anyone related to or held dear by him, or forcibly made to confess to the commission of a crime, or forced to consent to an act which is injurious to his interests.

VIII. Right to Protection of Honour and Reputation

Every person has the right to protect his honour and reputation against calumnies, groundless charges or deliberate attempts at defamation and blackmail.

IX. Right to Asylum

(a) Every persecuted or oppressed person has the right to seek refuge and asylum. This right is guaranteed to every human being irrespective of race, religion, colour and sex.

(b) Al-Masjid Al-Haram (the sacred house of Allah) in Mecca is a sanctuary for all Muslims.

X. Rights of Minorities

(a) The Qur'anic principle "There is no compulsion in religion" shall govern the religious rights of non-Muslim minorities.

(b) In a Muslim country religious minorities shall have the choice to be governed in respect of their civil and personal matters by Islamic Law, or by their own laws.

XI. Right and Obligation to Participate in the Conduct and Management of Public Affairs

(a) Subject to the Law, every individual in the community *(Ummah)* is entitled to assume public office.

(b) Process of free consultation *(Shura)* is the basis of the administrative relationship between the government and the people. People also have the right to choose and remove their rulers in accordance with this principle.

XII. Right to Freedom of Belief, Thought and Speech

(a) Every person has the right to express his thoughts and beliefs so long as he remains within the limits prescribed by the Law. No one, however, is entitled to disseminate falsehood or to circulate reports which may outrage public decency, or to indulge in slander, innuendo or to cast defamatory aspersions on other persons.

(b) Pursuit of knowledge and search after truth is not only a right but a duty of every Muslim.

(c) It is the right and duty of every Muslim to protest and strive (within the limits set out by the Law) against oppression even if it involves challenging the highest authority in the state.

(d) There shall be no bar on the dissemination of information provided it does not endanger the security of the society or the state and is confined within the limits imposed by the Law.

(e) No one shall hold in contempt or ridicule the religious beliefs of others or incite public hostility against them; respect for the religious feelings of others is obligatory on all Muslims.

XIII. Right to Freedom of Religion

Every person has the right to freedom of conscience and worship in accordance with his religious beliefs.

XIV. Right to Free Association

(a) Every person is entitled to participate individually and collectively in the religious, social, cultural and political life of his community and to establish institutions and agencies meant to enjoin what is right *(ma`roof)* and to prevent what is wrong *(munkar)*.

(b) Every person is entitled to strive for the establishment of institutions whereunder an enjoyment of these rights would be made possible. Collectively, the community is obliged to establish conditions so as to allow its members full development of their personalities.

XV. The Economic Order and the Rights Evolving Therefrom

(a) In their economic pursuits, all persons are entitled to the full benefits of nature and all its resources. These are blessings bestowed by God for the benefit of mankind as a whole.

(b) All human beings are entitled to earn their living according to the Law.

(c) Every person is entitled to own property individually or in association with others. State ownership of certain economic resources in the public interest is legitimate.

(d) The poor have the right to a prescribed share in the wealth of the rich, as fixed by Zakah, levied and collected in accordance with the Law.

(e) All means of production shall be utilised in the interest of the community *(Ummah)* as a whole, and may not be neglected or misused.

(f) In order to promote the development of a balanced economy and to protect society from exploitation, Islamic Law forbids monopolies, unreasonable restrictive trade practices, usury, the use of coercion in the making of contracts and the publication of misleading advertisements.

(g) All economic activities are permitted provided they are not detrimental to the interests of the community *(Ummah)* and do not violate Islamic laws and values.

XVI. Right to Protection of Property

No property may be expropriated except in the public interest and on payment of fair and adequate compensation.

XVII. Status and Dignity of Workers

Islam honours work and the worker and enjoins Muslims not only to treat the worker justly but also generously. He is not only to be paid his earned wages promptly, but is also entitled to adequate rest and leisure.

XVIII. Right to Social Security

Every person has the right to food, shelter, clothing, education and medical care consistent with the resources of the community. This obligation of the community extends in particular to all individuals who cannot take care of themselves due to some temporary or permanent disability.

XIX. Right to Found a Family and Related Matters

(a) Every person is entitled to marry, to found a family and to bring up children in conformity with his religion, traditions and culture. Every spouse is entitled to such rights and privileges and carries such obligations as are stipulated by the Law.

(b) Each of the partners in a marriage is entitled to respect and consideration from the other.

(c) Every husband is obligated to maintain his wife and children according to his means.

(d) Every child has the right to be maintained and properly brought up by its parents, it being forbidden that children are made to work at an early age or that any burden is put on them which would arrest or harm their natural development.

(e) If parents are for some reason unable to discharge their obligations toward a child it becomes the responsibility of the community to fulfill these obligations at public expense.

(f) Every person is entitled to material support, as well as care and protection, from his family during his childhood, old age or incapacity. Parents are entitled to material support as well as care and protection from their children.

(g) Motherhood is entitled to special respect, care and assistance on the part of the family and the public organs of the community *(Ummah)*.

(h) Within the family, men and women are to share in their obligations and responsibilities according to their sex, their natural endowments, talents and inclinations, bearing in mind their common responsibilities toward their progeny and their relatives.

(i) No person may be married against his or her will, or lose or suffer dimunition of legal personality on account of marriage.

XX. Rights of Married Women

Every married woman is entitled to:

(a) live in the house in which her husband lives;

(b) receive the means necessary for maintaining a standard of living which is not inferior to that of her spouse, and, in the event of divorce, receive during the statutory period of waiting (*'iddah)* means of maintenance commensurate with her husband's resources, for herself as well as for the children she nurses or keeps, irrespective of her own financial status, earnings, or property that she may hold in her own rights;

(c) seek and obtain dissolution of marriage (*Khul'a)* in accordance with the terms of the Law. This right is in addition to her right to seek divorce through the courts.

(d) inherit from her husband, her parents, her children and other relatives according to the Law;

(e) strict confidentiality from her spouse, or ex-spouse if divorced, with regard to any information that he may have obtained about her, the disclosure of which could prove detrimental to her interests. A similar responsibility rests upon her in respect of her spouse or ex-spouse.

XXI. Right to Education

(a) Every person is entitled to receive education in accordance with his natural capabilities.

(b) Every person is entitled to a free choice of profession and career and to the opportunity for the full development of his natural endowments.

XXII. Right of Privacy

Every person is entitled to the protection of his privacy.

XXIII. Right to Freedom of Movement and Residence

(a) In view of the fact that the World of Islam is veritably Ummah Islamia, every Muslim shall have the right to freely move in and out of any Muslim country.

(b) No one shall be forced to leave the country of his residence, or be arbitrarily deported therefrom without recourse to due process of Law.

Explanatory Notes

(1) In the above formulation of Human Rights, unless the context provides otherwise:

(a) the term "person" refers to both the male and female sexes.

(b) the term "Law" denotes the Shari'ah, i.e., the totality of ordinances derived from the Qur'an and the Sunnah and any other laws that are deduced from these two sources by methods considered valid in Islamic jurisprudence.

(2) Each one of the Human Rights enunciated in this declaration carries a corresponding duty.

(3) In the exercise and enjoyment of the rights referred to above every person shall be subject only to such limitations as are enjoined by the Law for the purpose of securing the due recognition of, and respect for, the rights and the freedom of others and of meeting the just requirements of morality, public order and the general welfare of the Community *(Ummah)*.

The Arabic text of this *Declaration* is the original.

NOTES

1   Rene Descartes, *Meditations on First Philosophy*, trans. John Cottingham (Cambridge University Press, 1986), 49.

2   Jean-Jacques Rousseau, *The Social Contract*, trans. Maurice Cranston (London: Penguin Books, 1968), 186.

3   Immanuel Kant, *Critique of Pure Reason*, trans. Norman Kemp Smith (New York: Macmillan, 1929), 640.

4   Friedrich Nietzsche, *Beyond Good and Evil* (New York: Vintage Books, 1966), 66.

5   Karl Marx, *The Marx-Engels Reader*, ed. Robert C. Tucker, 2d ed. (Newe York: W. W. Norton, 1978), 28.

6   Ibid., 74-75.

7   Ibid., 45.

8   Rashid al-Ghanoushi, *Al-Huriyyat al-`Ammah fi al-Dawlah al-Islamiyyah* [General Liberties in the Islamic State] (Beirut: Markaz Dirasat al-Wihdah al-`Arabiyyah, 1993), 258.

9   To review the full text of the Compact of Madinah, refer to Ibn Hisham, *Al-Sirah al-Nabawiyah* [The Biography of the Prophet], (Damascus: Dar al-Kunuz al-Adabiyah, n.d.), 1:501-2.

10   Ibid., 501.

11   Ibid.

12   See 9:97 and 49:14.

13   Ibn Hisham, *Al-Sirah*, 501.

14   Ibid.

15   Ibid.

16   Muhammad bin Ahmad al-Sarakhsi, *Sharh Kitab al-Siyar al-Kabir* (Pakistan: Nusrullah Mansour, 1405 AH), 4:1530.

17   Ibid.

18   `Ali bin Muhammad al-Mawardi, *Al-Ahkam al-Sultaniyyah* (Cairo: Dar al-Fikr, 1401/1983), 59.

19   Ibid., 20-23.

20   Ibid., 24.

21   See Ibn al-Qayim, *Sharh al-Shurut al-`Umariyyah* (Beirut: Dar al-`Ilm li al-Malayin, 1381/1961).

22   "What Allah has bestowed on His Messenger (and taken away) from the people of the townships belongs to Allah, to His Messenger and to kindred and orphans, the needy and the wayfarer; in order that it may not take a circuit (*li alla yakuna dulah*) between the wealthy among you" (59:7).

23   See, for instance, al-Mawardi, *Al-Ahkam al-Sultaniyah* (Cairo: Dar al-Fikr, 1401/1983); also Abu al-Hassan al-Shaybani, *Al-Siyar al-Kabir.*

24   For Ibn Khaldun's views on the state, see *Al-Muqaddimah,* (Beirut: Dar al-Kitab al-Lubnani, 1956), 3:121-44.

25   See for example 'Abd al-Qadir 'Awdah, *Al-Islam wa Awda'una al-Siyasiyah* (Beirut: Mu'assasah al-Risalah, 1984), 177; or Muhammad Fa-

ruq al-Nabhan, *Muhadarat fi al-Fikr al-Siyasi wa al-Iqtisadi fi al-Islam* (n.p.: n.d.), 35-58.

26   Abu al-Ma`ali al-Juwayni, *Ghiyath al-Umam* (Alexandria, Egypt: Dar al-Da`wah, n.d.), 47.

27   "If it had been your Lord's will, all those on earth would have believed; will you then compel mankind, against its will, to believe?" (10:99); also "Let there be no compulsion in religion: Truth stands out clear from error" (2:256).

28   See T. Walter Walibank, et al., *Civilization Past and Present*, 5th ed. (Glenview, IL: Scott Foresman and Company, 1965), 208.

29   See, for instance, Ibn Kathir's *Al-Bidayah wa al-Nihayah*, (n.p.: n.d.).

30   The Shari`ah's humane and global orientation is reflected in many verses of the Qur'an, such as: "We sent you not but as a mercy for humanity" (21:7). Its humanistic orientation has been articulated by Abu Ishaq al-Shatibi (d. 730 AH), who posits in his major work *Muwafaqat* five purposes of the Shari`ah: the protection of religion, life, progeny, property, and mind. For a detailed discussion on the subject, see his *Muwafaqat* (Cairo: al-Maktabat al-Tijariyah), 2:5-20.

31   See al-Mawardi (d. 450 AH), *Al-Ahkam al-Sultaniyah*, 6-9; also al-Juwayni, *Ghiyath al-Umam.*

32   Quoted in Ann K. Lambton, *State and Government in Medieval Islam* (Oxford: Oxford University Press, 1981), 81.

33   Al-Mawardi, *al-Ahkam al-Sultaniyah*, 6-9.

34   Al-Juwayni, *Ghiyath al-Umam*, 55-56.

35   Abu Hamid al-Ghazzali, *Fada'ih al-Batiniyah* (Cairo: al-Dar al-Qawmiyah, n.d.), 176-77.

36   See Muhammad Rashid Rida, *Al-Khilafah*; also Abu Ala Mauduidi's *Islamic State*, trans. Mazheruddin Siddiqi (Karachi: Islamic Research Academy, 1986).

37   See al-Mawdadi, *Islamic State*, 14-17.

38   The term "class" includes, but is not limited to, the economic sphere. It may also include social groups divided along political, ideological, or regional lines.

39   The Qur'an expresses in so many ways the obligation of the *ummah* to establish an equitable order in which human exploitation and abuse is prevented and human dignity is protected and promoted. See, for example, 4:135, 5:8, 16:90, 57:25, and 59:7.

40   See for instance Ibn Qutaybah, *Al-Imamah wa al-Siyasah* (Cairo: Maktabah Mustafa al-Babi, 1328/1963), 36-37.

41   Abu Hamid al-Ghazzali, *Tahafut al-Falasifah* (Cairo: Dar al-Ma`arif, n.d.), 65-67.

42   Ibid., 229-31.

43   Ibn Rushd, *Tahafut al-Tahafut* (Cairo: Dar al-Ma`arif, n.d.), 2:782-83.

44   Abu Hamid al-Ghazzali, *Al-Mustasfa min Usul al-Fiqh* (Cairo: al-Matab`ah al-Amiriyyah, 1322 AH), 1:3.

45   Abu Ishaq al-Shatibi, *Al-Muwafaqat fi Usul al-Shari`ah* (Beirut: Dar al-Ma`rifah, n.d.), vol. 1, 46.

46   Ibid., 51.

47   Ibid., 51-52.

48   The arguments presented in this, and the next two sections, are discussed in greater length in Part II of my book, *The Challenge of Modernity: The Quest for Authenticity in the Arab World* (Lanham, Maryland: University Press of America, 1994).

49   Abdul Rahman al-Rafi`i, `Asr Muhammad `Ali, 4th ed. (Cairo: Dar al-Ma`arif, 1982), 326-42.

50   Ibid., 406-8; see also Muhammad Latif al-Bahrawi, *Harakat al-Islah al-`Uthmani `Asr al-Sultan Mahmoud al-Thani (1808-1839)* (Cairo: Dar al-Turath, 1978), 118.

51   Ibid., 321.

52   Jamal al-Din al-Afghani, "Lectures on Teaching and Learning," in *An Islamic Response to Imperialism*, Nikkie R. Keddie, ed. (Berkeley, CA: University of California Press, 1968), 17.

53   Ibid., 18.

54   See Muhammad `Abduh, *Al-Islam Din wa Hayah*, edited by Tahir al-Tinaji (Cairo: al-Hilal, n.d.), 148.

55   Al-Afghani, "Lectures on Teaching and Learning," 17.

56   Muhammad `Abduh, *Al-Islam wa al-Nasraniyyah ma`a al-`Ilm wa al-Madaniyyah*, 7th ed. (Cairo: Dar al-Manar, 1367 AH), 140-41.

57   Ibid., 177-78.

58   Ibid. 134-37, and 154.

59   Quoted in John Esposito, *Islam in Transition: Muslim Perspective* (NY: Oxford University Press, 1982), 19.

60   Taha Hussein, *Mustaqbal al-Thaqafah fi Misr* (1938) in *The Collected Work of Taha Hussein* (Beirut: Dar al-Kitab al-Lubnani, 1973), 9:17.

61   Ibid., 20.

62   Ibid., 29.

63   Ibid., 32.

64   Ibid., 24.

65   Ibid., 25.

66   Ibid., 41.

67   Ibid., 44-45.

68   Parliamentary rule was abolished by Jamal Abdul Nasser on 23 July, 1952. It only took an executive order signed by Abdul Nasser to dismantle the Egyptian "democratic" experiment.

69   Ibid., 49.

70   Taha Hussein, *Mustaqbal al-Thaqafah*, 54.

71   Sayyid Qutb, *Ma`alim fi al-Tariq* (Beirut: Dar al-Shuruq, 1982), 166.

72   Ibid., 8.

73   Ibid., 54.

74   Sati al-Husari, *Abhath Mukhtara fi al-Qawmiyyah al-Arabiyyah* (Beirut: Dar al-Quds, 1974), 1:39.

75   Ibid., 42.

76   Ibid.

77   Ibid., 134.

[78] Elie Kedourie, *Nationalism* (New York: Frederick A. Praeger, 1960), 58-59.

[79] Quoted in ibid., 68.

[80] Ibid., 69.

[81] Ibid., 63-68.

[82] Ibid., 58.

[83] Daniel S. Papp, *Contemporary International Relations* (New York: Macmillan, 1988), 17

[84] Ibid., 19.

[85] Ibid., 20.

[86] Ibid., 134.

[87] Michel Aflaq, *Fi Sabil al-Ba`th* (Damascus, Syria: Dar al-Tali'ah, 1959), 27.

[88] Ibid., 29.

[89] Ibid., 76.

[90] Ibid., 97-98, 109-10.

[91] Ibid., 43.

[92] Ibid., 88.

[93] Rodinson, as quoted in Birch, ibid., 6.

[94] M. E. Yapp, *The Making of the Modern Near East* (London: Longman, 1987), 93.

[95] Gerard Chaliand, ed., *Minority People in the Age of Nation-States* (London: Pluto Press, 1989), 57.

[96] Ibid., 58; Zeine N. Zeine, *The Emergence of Arab Nationalism* (Beirut: Khayyats, 1966), 22.

[97] Halil Inalcik, *The Ottoman Empire: The Classical Age 1300-1600* (New Rochelle, NY: Aristide D. Caratzas Pub., 1973), 13.

[98] Zeine, *Emergence,* 7-8.

[99] Ibid., 10.

[100] Ibid., 11.

[101] Quoted in ibid., 16-17.

[102] Ibid., 9.

[103] Yapp, *The Making,* 3.

[104] Ibid., 39.

[105] Kedourie, *Nationalism*, 134.

[106] Chaliand, *Minority People*, 60.

[107] Kedourie, *Nationalism*, 25.

[108] Jamaluddin Afghani, *Al-A'mal al-Kamilah*, ed. Muhammad `Imara (Beirut: al-Mu'asasah al-`Arabiyah li al-Dirasat wa al-Nashr, 1979), 20, 29. The birthplace and sectarian origin of al-Afghani have been the subject of fierce debate. While many Sunni writers insist that he was born at Asadabad near Kabul in Afghanistan, Shi`i sources have maintained that he was born at As'adabad in Iran. Nikki Keddie, in her biographical work on al-Afghani, has made a persuasive argument in support of the latter version. See her work, *Sayyid Jamaluddin "Afghani": A Political Biography* (Berkeley: University of California Press, 1972), and *An Islamic Response to Imperialism: Political and Religious Writings of Sayyid Jamaluddin*

"al-Afghani" (Berkeley: University of California Press, 1983); also the collection of al-Afghani's works, *al-A`mal al-Kamilah*, edited by Muhammad `Imara.

[109] Muhammad Abduh, *Al-Islam Din wa Hadarah*, 148.

[110] Jamaluddin al-Afghani, "Lectures on Teaching and Learning," 17.

[111] Afghani, *Al-A`mal al-Kamilah*, 334-39.

[112] Afghani, "The Benefit of Philosophy," in Keddie, *An Islamic Response to Imperialism*, 120-21.

[113] Afghani, "Islamic Solidarity," in *Islam in Transition: Muslim Perspectives*, eds. John J. Donohue and John L. Esposito (New York: Oxford University Press, 1982), 19.

[114] Ibid., 24; and Afghani, "Commentary on the Commentator," in Keddie, *An Islamic Response to Imperialism*, 123.

[115] Afghani, *Al-A`mal al-Kamilah*, 28-33.

[116] Afghani, "Islamic Solidarity," 23.

[117] Afghani, *Al-A`mal al-Kamilah*, 35.

[118] Charles C. Adams, *Islam and Modernism in Egypt* (New York: Russell & Russell, 1968), 7.

[119] Afghani, *Al-A`mal al-Kamilah*, 16.

[120] Ibid., 329.

[121] Afghani, "Islamic Solidarity," 21.

[122] Hasan al-Banna, *Mabadi' wa Usul fi Mu'tamarat Khassah* (Cairo: al-Mu'ssasah al-Islamiyah li al-Tiba`ah wa al-Nashr, 1979). 90; also Hasan al-Banna, *Majmu`at Rasa'il al-Imam al-Shahid Hasan al-Banna* (Cairo: Darul Hadarah al-Islamiyyah, n.d), 225.

[123] Asaf Hussain, *Islamic Movements in Egypt, Pakistan, and Iran: An Annotated Bibliography* (London: Mansell Publishing Limited, 1983), 6-7.

[124] Mahmoud `Abd al-Halim, *Al-Ikhwan al-Muslimun: Ahdath Sana`at al-Tarikh* (Alexandria, Egypt: Dar al-Da`wah, 1981), 2:221, 224.

[125] Al-Banna, *Mabadi' wa Usul*, 47-48, 57-58.

[126] Ibid., 49.

[127] Tariq Y. Ismael and Jacqualine S. Ismael, *Government and Politics in Islam* (London: Frances Pinter, 1985), 60-65.

[128] Quoted in ibid., 61.

[129] Ibid., 61-62; See also al-Banna, *Mabadi' wa Usul*, 50.

[130] `Abd al-Halim, *Al-Ikhwan al-Muslimun*, 2:258-59.

[131] Ibid., 2:71, 211, 213.

[132] Ibid., 2:493-94

[133] Ibid., 2:203.

[134] Ismael and Ismael, *Government and Politics*, 70-76.

[135] Ibid., 65; See also Abd al-Halim, *al-Ikhwan al-Muslimun*, vol. 2, 122.

[136] Quoted in Ismael and Ismael, *Government and Politics*, 65.

[137] Al-Banna, *Mabadi' wa Usul*, 91, 104.

[138] Al-Banna, *Majmu`at al-Rasa'il*, 374.

[139] Al-Banna, *Mabadi' wa Usul*. 69..

[140] Saleh al-`Ashmawi, *Al-Ikhwan wa al-Thawrah* (Cairo: al-Maktab al-Misri al-Hadith, 1977), 69.

[141] Jabir Rizq, *Madhabih al-Ikhwan fi Sujun Nasir* (Cairo: Dar al-Nasir li al-Tiba`ah al-Islamiyyah, 1987), 21.

[142] Al-`Ashmawi, *Al-Ikhwan wa al-Thawrah*, 74.

[143] Ibid., 69, 76.

[144] Rizq, *Madhabih al-Ikhwan*, 145.

[145] Alex Cudsi and Ali E. Hillal Dessouki, *Islam and Power* (Baltimore: The Johns Hopkins University Press, 1981), 8; also Hussain, *Islamic Movements*, 95-96.

[146] Unlike Marxists, Islamists define imperialism in light of the concept of *jahiliyah*, rather than in connection to capitalism.

[147] John L. Esposito, *Islam and Politics* (NewYork: Syracuse University Press, 1984) 137.

[148] Ibid., 13; Rudi Matthee, "The Egyptian Opposition on the Iranian Revolt." in *Shi`ism and Social Protest*, ed. Juan R. Cole and Nikki R. Keddie (New Haven: Yale University Press, 1986) 225.

[149] Qutb, *Hadha al-din*, 13.

[150] Ibid., 7.

[151] Hussain, *Islamic Movements, 95.*

[152] Rizq, *Madhabih al-Ikhwan*, 146.

[153] Qutb, *Hadha al-din*, 35.

[154] Qutb, *Milestones*, 47.

[155] Ibid., 140.

[156] Ibid., 125.

[157] Ibid.

[158] Matthee, "The Egyptian Opposition," 249; Saad Eddin Ibrahim, "Islamic Militancy as a Social Movement: The Case of Two Groups in Egypt," in *Islamic Resurgence in the Arab World*, ed. Ali E. Hillal Dessouki (New York: Praeger Publisher, 1982) 18; and Ismael and Ismael, *Government and Politics*, 109.

[159] Ismael and Ismael, *Government and Politics*, 109-10.

[160] Ibid., 117.

[161] Hussain, *Islamic Movements*, 14.

[162] Ibid.; Ismael and Ismael, *Government and Politics*, 119.

[163] "How oft, by God's will, has a small force vanquished a big one" (2:249).

[164] Johnnes J. G. Jansen, *The Neglected Duly: The Creed of Sadat's Assassins and Islamic Resurgence in the Middle East* (New York: Macmillan, 1986), 186.

[165] Quoted in ibid., 184.

[166] Ibid., 185.

[167] Cudsi and Dessouki, *Islam and Power*, 19.

[168] Abd al-Wahab Khalaf, *`Ilm Usul al-Fiqh*, 8th ed. (Kuwait: Dar al-Kuwaytiyyah, 1388/1978); Fazlur Rahman, *Islam,* 2nd ed. (Chicago: University of Chicago Press, 1979), 84.

[169] Iredell Jenkins, *Social Order and Limits of Law: A Theoretical Essay* (Princeton, N.J.: Princeton University Press, 1980), 35.

[170] Majid Khadduri, *The Islamic Concept of Justice* (Baltimore: The Johns Hopkins University Press, 1984), 135.

[171] Rabman, *Islam,* 37-38.

[172] Muhammad bin Ahmad al-Sarakhsi, *Usul al-Sarkhasi,* Vol. 1 (Beirut: Dar al-Ma'rifah, 1393/1973), 114-15; 'Abd al-Karim Zaydan, *Madkhal li-Dirasat al-Shari'ah al-Islamiyah,* 5th ed. (Beirut: Mu'assasat al-Risalah, 1397/1976), 108-18; and 'Abd al-Majid *Mahmiid, Al-Madrasah al-Fiqhiyyah li al-Muhadithin* (Cairo: Dar al-Shabab, 1972), 4-5. See also Rahman, *Islam,* 56-61.

[173] There are four major schools of law in the Sunni branch of Islam: Hanafi, Maliki, Shafi'i, and Hanbali.

[174] See Ibrahim bin Musa al-Shatibi, *Al-Muwafaqat fi Usul al-Shari'ah* (Cairo: Al-Maktabah al-Tijariyah, n.d.), 4:6-7; Taqi al-Din bin Taymiy-yah, Raf' al-Mallam 'an al-A'immah al-A'lam (Damascus: Al-Maktab al-Islami, 1382 AH), 49-52; and Al-Sarakhsi, *Al-Muwafaqat,* 340-42.

[175] Muhammad bin Idris al-Shafi'i, *Al-Risalah,* 2nd ed. (Cairo: Dar al-Turath, 1399/1979), 88-92.

[176] See al-Shatibi, *Al-Muwafaqat,* 4:8-9. Al-Shafi'i does not permit the abro-gation of the Qur'an by the Hadith, nor the Hadith by the Qur'an; see his *Al-Risalah,* 110-13. And for a discussion of the rules of *naskh* (abrogation) see Salih bin 'Abd al-'Aziz al-Mansur, *Usul al-Fiqh wa Ibn Taymiyyah* (n.p.: 1400/1980).

[177] See al-Shafi'i, *Al-Risalah,* 401-3, 471-72, 531-35; N. J. Coulson, *A History of Islamic Law* (Edinburgh: Edinburgh University Press, 1964), 59; and Joseph Schacht, *The Origins of Muhammadan Jurisprudence* (Oxford: Clarendon Press, 1950), 64.

[178] Quoted in Rahman, *Islam,* 14; Al-Shatibi, *Al-Muwafaqat,* 3:19-21; and 'Abd al-Malik bin 'Abdullah al-Juayni, *Al-Burhan fi Usul al-Fiqh* (Cairo: Dar al-Ansar, 1400 AH), 624-25, 599-611.

[179] Al-Shafi'i, *Al-Risalah,* 505.

[180] Ibid., 507; see also Malcolm Kerr, *Islamic Reform: The Political and Legal Theories of Muhammad Abduh and Rashid Rida* (Berkeley, CA: University of California Press, 1966), 90; Coulson, *History of Islamic Law,* 40.

[181] Al-Shatibi, *Al-Muwafaqat,* 2:8-22.

[182] Rahman, *Islam,* 78.

[183] Schacht, *Muhammadan Jurisprudence,* 73.

[184] Rahman, *Islam,* 78-79.

[185] Schacht, *Muhammadan Jurisprudence,* 73.

[186] For further discussion on this point see Jenkins, *Social Order,* 333-35.

[187] Haroon Khan Sherwani, *Studies in Muslim Political Thought and Administration* (Philadelphia: Porcupine Press, 1977), 102-3.

[188] Ibid.

[189] Kerr, *Islamic Reform,* 10

[190] Khadduri, *Islamic Concept of Justice,* 151; see also Coulson, *History of Islamic Law,* 140.

[191] Jamal al-Din al-Afghani, "The Benefit of Philosophy," in Keddie, ed. *An Islamic Response to Imperialism,* 120-21.

[192] Quoted in Kerr, *Islamic Reform,* 114.

193   The world "Shari`ah" in this work refers to the various rules and doctrines derived from Islamic sources by jurists, and not the sources themselves. The historical shari`a thus signifies rules derived by classical Muslim jurists.

194   Ann Elizabeth Mayer, *Islam and Human Right: Tradition and Practice*, 2d ed. (Boulder, CO: Westview Press, 1995), 64-5.

195   Ibid., 89.

196   Heiner Biefeldt, "Muslim Voices in the Human Rights Debate," *Human Rights Quarterly* 17, no. 4 (1995): 596.

197   Rhoda Howard, *Human Rights and the Search for Community* (Boulder, Co: Westview Press, 1995), 93.

198   Ibid., 94.

199   Ibid.

200   Abdullahi Ahmad An-Na`im, *Toward an Islamic Reformation* (Syracuse: NY: Syracuse University Press, 1990), 52-56.

201   The "Makkan Qur'an" refers to the Qur'an which was revealed in the city of Makkah (or Mecca), prior to the Prophet's migration to the city of Madinah, where the "Madinan Qur'an" was revealed.

202   Ibid., 176.

203   Ibid., 49.

204   Ibid., 180.

205   Mayer, *Islam and Human Rights*, 7.

206   See for example Reza Afshari, "An essay on Islamic Cultural Relativism in the Discourse of Human Rights," *Human Rights Quarterly* 16 (1994): 235-76.

207   Natural rights thinkers, such as Hobbes, Locke, or Rousseau, perceived society to be composed of free and equal individuals. The cultural homogeneity of members of society is taken for granted, and assumed in the notion of the state of nature.

208   The attitude of early Muslim jurists toward the moral autonomy of non-Muslims is illustrated in the next section.

209   Immanuel Kant, *Groundwork of the Metaphysics of Morals* (London: Routledge, 1993), 84.

210   See for, example, 2:194 and 55:60.

211   Muhammad bin Ahmad al-Sarakhsi, *Sharh Kitab al-Siyar al-Kabir* (Pakistan: Nasrullah Mansur, 1405 AH), 4:1530.

212   Ibid.

213   Al-Mawardi, *Al-Ahkam al-Sultaniyyah,* 59.

214   Ibid., 20-23.

215   Ibid., 24.

216   See Ibn al-Qayim, *Sharh al-Shurut al-`Umariyyah* (Beirut: Dar al-`Ilm li al-Malayin, 1381/1961).

217   Muhammad bin Ahmad bin Rushd (d. 595), *Bidayat al-Mujtahid wa Nihayat al-Muqtasid* (Beirut: Dar al-Ma`rifah, 1406/1986), 2:5.

218   Ibid., 8.

219   Ibid., 66-68.

220   Ibid., 40; see also al-Mawardi, *Al-ahkam al-Sultaniyyah,* 59.

221   For further elaboration on this point, see Louay M. Safi, "Islamic Law and Society," *The American Journal of Islamic Social Sciences* 7, no. 2 (September 1992): 177-92

222   Muhammad bin Idris al-Shafi`i, *Al-Risalah* (Beirut: Dar al-Kutub al-`Ilmiyyah, n.d), 401-76.

223   Ibid.

224   For elaboration of Hanbali principles of jurisprudence, see Ibn al-Qayim, *A`lam al-Muwaqi`in* (Beirut: Dar al-Kutub al-`Ilmiyyah, 1411/1991), 1:24-26.

225   Shi`a jurists imposed, by far, fewer restrictions on *ijtihad*.

226   I have elsewhere expounded this approach under the title "The Methodology of Comparative Rules," See also Louay M. Safi, *I`mal al-`Aql* (Damascus, Dar al-Fikr, 1998), chapter 4.

227   "He [Noah] said: 'O my people! See if I have a clear sign from my Lord, and that he has sent mercy unto me, but that the mercy has been obscured from your sight? Shall we compel you to accept it when you are averse to it!'" (11:28); and "The message of freedom of belief and conviction, and the call to religious tolerance is reiterated time and again through various Prophets: And if there is a party among you that believes in the message with which I have been sent, and a party which does not believe, hold yourselves in patience until Allah does decide between us: for He is the best to decide. The leaders, the arrogant party among his people, said: 'O Shu'ayb! We shall certainly drive you out of our city, and those who believe with you, or else you shall have to return to our ways and religion.' He said: 'What! Even though we do not wish to do so'" (7:86-87).

228   "Say: 'O my people! Do whatever you may: I will do (my part). But soon will you know on whom an anguish of ignoring shall be visited, and on whom decends an anguish that abide.'" (39:39-40); and "Say: 'Everyone acts according to his own disposition: But your Lord knows best who it is that is best guided on the way'" (17:84).

229   "O you who believe! Guard your own souls: If you follow (right) guidance, no hurt can come to you from those who stray. The goal of you all is God: It is He that will show you the truth of all that you do." (5:105); and "So if they dispute with you, say: 'I have submitted my whole self to God and so have those who follow me.' And say to the People of the Book and to those who are unlearned: 'Do you (also) submit yourselves? If they do, they are in right guidance. But if they turn back, your duty is to convey the Message.' And in God's sight are (all) His servants" (3:20).

230   In fact, one cannot find in the Qur'an any support for the *ridda* penalty. The Qur'an makes two references to *ridda*: "Nor will they cease fighting you until they turn you back from you faith if they can. And if any of you turn back (commit *ridda*) from their faith and die in unbelief, their works will bear no fruit in this life; and in the Hereafter they will be Companions of the fire and will abide therein" (2:217); and, "O you who believe! If any from among you turn back (commits *ridda*) from his faith, soon will God produce a people whom He will love as they will love Him – humble with the believers mighty against the disbelievers, thriving in the way of God,

and never afraid of the reproaches of detractors. That is the grace of God. He bestows it on whom He pleases; and God encompasses all and knows all things" (5:54). In both cases, the Qur'an does not specify any physical punishment here and now, let alone a death penalty. It rather warns those who renounce their faith of disgrace and ill-fate. To the countrary, the Qur'an provides a direct evidence, albeit open to interpretation, that *ridda* is not punishable by death: "Those who believe then disbelieve, then believe again, then disbelieve and then increase in their disbelief – God will never forgive them nor guide them to the path" (4:137).

231 See al-Shatibi, *Al-Muwafaqat*, 3:15-26.

232 Ibn Hisham, *Al-Sirah al-Nabawiah* (Cairo: Mustafa Halabi Press, 1375/1955), 2:409.

233 For an elaborate discussion of this point, see Mohamad Hashim Kamali, *Freedom of Expression In Islam* (Kuala Lumpur: Ilmiah Publishers, 1998), 87-106.

234 See, for example, Abu Hamid al-Ghazzali, *Fada'ih al-Batiniyyah* (Amman, Jordan: Dar al-Bashir, 1413/1993), 95-97.

235 See, for instance, Al-`Iz bin `Abd al-Salam (d. 660 AH), *Qawa'id al-Ahkam* [The Basis of Rules] (n.p.: n.d.): 1:113-21; Al-Shatibi, *Al-Muwafaqat*, 2:318-20.

236 The Qur'an repeatedly points out that people's neglect of its commandments has no consequences on the divine whatsoever – be it good on evil – but only on themselves: See, for example, 2:57, 7:160, 3:176-77, and 47:32.

237 The execution of Ghaylan al-Dimanshqi by the order of Caliph `Abd al-Malik bin Marwan, and Ahmad bin Nasir by the order of Caliph al-Wathiq, after being accused of heresy are cases in point.

238 See Ibn al-Qayim, *Al-Shurut al-`Umariyyah*; also Ibrahim bin Nujaym (d. 970 AH), *Al-Ashbah was al-Naza'ir* (Damascus; Dar al-Fikr, 1403/1988), 386-88. Ibn Nujaym belongs to the more tolerant school of the Hanafi.

239 "Not all of them are alike! Of the People of the Book are a portion that stand (for the right); they rehearse the signs of God around the night, and they postrate themselves in adoration. They believe in God and the last day; they enjoin the right and forbid the intolerable (*munkar*); and they hasten in (all) good works: they are in the rank of the righteous. Of the good that they do, nothing will be rejected of them; for God knows well those that do right" (3:113-5); and "And there are certainly among the People of the Book those who believe in God, in the revelation to you, and in the revelation to them, bowing in humility to God. They will not sell the signs of God for a miserable gain! For them is a reward with their Lord, and God is swift in account" (3:199).

240 "Those who believe (in the Qur'an), those who follow the Jewish (scriptures), and the Sabians and the Christians – any who believe in God and the Last Day, and work righteousness – on them shall be no fear, nor shall they grieve" (5:69); "The Qur'an goes even further to make it abundantly clear that no religious community has the right to claim monopoly on righteousness or salvation: The Jews say: The Christians have naught (to

stand) upon; and the Christians say: The Jews have naught (to stand) upon. Yet they (Profess to) study the (same) book. Like unto their work is what those say who know not; but Allah will judge between them in their quarrel on the Day of Judgement" (2:113); and "Indeed the Qur'an rebuke those of the People of the Book who justify the violation of their moral code when dealing with people who belong to another faith: Among the people of the book are some who, if entrusted with a hoard of gold, will (readily) pay it back; others, who, if entrusted with a single silver coin, will not repay it unless you constantly stood demanding, because they say: there is no call on us (to keep faith) with these ignorant (pagans). But they tell a lie against god, and (well) they know it" (3:75).

[241]   See, for example, 2:8-20 and 4:142-43.

[242]   "Those who believed, and migrated, and fought for the faith, with their property and their persons, in the cause of God, as well as those who gave (them) asylum and aid – these are (all) friends and protectors, one of another. As to those who believed but chose not to migrate, you owe no duty of protection to them until they migrate; but if they seek your aid in religion, it is your duty to help them, except against a people with whom you have a treaty of mutual alliance. And (remember) God sees all that you do. The unbelievers are protectors, one of another: unless you do this (protect each other), there would be oppression and commotion on earth, and great mischief" (8:72).

[243]   See Ibn Hisham, *Al-Sirah al-Nabawiyah*, 1:501.

[244]   Reported by Bukhari, al-Tirmidhi, and al-Tabarani.

[245]   Empowering women through public work, education, and legal reform addresses cases of injustice steaming from polygamy, while separating moral from legal obligations addresses interrelagious marriage. Unequal inheritance, on the other hand, is connected with exempting women from any obligation to spend on the household, even when they enjoy high income, and hence must be dealt with in any legal reform by considering both rights and obligations within the family.

[246]   The works of Abdullahi A. An-Na'im represent the views of the proponents of cross-cultural dialogue, while the writings of Rhoda Howard represent those of its opponents.

[247]   For an excellent discussion on strategic formation, see Edward Said, *Orientalism*, (New York: Vintage Books, 1979).

[248]   One such example of an openly prejudicial argument against Islam's capacity to recognize human rights can be found in the following argument by the eminent Italian scholar Lurgi Bonanate, who suggests that a non-Muslim is automatically considered an enemy in an Islamic state: "That the state may recognize other states as different from itself is one thing: the protection of the wellbeing of a human being who, regardless of his flag, is entitled to the same guarantees that the state offers its nationals is another. *(The only exception to this idea of the state in the contemporary world is the Islamic one*, in which the *foreigner is an enemy in so far as he is an infidel*, not because he was born under a different sky!)" See Lurgi

Bonanate, *Ethics and International Politics*, trans. John Irving (Cambridge, UK: Polity Press, 1995), 108. (Emphasis added.)

[249] Ann Elizabeth Mayer, *Islam and Human Rights*.

[250] Ibid., 70.

[251] Ibid.

[252] Ibid.

[253] Ibid., 11.

[254] Al-Sarakhsi, *Sharh Kitab al-Siyar al-Kabir*, 4:1530.

[255] Ibid., 4:1531.

[256] Bassam Tibi, "Islamic Law/Shari`ah, Human Rights, Universal Morality and International Relations," *Human Right Quarterly* 16 (1994): 284.

[257] Ibid., 286.

[258] I return to examine Tibi's arguments more closely in subsequent section.

[259] Reza Afshari "An Essay on Islamic Cultural Relativism, 235-76.

[260] Ibid., 254.

[261] Ibid., 253.

[262] See John O. Voll, *Islam: Continuity and Change in the Modern World*, 2d ed. (Syracuse, NY: Syracuse University Press, 1994), 339.

[263] Ibid., 256.

[264] Rhoda Howard "Dignity, Community, and Human Rights," in Abdullah An-Na'im, ed., *Human Rights in Cross-Cultural Perspectives* (Philadelphia: University of Pennsylvania Press, 1992), 83.

[265] Ibid., 94.

[266] Immanuel Kant, *Groundwork*, 96.

[267] Ibid.

[268] Howard, "Dignity, Community, and Human Rights," 94.

[269] Afshari, "An Essay on Islamic Cultural Relativism," 256.

[270] Daniel Pipes, Oliver Roy, and Fuad Ajami are well-known representatives of this approach.

[271] See Fuzlur Rahman, *Roots of Islamic neo-Fundamentalism*; Fred Halliday, *The Politics of Islamic Fundamentalism*; John Epositio, *Islam and Politics;* and Leonard Binder, *Islamic Liberalism* (Chicago: The University of Chicago Press, 1988).

[272] Mayer, *Islam and Human Rights*, 177.

[273] See, for instance, Muhammad Abduh, "Islam, Reason, and Civilization," in John J. Donohue and John L. Esposito, *Islam in Transition* (New York: Oxford University Press, 1982), 24-8.

[274] Muhammad Rashid Rida, *Huquq al-Nisa' fi al-Islam* [Women's Rights in Islam] (Beirut: Dar al-Hijra, 1987), 12-14.

[275] `Abd al-Rahman al-Kawakibi, "Umm al-Qura," in *Al-A`mal al-Kamilah*, ed. Muhammad `Imarah (Cairo: al-Hay'ah al-Misriyyah al-`Ammah, 1970), 261-64. For discussion of the views of early contemporary Muslim reformists, see Louay M. Safi, *The Challenge of Modernity* (Lanam, MD: University Press of America, 1994), 111-32.

[276] See for example, Muhammad Al-Ghazali, *Huquq al-Insan fi al-Islam* (n.p.: n.d.).

[277] Fahmi Huwaydi, *Muwatinun la Dhimmiyun* (Cairo: Dar al-Shuruq, 1985).

278   Rashid al-Ghanoushi, *Al-Huriyyat al-`Ammah fi al-Dawlah al-Islamiyyah* [Public Rights in the Islamic State] (Beirut: Markaz Dirasat al-Wihdah al-Arabiyyah, 1993), 135.

279   Ibid., 132. The list of eminent Muslim scholars and leaders who have adopted reformist views includes, just to cite few highly influencial people, Fahti Osman, Muhammad Salim al-Awwa, Tariq al-Bishri, Ridwan al-Sayyed, Ishaq Farhan, Anwar Ibrahim, Khalisnur Majid, and Chandra Muzaffar.

280   See Zaki Milad, "Al-Fikr al-Islami wa Qadayyah al-Mar'ah" *Al-Kalimah* 21 (1998): 9-24.

281   Bassam Tibe, "Islalmic law/Shari`a, Human Rights, Universal Morality and International Relations," Human /rights Quarterly 16 (1994): 280.

282   Jack Donnelly, *Universal Human Rights in Theory and Practice* (Ithaca, NY: Cornell University Press, 1989), 51.

283   Al-Mawardi, *Al-Ahkam al-Sultaniyyah*, 53.

284   Ibid., 71-72.

285   See Ann Belinda Prais, "Human Rights as Cultural Practice," *Human Rights Quarterly 18* (1996) 288; also Donnelly, *Universal Human Rights*, 109-12.

286   See Max Weber, *Economy and Society* (Berkeley: University of California Press, 1978), 1:1121-56; also Alasdair MacIntyre, *Whose Justice? Which Rationality?* (London: Duckworth,1990).

287   Donnelly, *Universal Human Rights*, 110.

288   See Ibid., 117-8; also Abdullah An-Na'im, "Toward a Cultural Approach to Defining International Standards of Human Rights," in A. An-Na'im (ed.), *Human Rights in Cross Cultural Perspective* (Philadelphia: University of Pennsylvania Press, 1992), 25.

289   Richard Falk, "Cultural Foundation for the International Protection of Human Rights," in ibid., 44.

290   Leonard Binder, *Islamic Liberalism* (The University of Chicago Press, 1988), 9.

291   The unilinear conception of history derives its intellectual force from Hegel's *Philosophy of History.*

292   Howard, "Dignity, Community, and Human Rights," in Abdullahi An-Na'im (ed.), *Human Rights in Cross-Cultural Perspective*, 99.

293   For an excellent discussion on the impact of social context on the implementation of human rights, see Daniel A. Bell, "The East Asian Challenge to Human Rights: Reflection on an East West Dialogue," *Human Rights Quarterly* 18 (1996): 641-67.

294   Bassam Tibi, "Islamic Law/Shari`ah," 280.

295   Ibid., 280.

296   Ibid.

297   Ibid., 293.

298   Binder, *Islamic Liberalism*, 9.

299   See Jurgen Habermas, *Moral Consciousnes and Communicative Action*, trans. Chistian Lannardt and Shierry Weber Nicholsen (Cambridge, UK: Polity Press, 1990), 58.

[300]   In stipulating objective universalism as a preconditon of a true dialogue, I am drawing on Habermas's argument for Discourse Ethics. See Habermas, *Moral Consciousness*, 68.

[301]   Kant, *Groundwork*, 84.

[302]   Thomas McCarthy, *The Critical Theory of Jurgen Habermas* (Cambridge, MA: Cambridge University Press, 1978), 326.

[303]   Richard Falk, "Cultural Foundations," 57-59.

[304]   See J. M. Roberts, *Europe 1880-1945* (London: Longman, 1989), 321-49. Out of the 32 nations that constituted the League, 22 were non-European.

[305]   See for example, John L. Esposito, *The Islamic Threat: Myth or Reality* (New York: Oxford University Press, 1999), and Bruce B. Lawrence, *Shattering the Myth* (Princeton, NJ: Princeton University Press, 2000)

[306]   Daniel Lemer, *The Passing of Traditional Society* (Glencoe, ILL, The Free Press, 1958), 45.

[307]   Francis Fukuyama, *The End of History and the Last Man* (New York: Avon Books, 1992), 45-46.

[308]   Zbigniew Brzezinski, *Out of Control: Global Turmoil on the Eve of Twenty-first Century* (New York: Maxwell Macmillan, 1993), 159.

[309]   Samuel Huntington, "The Clash of Civilizations," *Foreign Affairs* 72 (summer 1993): 22-49.

[310]   Ibid., 49.

[311]   Quoted in Samuel Huntington, "The Lone Superpower," *Foreign Affairs* 78:2 (March/April 1999): 38.

[312]   John Dewey, "Imperialism Is Easy," *The New Republic* 50 (23 March 23, 1927).

[313]   Ibid.

[314]   Kim Holmes and Thomas Moore (eds.), *Restoring American Leadership: US Foreign Policy and Defense Blueprint* (Washington, DC: The Heritage Foundation, 1996), vii.

[315]   Woodrow Wilson, *President Wilson's Great Speeches* (Chicago: Stanton and Von Vliet, 1917).

[316]   Henry Steele Commager, *Documents of American History* (New York: Appleton-Century-Crofts, 1963).

[317]   Ibid.

[318]   Ibid.

[319]   Harry Truman, "Fundamentals of American Foreign Policy (1945)," in Michael B. Levy, *Political Thought in America* (Homewood, IL: The Dorsey Press, 1982), 428-9.

[320]   Ibid.

[321]   Holmes and Moore (eds.), *Restoring American Leadership*, 2

[322]   Ibid.

[323]   Ibid.

[324]   Ibid.

[325]   Ten years of economic sanctions have devastated the Iraqi population, and brought untold sorrow and misery to ordinary Iraqis, particularly the most vulnerable. UNICEF reported that 18% in 1991 to 31% in 1996 of all children under five suffer from "chronic malnutrition (stunting); 9% to 26%

with underweight malnutrition; 3% to 11% with wasting (acute malnutrition), an increase in over 200%. By 1997, it was estimated about one million children under five were [chronically] malnourished." See UNICEF 1998 Report.

[326] UN Resolutions 242 and 338 require that Israel withdraw from territories it occupied during 1967 War with Egypt, Jordan, and Syria, including the West Bank, Gaza, and the Golan Heights of Syria.

[327] For a complete list of the 34 resolutions, see the Jewish Virtual Library, url: http://www.us-israel.org/jsource/UN/usvetoes.html.

[328] Ibid.

[329] Robert H. Pelletreau, Jr., US Assistant Secretary of State for Near Eastern Affairs, stated, at a symposium entitled "Resurgent Islam in the Middle East," sponsored by the Middle East Policy Council and held in Washington D.C. in May 1994, that "we, as a government, have no quarrel with Islam." He goes on to argue that "certain manifestations of the Islamic revival are intensely anti-Western. They aim not only at elimination of Western influences, but at resisting any form of cooperation with the West." He concludes that "such tendencies are clearly hostile to US interests." See "Symposium: Resurgent Islam in the Middle East," *Middle East Policy* 3, no. 2.

[330] See "Turkey's Pro-Islamic Party Banned," *Middle East Times*, 22 June 2001.

[331] "Jolyan Naegele, Turkey: Military Upholds Secularist Trandition." Online at: www.rferl.org/nca/features/1998/08/F.RU.980804131658.html.

[332] While Christian Right and pro-Israeli writers such as Pall R. Pillar, Judith Miller and Daniel Pipes continue to treat Islamically-inspired political groups as monolithic groups, other Middle East experts reject such simplistic views. In a commentary that appeared in the CATO Institute's daily dispatches, Peter Orvetti argued that "neither Islam nor Islamic fundamentalism is by definition 'anti-Western.' As noted, the anti-American attitudes of Islamic groups and movements in the Middle East are not directed against Christianity or Western civilization *per se*. They are instead a reaction to US policies, especially Washington's support for authoritarian regimes and the long history of US military intervention." See for instance, Peter J. M. Orvetti, *CATO Daily Dispatch* (Washington, DC: The CATO Institute, 17 November 1999). Online at: www.cato.org/dispatch/11-17-99d.html. See also Leon H. Hadar, "The Green Peril: Creating the Islamic Fundamentalist Threat," *Policy Analysis No. 177* (27 August 1992); Esposito, *The Islamic Threat: Myth or Reality?*, and Ryoji Tateyama, "Political Islam: Pluralism Denied," *NIRA Review* (winter 1995), published by the National Institute for Research Advancement (NIRA), Tokyo, Japan.

Glossary

`Ahd` (covenant): an oath taken by individuals or group representatives to abide by a written or verbal agreement.

`Amm` (general): a statement or rule that is true or applicable for the total population.

`Aql` (reason): the rational capacity of humans.

Ahl al-Hall wa al-`Aqd (people who loosen and bind): individuals with political clout; political leaders and leaders of public opinion.

Akhlaq: moral values. The term very often used in reference to individual moral traits.

Ansar (supporters): the Muslims of Madinah who supported the Prophet and gave shelter to Muslim immigrants of Makkah.

`Asabiyyah` (group solidarity): solidarity among natural groups, such as families, tribes, or ethnic groups.

Batil: a Qur'anic term refers to a state of corruption and deviance.

**Bay`ah**: a declaration of allegiance to political leadership. In classical Muslim political theory, bay`ah is the consent of the ruled given to political authority.

Companions: the close associates of the Prophet.

Dalil: Evidence that support a claim. In Islamic jurisprudence, it references an authentic Islamic text supporting a jurist rule or proposition.

Dalil qat`i: a firm jurist ruling based on incontrovertible evidence.

Dalil zanni: a juristic ruling that lacks conclusive evidence, and is, hence, open to disagreement among jurists.

Dawlah: a political state; polity.

Dhimmi: a covenanter. In classical Islamic jurisprudence, a non-Muslim who entered into a peace covenant with the Muslim community.

Dulah: circulation of wealth among a social group or class.

Falasifah: philosophers.

Fiqh: the body of legal and ethical principles and rules in Islamic law.

Fuqaha': Muslim jurists.

Ghazi: a Muslim warrior who, historically, participated expeditions against the enemies of the Muslim community.

Hadith: a narration by a Companion of the Prophet concerning the Prophets' statements and action. Hadith is a major source of Islamic law.

Hajj (pilgrimage): an annual visit to Makkah, and one of the pillars of Islam. Muslims who have the financial means are required to visit Makkah once in a lifetime during the twelfth month of the Muslim calendar to perform the rituals of hajj.

Haqq: what is true and right; the principle upon which the natural and human orders rest.

Haram: attitudes and actions prohibited by divine revelation.

Hiyal shar`iyyah: legal devices or tricks introduced by late Muslim jurists to sidestep the rulings of Islamic law.

Hudud (limits): the upper limits of punishments in Islamic penal code.

Huquq: plural of Haqq (see above).

Huquq al-`Ibad: legal protections of individual rights in Islamic law.

Huquq Allah: individual obligations towards Allah.

`Ibadat (rituals): acts of worship, such as prayer, fasting, etc.

**Ijma`** (consensus): a Shari`ah ruling that receives wide support by different Muslim jurists.

Ijtihad: the intellectual efforts exerted by a scholar to arrive at Shari`ah ruling, as well as the outcome of those efforts.

Ikhtiyar: the process by which the ruler is selected, the concept was developed by Sunni scholars to counter the Shi`ah claims that the Prophet designated his cousin `Ali bin Abu Talib as his successor.

Iman: the state of being faithful.

Jihad: exertion of one effort to adhere to and promote divine principles. Jihad spans a variety of activities, including self-control, seeking knowledge, community service, and fighting to repel aggression and defend the oppressed.

Juz'i (particular): a juristic rule that affect a particular category of people of actions. Opposite of kulli.

Kafir (infidel): a person who rejects divine revelation, and oppose its followers.

Khass (specific): a juristic rule that affect a specified category of people of actions. Opposite of `amm.

Khalifah (caliph): the title that was historically given to the highest political office in the territories ruled by Muslims.

Khulafa': plural of khalifah.

Kufr (infidelity): the mental and practical state of rejecting divine revelation.

Kulli (universal): a juristic rule that affect all peoples of categories of action. Opposite of juz'i.

Ma`ruf: actions that are commonly acceptable and agreeable in society. Opposite of munkar.
Makkan: the adjective form of Makkah. The birthplace of the Prophet, and the holiest site in the world of Islam. Also Mecca.

Makruh: reprehensible actions. A category of Islamic law.

Mandub: recommended actions. A category of Islamic law.

Maqasid (purposes): The purpose for which a divine directive was revealed, and the purpose of actions. A category of Islamic law.

Masalih: public interests and common good. A category of Islamic law.

Millah or Millet: a religious community, and the political system implemented historically by Muslim states that recognizes the moral autonomy of religious communities.

Milli: an adjective form of millah (see above).

Mu`amalat (transactions): the branch of fiqh that regulates trade and commercial transactions.

Mubah (permissible): actions that are neither recommended or commanded. A category of Islamic law.

Muhajirun: the early Muslim who immigrated from Makkah to Medina to join the Ansar and form the first Muslim community.

Munkar: the subversive and anti-social behavior that the overwhelming majority find reprehensive.

Mutakallimun: Muslim theologians. The singular form is mutakallim.

Naskh (abrogation): a procedure in Islamic jurisprudence by which a latter pronouncement is used to abrogate an earlier rule or principle. The procedure is controversial and far from being accepted by Muslim jurists.

Nass (text): a written statement that belongs to Islamic authoritative text, more often a Qur'anic text or a Prophetic statement of hadith.

Nass qat`i: an authoritative Islamic text whose authenticity is not in dispute.
Nass zanni: an authoritative Islamic text whose authenticity is disputed by Muslim scholars.

Qahr (domination): a state in which the ruling elites have overwhelming coercive power to render any opposition to their rule ineffective.

Qawamah: a Qur'anic concept that connotes authority, responsibility, and protection.

Qawwamun: individual who possess authority and are responsible of the well-being of others.

Qiyas (analogy): a procedure in Islamic jurisprudence that allows the jurist to extent the application of a rule to similar cases. Unlike the deductive procedure used in formal logic, the expansion of the rule does not require a general premise, but is done by employing particular premises.

Ra'i (opinion): a conclusion reached by an individual jurist or scholar. Unless it is baked by other jurist, the conclusion reflects the personal understanding of the jurist, and has less weight than a conclusion that received wider support or the consensus of the scholarly community.

Ra'iyyah: the individuals under the authority of a governor or a ruler.

Ridda (apostasy): the act of renouncing one's faith.

Shari`ah (Islamic law): the word refers to the different pronouncements and directives in Islamic revelation. It is often used in reference to the fiqh rulings.

**Shi`a**: the term was originally used to refer to the followers of Ali bin Abi Talib, the cousin of the Prophet, and the forth Khalifah. By the fifth Islamic century, Shi`a took the form of an Islamic sect with distinct doctrines and rituals that set them apart from the Muslim majority, the Sunni.

**Shi`i**: The adjective form of Shi`a. Also used as noun to denote the follower of Shi`a.

Siyasah: politics or the science of politics.

Sunnah: the term used to denote both the main branch of Islam and the practice the Prophet.

Tafsir: the scholarly interpretation of the Qur'an. It is also used to denote the act of interpretation in general.

Takfir: excommunicating a Muslim or a group of Muslims by other fellow Muslims. Rejected by many Muslim scholars and jurists, because it is considered to be a divine prerogative, and since none within the Muslim community can claim to speak on behalf of the divine.

Ulama: Muslim scholars, particularly those trained in Shari`ah sciences.

Ummah: the Muslim community.

Usul: roots of basic principles.

Usul al-fiqh: the principles of Islamic jurisprudence, consisting of methodological questions and procedures.

Wajib (duty): actions obligatory to Muslims. A category of Islamic jurisprudence.

Wazir (minister or secretary): a public official empowered by the ruler or sultan to oversee a particular area of public policy, or act on behalf of the ruler.

Zandaqah: heresy.

Zann (conjecture): a statement whose reality cannot be ascertained. Knowledge that is less than certain, and whose truth range between the possible and the probable.

Bibliography

Abduh, Muhammad. *Al-Islam Din wa Hayah*, ed. by Tahir al-Tinaji. Cairo: al-Hilal, n.d.

Abduh, Muhammad. *Al-Islam wa al-Nasraniyyah ma`a al-`Ilm wa al-Madaniyyah*, 7th ed. Cairo: Dar al-Manar, 1367 AH.

Abduh, Muhammad. *Al-Islam Din wa Hadarah*, ed. Tahir al-Tinaji. Cairo: al- Hilal, n.d.

Abu Hamid al-Ghazzali, *Al-Mustasfa min Usul al-Fiqh*. Cairo: al-Matab`ah al-Amiriyyah, 1322 AH.

Abu Hamid al-Ghazzali, *Fada'ih al-Batiniyyah*. Amman, Jordan: Dar al-Bashir, 1413/1993.

Afghani, Jamal al-Din al-. *Al-A`mal al-Kamilah*, ed. Muhammad `Imara. Beirut: al-Mu'asasah al-`Arabiyah li al-Dirasat wa al-Nashr, 1979.

Afghani, Jamal al-Din al-. *An Islamic Response to Imperialism*, ed. by Nikkie R. Keddie. Berkeley, CA: University of California Press, 1968.

Aflaq, Michel. *Fi Sabil al-Ba`th*. Damascus: Dar al-Tali`ah, 1959.

An-Na`im, Abdullahi, ed. *Human Rights in Cross Cultural Perspective*. Philadelphia: University of Pennsylvania Press, 1992.

Ashmawi, Salih al-. *Al-Ikhwan wa al-Thawrah*. Cairo: al-Maktab al-Misri al-Hadith, 1977.

Awdah, `Abd al-Qadir. *Al-Islam wa Awda`una al Siyasiyah*. Beirut: Mu'assasah al Risalah, 1984.

Bahrawi, Muhammad Latif al-. *Harakat al-Islah al-`Uthmani `Asr al-Sultan Mahmoud al-Thani. 1808-1839*. Cairo: Dar al-Turath, 1978.

Banna, Hasan al-. *Mabadi' wa Usul fi Mu'tamarat Khassah*. Cairo: al-Mu'ssasah al-Islamiyyah li al-Tiba`ah wa al-Nashr, 1979.

Banna, Hasan al-. *Majmu`at Rasa'il al-Imam al-Shahid Hasan al-Banna*. Cairo: Darul Hadarah al-Islamiyyah, n.d.

Binder, Leonard. *Islamic Liberalism*. Chicago, IL: The University of Chicago Press, 1988.

Bonanate, Lurgi. *Ethics and International Politics*, trans. John Irving. Cambridge, UK: Polity Press, 1995.

Brzezinski, Zbigniew. *Out of Control: Global Turmoil on the Eve of Twenty-first Century*. New York: Maxwell Macmillan, 1993.

Chaliand, Gerard, ed. *Minority People in the Age of Nation-States*. London: Pluto Press, 1393/1973.

Coulson, N. J. *A History of Islamic Law*. Edinburgh, UK: Edinburgh University Press, 1964.

Daniel Lerner, *The Passing of Traditional Society*. Glencoe, IL: The Free Press, 1958.

Descartes, Rene. *Meditations on First Philosophy*, trans. John Cottingham. Cambridge, UK and New York: Cambridge University Press, 1986.

Dessouki, Ali E. Hillal. ed. *Islamic Resurgence in the Arab World*, ed. New York: Praeger Publisher, 1982.

Donnelly, Jack. *Universal Human Rights in Theory and Practice*. Ithaca, NY: Cornell University Press, 1989.

Donohue, John J. and John L. Esposito, *Islam in Transition*. New York: Oxford University Press, 1982.

Esposito, John L. *Islam and Politics*. New York: Syracuse University Press, 1984.

Esposito, John L. *Islam in Transition: Muslim Perspective*. New York: Oxford University Press, 1982.

Esposito, John L. *The Islamic Threat: Myth or Reality?* New York: Oxford University Press, 1999.

Fazlur Rahman, *Islam*, 2d ed. Chicago: University of Chicago Press, 1979.

Fukuyama, Francis. *The End of History and the Last Man*. New York: Avon Books, 1992.

Ghanoushi, Rashid al-. *al-Huriyyat al-Ammah fi al-Dawah al-Islamiyyah* [Public Rights in the Islamic State]. Beirut: Markaz Dirasat al-Wihdah al-Arabiyyah, 1993.

Ghazzali, Abu Hamid al-. *Tahafut al-Falasifah*. Cairo: Dar al-Ma'arif, n.d.

Habermas, Jurgen. *Moral Consciousness and Communicative Action*, trans. Chistian Lannardt and Shierry Weber Nicholsen. Cambridge, UK: Polity Press, 1990.

Holmes, Kim and Thomas Moore. eds., *Restoring American Leadership: US Foreign Policy and Defense Blueprint*. Washington, DC: The Heritage Foundation, 1996.

Howard, Rhoda. *Human Rights and the Search for Community*. Boulder, CO: Westview Press, 1995.

Husari, Sati al-. *Abhath Mukhtara fi al-Qawmiyyah al-Arabiyyah*, vol. 1. Beirut: Dar al-Quds, 1974.

Hussain, Asaf. *Islamic Movements in Egypt, Pakistan, and Iran: An Annotated Bibliography.* London: Mansell Publishing Limited, 1983.

Hussein, Taha. "Mustaqbal al-Thaqafah fi Misr." 1938. In *The Collected Work of Taha Hussein.* Beirut: Dar al-Kitab al-Lubnani, 1973.

Huwaydi, Fahm. *Muwatinun la Dhimiyun.* Cairo: Dar al-Shuruq, 1985.

Ibn al-Qayim, *A`lam al-Muwaqi`in.* Beirut: Dar al-Kutub al-`Ilmiyyah, 1411/1991.

Ibn al-Qayim, *Sharh al-Shurut al-`Umariyyah.* Beirut: Dar al-`Ilm li al-Malayin. 1381/1961.

Ibn Hisham, *Al-Sirah al-Nabawiyyah.* Cairo: Mustafa Halabi Press, 1375/1955.

Ibn Khaldun, *Al-Muqaddimah,* chapter 3. Beirut: Dar al-Kitab al Lubnani, 1956.

Ibn Nujaym, Ibrahim. *Al-Ashbah wa al-Naza'ir.* Damascus: Dar al-Fikr, 1403/1988.

Ibn Qutaybah, *Al-Imamah wa al-Siyasah.* Cairo: Maktabat Mustafa al-Babi, 1328/1963.

Ibn Rushd, Muhammad bin Ahmad. *Bidayat al-Mujtahid wa Nihayat al-Muqtasid.* Beirut: Dar al-Ma`rifah, 1406/1986.

Ibn Rushd, *Tahafut al-Tahafut.* Cairo: Dar al-Ma`arif, n.d.

Ibn Taymiyah, Taqi al-Din. *Raf` al-Mallam `an al-A'immah al-A`lam.* Damascus: Al-Maktab al-Islami, 1382.

Inalcik, Halil. *The Ottoman Empire: The Classical Age 1300-1600.* New Rochelle, NY: Aristide D. Caratzas Pub., 1973.

Jansen, Johnnes J. G. *The Neglected Duly: The Creed of Sadat's Assassins and Islamic Resurgence in the Middle East.* New York: Macmillan, 1986.

Juayni, `Abd al-Malik bin `Abdullah al-. *Al-Burhan fi Usul al Fiqh.* Cairo: Dar al-Ansar, 1400.

Juwayni, Abu al Ma'ali al-. *Ghiyath al Umam.* Alexandria, Egypt: Dar al-Da`wah, n.d.

Kamali, Mohamad Hashim. *Freedom of Expression In Islam.* Kuala Lumpur: Ilmiah Publishers, 1998.

Kant, Immanuel. *Critique of Pure Reason,* trans. Norman Kemp Smith. New York, Macmillan, 1929.

Kant, Immanuel. *Groundwork of the Metaphysic of Morals.* London: Routledge, 1993.

Kawakibi, `Abd al-Rahman al-. *Umm al-Qura.* In *Al-A`mal al-Kamilah,* ed. Muhammad 'Imarah. Cairo: al-Hay'ah al-Misriyyah al-`Ammah, 1970.

Keddie, Nikki. *Sayyid Jamaluddin "Afghani": A Political Biography.* Berkeley: University of California Press, 1972.

Kedourie, Elie. *Nationalism.* New York: Frederick A. Praeger, 1960.

Kerr, Malcolm. *Islamic Reform: The Political and Legal Theories of Muhammad Abduh and Rashid Rida.* Berkeley: University of California Press, 1966.

Khadduri, Majid. *The Islamic Concept of Justice.* Baltimore: The Johns Hopkins University Press, 1984.

Khalaf, `Abd al-Wahab. *'Ilm Usul al-Fiqh,* 8th ed. Kuwait: Dar al-Kuwaytiyyah, 1388/1978.

Lambton, Ann K. *State and Government in Medieval Islam.* Oxford: Oxford University Press, 1981.

Lawrence, Bruce B. *Shattering the Myth.* Princeton, NJ: Princeton University Press, 2000.

MacIntyre, Alasdair. *Whose Justice? Which Rationality?* London: Duckworth, 1990.

Mahmud, `Abd al-Majid. *Al-Madrasah al-Fiqhiyyah li al-Muhadithin.* Cairo: Dar al-Shabab, 1972.

Mansur, Salih bin 'Abd al-'Aziz al-. *Usul al-Fiqh wa Ibn Taymiyah.* n.p.: 1400/1980.

Matthee, Rudi. "The Egyptian Opposition on the Iranian Revolt." in *Shi`ism and Social Protest.* eds. Juan R. Cole and Nikki R. Keddie. New Haven, CT: Yale University Press, 1986.

Maudud, Abul Ala. *Islamic State,* trans. Mazheruddin Siddiqi. Karachi: Islamic Research Academy, 1986.

Mawardi, `Ali bin Muhammad al-. *Al-Ahkam al-Sultaniyyah.* Cairo: Dar al-Fikr, 1983/1401.

Mayer, Ann Elizabeth. *Islam and Human Right: Tradition and Practice.* 2d ed. Boulder, CO.: Westview Press, 1995.

McCarthy, Thomas A. *The Critical Theory of Jurgen Habermas.* Cambridge, MA: MIT Press 1978.

Nietzsche, Friedrich. *Beyond Good and Evil.* New York: Vintage Books, 1966.

Papp, Daniel S. *Contemporary International Relations.* New York: Macmillan, 1988.

Rafi`i, `Abd al-Rahman al-. *`Asr Muhammad `Ali,* 4th ed. Cairo: Dar al-Ma`arif, 1982.

Rida, Muhammad Rashid. *Huquq al-Nisa' fi al-Islam* [Women's Rights in Islam]. Beirut: Dal al-Hijrah, 1987.

Rousseau, Jean-Jacque. *The Social Contract*, trans. Maurice Cranston. London: Penguin Books, 1968.

Said, Edward. *Orientalism*. New York: Vintage Books, 1979.

Sarakhsi, Muhammad bin Ahmad al-. *Sharh Kitab al-Siyar al-Kabir*. Pakistan: Nusrullah Mansour, 1405 AH.

Schacht, Joseph. *The Origins of Muhammadan Jurisprudence*. Oxford: Clarendon Press, 1950.

Shafi'i, Muhammad bin Idris al-. *Al-Risalah*. 2d ed. Cairo: Dar al-Turath, 1399/1979.

Shatibi, Abu Ishaq al-. *Al-Muwafaqat fi Usul al-Shari'ah*. Beirut: Dar al-Ma'rifah, n.d.

Sherwani, Haroon Khan. *Studies in Muslim Political Thought and Administration*. Philadelphia: Porcupine Press, 1977.

Voll, John O. *Islam: Continuity and Change in the Modern World*. 2d ed. Syracuse, NY: Syracuse University Press, 1994.

Walibank, T. Walter, et al. *Civilization Past and Present*. 5th ed. Glenview, IL: Scott Foresman and Company, 1965.

Weber, Max. *Economy and Society: An Outline of Interpretive Sociology*. Berkeley: University of California Press, 1978.

Wilson, Woodrow. President *Wilson's Great Speeches*. Chicago: Stanton and Von Vliet, 1917.

Yapp, M. E. *The Making of the Modern Near East*. London: Longman, 1987.

Zaydan, Abdul Karim. *Madkhal li-Dirasat al-Shari'ah al-Islamiyah*, 5th ed. Mu'assasat al-Risalah, 1397/1976.

Zeine, Zeine N. *The Emergence of Arab Nationalism*. Beirut: Khayyats, 1966.

Index

About the Author

Dr. Louay Safi is a recognized authority on Islam and the Middle East. He has published seven books and numerous academic papers on such issues as sociopolitical development, modernization, democracy, human rights, and Islamic resurgence. Among his books are *The Challenge of Modernity* (Lanham, MD: University Press of America, 1994) and *Al-Aqida wa al-Siyasah* [Creed and Politics] (Herndon, VA: International Institute of Islamic Thought, 1996). His work *Peace and the Limits of War* is on Amazon's best-seller list. He has lectured on Islam and the Middle East on five continents.

Dr. Safi received his Ph.D. in political science from Wayne State University (Detroit, MI) in 1992. He has served as dean of research and associate professor of political science at the International Islamic University of Malaysia, editor of the *American Journal of Islamic Social Sciences* (AJISS), director of research at the International Institute of Islamic Thought (IIIT), and visiting professor at George Washington University.

In addition, he is president of the Association of Muslim Social Scientists (AMSS), a founding board member of the Center for the Study of Islam and Democracy (CSID), and serves on the board of several leading Muslim organizations, including the Islamic Society of North America (ISNA), the Crescent University Foundation (CUF), and the Muslim Women Lawyers for Human Rights (KARAMAH).